FEMININE GYMNASTICS

third edition

PHYLLIS COOPER

illustrated by
A. BRUCE FREDERICK

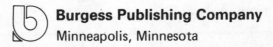

Burgess Publishing Company
Minneapolis, Minnesota

Editorial: Wayne Schotanus
Art: Joan Gordon, Adelaide Trettel
Production: Morris Lundin, Pat Barnes
Composition: Dennis Tasa

Cover design: Adelaide Trettel

Burgess Publishing Company
7108 Ohms Lane
Minneapolis, Minnesota 55435

0 9 8 7 6 5 4 3 2 1

PREFACE

Feminine Gymnastics was written to serve as a guide for teachers and coaches of gymnastics in schools, private clubs, and community organizations. The material covered provides the novice and skilled instructor with methods of teaching, skill analyses, spotting techniques, common errors that are made when students perform skills for the first time, and methods of evaluation for use in the school curriculum.

This new edition includes the following:

- Chapter on mechanical analysis
- Chapter on conditioning
- Suggested curriculum K-12
- More advanced skills in all events
- General competitive requirements
- Where to receive the latest information on judging

The new chapter on mechanical analyses will be particularly helpful to those teachers new to the sport of gymnastics and will enable present coaches to analyse the more difficult skills they cannot personally perform for their students.

Since conditioning plays a very important role in learning gymnastics skills safely and efficiently, all aspects are covered with suggested exercises for developing strength, flexibility, coordination, balance, and endurance. Diet and rest are also discussed, since they are an important part of total fitness.

Suggestions for class procedures and program planning have been included with the hope that they will serve as guidelines when developing a program to fit the needs of your particular school or club. A curriculum for gymnastics in K-12 is included. This curriculum can be easily adapted to most school programs.

The area of competitive gymnastics is also discussed, along with instructions or suggestions for running a gymnastics meet. Since the rules of competitive requirements change often, however, some of the judging information has been deleted with reference given to where the latest information can be obtained.

Gymnastics is a popular sport for both participants and spectators, and there is no doubt as to the values this activity offers individual gymnasts and its importance in the total school curriculum.

TO THE READER

Many of the skills have been described to one side (e.g., left foot or left hand leading). To perform the skill to the other side, reverse the directions for movement of the hands or feet.

For spotting, the *inside hand* (near) is the one closest to the performer, and the *outside hand* (far) is the one away from the performer. If the spotter is standing directly beside a performer, the inside hand is the hand closest to the part of the body that initiates the movement. There are also other spotting methods for each skill, but the one(s) presented have been proven successful by the author.

The code used throughout the book is as follows:

SL Skill Level
PT Performance Technique
SP Spotting Technique
CE Common Errors made by beginners
MO Movements out of the skill described
VA Variations of the skill
PB Position on bed of trampoline

Each group of skills has been described in a general order of progression. However, this is not the only progression that can or should be used, because individuals and groups have varied capacities for learning.

The skills have also been coded in the following manner:

L Locomotor
B Balance beam
F Floor exercise
U Uneven bars
T Tumbling
TR Trampoline
V Vaulting
C Conditioning

A PHILOSOPHY

Those things that are built on a solid foundation will last longer, and the final results are more rewarding. Building a strong foundation in gymnastics begins by learning the fundamental skills well so they may be executed efficiently. When this is done, success comes often and frustration seldom occurs.

It is important to know where the body is at all times in relation to space (kinesthetic sense) from the very beginning in gymnastics. Some people are gifted with a great amount of kinesthetic awareness, while others must learn every step of the way. Therefore, it is essential for a student to feel her body in motion on the mat (e.g., doing a forward roll) before attempting motion in the air without support of the hands or feet.

As we look around us, we see individuals of many shapes and sizes. Some are strong, some weak; some flexible, some not so flexible; some are agile, while others move a bit slower; and some have more interest and drive than others. All of these individuals cannot excel in gymnastics, but all can have success to some degree at some level. As you teach the sport, keep in mind that everyone in a given group can do only what her mind and body will allow, and she should be evaluated accordingly.

FOREWORD: GYMNASTICS—MORE STRAIGHT THAN EVER

Today's gymnastic skills are quite different from those of the sixties. No longer is the arched handstand in vogue or the undercut backhandspring a "neat trick."

With more knowledge in the area of kinesiology and mechanical analysis, today's gymnasts are reaping the benefits.

Most skills rely on a tight body position for efficient execution with least resistance. If students are taught the meaning of straight body (stretched body-tight body-taut body) in the initial stages of their encounter with gymnastics, they will find success comes more easily as they progress.

A body performs a skill to the fullest when its various muscle groups are functioning at maximum. The body or body parts must be in the right position and receiving proportionate impetus in the beginning, middle, and end of a skill in order to be successfully completed. The student or gymnast must know where the body is and what it is doing (kinesthetic awareness) in order to complete a skill successfully.

My favorite comparison for explaining body-control awareness is cooked and uncooked spaghetti. Students of all ages understand that example in most body positions. The following will show "cooked" and "uncooked" spaghetti in various body positions.

Squat

Open pike

Closed pike

Inverted pike

Straddle

Handstand

CONTENTS

LIST OF ILLUSTRATIONS

UNEVEN PARALLEL BARS (Figures U-1 to U-97)

chapter one

MECHANICAL ANALYSIS OF MOVEMENT

Too often in the learning process of teaching and spotting skills, one is confronted with many questions. Why did that happen? Why can't I get around? What am I doing wrong? To a novice sometimes these questions are often frustrating, and no matter what he or she may say, the student still fails to perform the skill properly. It is hoped that this chapter will help alleviate many problems for the novice by offering a basic understanding of the mechanical principles of movement by which skills can be taught and spotted more effectively and efficiently. Understanding movement is also the key to identifying performance errors, and spotting becomes a relatively easy job if one knows how, when, and where to apply force.

The following vocabulary discussed briefly below will be used:

Center of gravity—that point at which stability may occur
Base of support—body part or parts which support the body weight
Motion—an observable change in position of the entire body or its parts
    Sustained—slow movement
    Percussive—quick or rapid movement
    Translatory—movement through a continuing plane
    Rotatory—movement about or around a central point
    Curvilinear—movement as a whole in a circular path
Axis—point about which movement revolves
Force—an influence which produces or tends to produce motion or a change of motion
Inertia—properties remaining at rest or in motion unless acted upon by an outside force
Acceleration— resulting change in speed is directly proportional to the force producing it and inversely proportional to the mass
Action-reaction—for every action force there is an equal and opposite reaction force
Angle of rebound—direction of rebound as determined or altered by the degree of resistance

CENTER OF GRAVITY may be defined as that point at which stability may occur. In an individual standing erect with arms at the sides, the center of gravity (c of g) falls between the hip and waist areas. Examples below describe how the center of gravity moves with movement of the body or body parts.

In order for motion to occur, force must be applied to displace the center of gravity past the base of support in the desired direction, thus overcoming inertia. Three basic principles to keep in mind regarding center of gravity are:

1. The closer the center of gravity is to the base of support, the more stable the object (A is more stable than C).
2. The closer the center of gravity is to the radius of rotation, the faster the object will move (D).
3. The higher the center of gravity upon landing on a vault, a tumbling skill, or a dismount, etc., the lighter and more controlled the landing will be (F).

As a person stands erect, the feet are the base of support (A). If the body is to move forward with the feet stationary, then the upper body must lean forward, forcing the c of g forward of the feet.

If the body is to move forward as in walking, the first foot lifts up, then the push down backward of the rear foot moves the center of gravity forward to the new base or forward foot (B).

The BASE OF SUPPORT is the body part or parts that support the total body weight. In a normal standing position the base of support is the feet; in a handstand the hands are the base of support; and on the uneven bars in a front support position, the hands and hips on the bars are the bases of support. Understanding the relationship of the center of gravity to the base of support (one could think of it as proper body alignment) is of utmost importance in teaching and spotting effectively.

In a back hip circle (refer to page 183 for total description) the student starts in a front support position (A, opposite page). In the process of moving the legs forward to prepare for the cast, the shoulders should remain forward (B). If the shoulders should move backward as the feet move forward and begin to cast, the body will be forced backward away from the bar (C). This is caused by moving the center of gravity past the base of support.

Completing a back walkover (refer to page 60) on the beam or floor is often a problem because of poor body alignment *or* relationship of c of g to base of support. In the initial stages the c of g is slightly above the hip area because the arms are raised (A, below). It should remain in this area throughout the skill because of the position of the arms. For stability throughout, the body must go from its first base of support (feet) to its second base of support (hands) to finish on the feet in one sustained movement. This can happen only if the split of the legs, flexibility of the back, and kick push of the leg action is adequate for the particular individual's body weight. The body generally collapses or the spotter must push with a great deal of effort at the point when the hands contact the floor if the center of gravity is not directly over the base of support (hips and shoulders not over hands) (C). After the first foot contacts the floor, the second leg must remain straight (D) so that the line will not be broken at the hip area (E). The line from the fingertips to the toe of the second foot must remain straight until the final lunge (F) or low arabesque position (G) has been reached.

| A | B | C | D | E | F | G |

Wrong finish   Right finish

If the relationship of the c of g to the base of support is clearly understood and can be applied to performance, analyses, and spotting of gymnastics skills, then we can say that Newton's Laws of Motion have been observed and practiced.

MOTION is usually thought of as an observable change in position of the entire body or its parts. *Sustained motion* occurs when the body parts move slowly in a given direction or position, e.g., stretching upward to a stand from a forward roll; stretching of the body into the glide before a kip on the bars; or constant muscle tensing to maintain the vertical position in a handstand.

Percussive motion consists of sharp or rapid movement of the body or its parts from one position to another, e.g., the kipping action of the hips and push of the arms on the back roll extension; or the immediate rebound (punch) from the reuther board before execution of a vault.

There are two basic types of motion, translatory (linear) and rotatory (angular). *Translatory motion* involves an object or body moving through a continuing plane at a constant rate. The best example of this would be a body moving forward while seated in an automobile or the body moving in air off a ski jump. *Rotatory motion*

AB   CD   EF

3

involves an object or body moving about or around a central point or axis. This axis could be part of the body, e.g., the body rotating around the bar on a back hip circle. A front or back somersault would be classified as a *curvilinear* motion as the object is moving as a whole in a circular path.

Rotatory motion may take place around one of three axes (page 3). The *longitudinal axis* (AB) runs the length of the object; the *transverse axis* (CD) runs across the object at any level in its entire length; and the *sagittal axis* (EF) goes from front to back at any level of the body.

In a freely suspended body, the axis rotation is at the point that is the center of gravity of the object at that moment. In a supported object, one in contact with another surface, the axis is at the contact point or in a nearby articulation.

A great deal of movement is a combination of linear and rotatory motion, e.g., running for a vault. The leg action is rotatory while the body as a whole moves linearly.

Two factors determine the type of motion that will result when force is applied: (1) *the point at which force is applied,* and (2) *the pathway available for the object to move in.* If force is applied through the center of gravity or totally to one whole side, translatory (linear) motion will result. If force is applied away from the center of gravity, rotatory (angular) motion will result. For example, a pencil resting on its side if pushed at midpoint should move directly forward. If force is applied at one end the movement would be in an arc. Therefore, the farther the force is applied from the center of gravity of an object, the greater the effectiveness of that force for rotation about the center (see example A). This tendency of a force to produce rotation is called *moment of rotation* or *rotatory force.* Understanding this factor is of utmost importance to the spotter. If the spotter knows exactly at what point and in what direction to apply force, she will use less physical effort in assisting skill performance, and skills will be learned more efficiently (example B).

Example A: Mill circle on bars; (refer to page 184 for total skill)
    If the inside hand spots the upper arm (B) instead of the wrist area (A), the amount of force that can be developed is greater; therefore, the spotter can force the body around the bar with less effort.

Example B: In a back sommie, if force is applied on the upper back in a forward direction at the same time force is applied to the hips in the direction of the turn, the movement would be constant and would result in a fall of the body downward (B, page 5). In order to be successful, force applied to the back should be upward (helping to gain height) while the force on the back of the legs and hip area should be up and rotating backward in the direction of the desired turn (A).

4

A   B

Force in some form is required to produce all motion. The word *force* is often used freely without any understanding of what it is, how it works, where it comes from, and how to control it. There are basically three types of force: muscular, frictional, and gravitational.

Force needed to initiate and perform skills of a physical nature comes from within the muscular structure of our body reacting among each other or an outside object such as the apparatus. If muscular force is used at the right time in performing skills, there will be less gravitational pull. Muscle tension accounts for part of the difference over which the force is applied, speed developed and the final outcome or performance of the skill. Therefore, if the muscles involved are brought into play at 50 percent, the skill will be executed at 50 percent of the performer's potential.

The force needed to keep the body in a straight handstand position is total body muscular contraction directed vertically.

The relative degree of tension and contraction affects the way the muscles function. When a muscle is taut it will go into quicker and smoother action.

Incorrect body position

Good body position

A

If the muscles relax three quarters of the way through a back layout, the body will come to a landing position in a pike (A) rather than an extended vertical position (B). This action of the body causes the moving arc to be changed and the c of g lowered.

5

B

FRICTION comes into play mainly on the bars. Because most of the skills are performed with some type of hand grip, the degree of tension in the grip will directly affect the outcome of the skill being performed. Friction is a menace to the beginner, who tends to grip tightly so as not to fall off.

In a mill circle if the grip is too tight, the last third of the skill will be greatly affected. Since momentum is decreased on the way down from what it could have been with a loose grip, gravity will pull on the body and make it difficult to return to the original position to complete the skill.

In skills such as the sole circle, two points of friction work against the performer. If the legs are totally extended and pushing against the bar, the radius of rotation is increased (distance from hip to bar), and if the arms are totally extended and the grip controlled, the body will develop more momentum on the way down, therefore making it easier to complete the skill and go into the next move. The body position will also affect momentum and friction. If the body is compressed (close together), there will be less air resistance and less friction.

GRAVITY acts on all objects (including humans) at all times. The gravitational force is always exerted in a downward vertical direction. Thus, on some skills or parts of skills, we can use gravity to our advantage. Gravity can assist on the first phase of skills such as mill circles, seat circles, and sole circles. The longer the radius of rotation (the higher the hips) and the more compressed the body (the closer the center of gravity to the base of support), the faster the movement on the first phase.

If the body continues in this position with the same speed, it will overcome the gravitational pull and return to the top of the bar to the original position.

6

On the other hand, gravity can act against the last part of these same skills by trying to pull the body down after it has passed midpoint. If the body is not compressed sufficiently, the grip too tight, and the initial force forward inadequate, gravity can easily overcome the motion after midpoint.

Newton's Laws of Motion

Inertia—A body at rest tends to remain at rest unless acted upon by an outside force. Likewise, a body in motion tends to remain in motion unless acted upon by an outside force. An outside force may be another person, object, gravity, or friction making contact with the body, or it may be muscular movement from within the body.

For instance, a body held in a stride position for a mill circle on the bars will remain in that position until the upper body and hip extend forward, moving the body weight forward (therefore moving c of g past the base of support).

A body spinning around the bars as in a mill circle could continue forward at the completion, unless the grip was tightened (friction) and the shoulders and chest were lifted upward at the completion of the skill to force the c of g directly over the base of support.

A body turning around the bar in a back hip circle could continue a second or third time (depending on momentum developed) unless the body moved from a pike to a layout (front support) position.

Too open

Good compression

Pattern of correct movement

Acceleration—When a body is acted upon by a force, its resulting change is speed. Acceleration is directly proportional to the force producing it and inversely proportional to the mass. Given an object of a certain weight, the greater the force applied to it the greater the speed of the object. Given a certain force applied, the greater the weight of an object, the less the speed of movement.

Therefore, the tighter the tuck the faster the spin (if equal force is applied), and the closer the c of g is to the radius of rotation, the faster the spin.

c of g

c of g

c of g

Faster spin

A

B

C

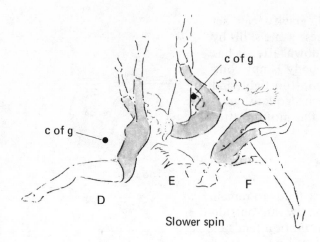

Slower spin

If two people punched the reuther board with equal force, the one weighing less would be projected farther.

50 lbs. force

Landing

50 lbs. force

Landing

If two people weighing the same punched the board with different amounts of force, the one producing the greater force would be projected farther.

100 lbs.

25 lbs. force

Landing

100 lbs.

50 lbs. force

Landing

If force opposes the direction of motion, a decrease in acceleration will occur; and if the force is in line with the motion, there will be an increase in momentum. This could be applied to the handstand (A, page 9) and front handspring (B). From a standing position, the two skills have identical movement beginnings. The initial force (kick, push action of legs) for the handstand, of course, is less than for a handspring. When the vertical position is reached in the handstand, the muscles tighten and force the body upward in order to stop forward movement. If the force from the initial kick push action is great enough, the body will pass through the vertical position, and with the secondary muscular force and hand push from the mat should return to an upright position.

A

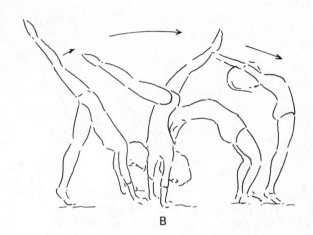

B

Action-reaction—For every action force there is an equal and opposite reaction.

In order to spring vertically for a sommie, the initial movement must be downward against the mat and floor. The more forceful the punch or lift from the floor, the higher the lift proportionate to body mass.

When the hip and upper body are extended forward in a mill circle, the center of gravity is pushed past the base of support; therefore, the body will move forward with proportional speed.

The body coming to a stand after a forward roll is the resultant force of pushing downward against the mat and floor by extending the legs and upper body in a vertical direction.

Angle of rebound—When a moving body or object comes in contact with a resistance greater than its own momentum, it will rebound from that resistance. The angle of rebound is altered by the degree of resistance. Gymnastics is mainly concerned with rebound techniques for tumbling and vaulting.

The position of the feet making contact with the mat out of a round-off is different for a back handspring and a back sommie or layout. A represents the proper position for a round-off back handspring. The feet come in closer to the hands for a back handspring than for a back sommie. This is necessary as the move out of the round-off should be on a 45° angle up and back. The position of the feet out of a round-off for a back sommie should be farther away from the hands than for a back handspring (B). The object here is to hit or punch the mat slightly back, so that by the time the upper body has pushed from the mat, the total body can be in a vertical flight pattern with the upward and backward momentum. The force from the knees driving to the chest will force the center of gravity past the base of support, thereby allowing a 360° turn slightly past the vertical position.

Looking back at the angle of projection, you can now see why it is more efficient and effective to contact the reuther board with the feet slightly in front of the shoulders. At the angle of impact, if the arms are lifted forcefully to an overhead position and full body extension occurs, the body, being shot as a missile, will rebound on an upward inverted flight. Total body inversion cannot occur unless the lower body and hip muscles are taut.

Body will be projected up and forward over or onto horse

Body will be projected forward into horse

10

In twisting and rotatory moves, once the body is free of the supporting surface it can no longer increase or decrease the initial force. However, a body can increase (by tucking) or decrease (by laying out) the speed of rotation. This is basically shortening or lengthening the radius of rotation.

On a front sommie, once the feet have left the ground the height gained in air will be equal to the push from the feet and legs. If the height is adequate and the performer proficient, the skill can be executed properly. If the height is inadequate and the performer proficient, the skill can be performed with less amplitude, and landing might occur in a squat position.

- The higher the angle of projection, the more time available to complete the rotation.
- Takeoff should be slightly less than 90° vertical since all rotatory movement takes place when the body is in a position of imbalance.
- In all layout and twisting moves, the body must be totally extended on takeoff and remain totally extended throughout. The example below shows a very relaxed body throughout—a typical beginner, anxious to get the feet on the mat as quickly as possible.

Hips should not flex at this point
Total body should be tight

Body not tight here at beginning

11

chapter two

CONDITIONING

The purpose of any conditioning program is to prepare the body to perform skills effectively and efficiently. The suggested program will be divided into component groups. Not all exercises in each group must be done; however, no group should be skipped in its entirety. Some exercises suggested will develop more than one component simultaneously, and exercises may be varied weekly or daily to avoid boredom.

GROUP I CARDIOVASCULAR EXERCISES

The muscle tissues must have an adequate blood supply to perform efficiently. Exercises that enhance this body function are called cardiovascular exercises and generally involve moving the body parts quickly.

Suggested cardiovascular exercises:

1. *Jumping jacks.* Arm and leg movements may be varied from day to day. (Fig. C-1)

2. *Running.* In place, running laps, or running a distance. Try to keep an even pace or rhythm and do not allow the upper body to sag. (Fig. C-2)

Figure C-1

Figure C-2

3. *Squat thrusts.* Generally ten are sufficient to develop some degree of cardiovascular fitness if done daily. (Fig. C-3)

Figure C-3

4. *Jump rope.* Jumping rope is an excellent form of cardiovascular exercise. You should start with one minute, then increase to ten. Ten minutes of jumping daily would almost insure that a gymnast could complete her floor routine without vigorous breathing. (Fig. C-4)

Figure C-4

5. *Locomotor skills.* Combine locomotor skills in a circular or line pattern. Perform at least five of each skill before going to next. (Fig. C-5)

Figure C-5

13

GROUP II STRENGTH

The gymnast needs total body strength to maneuver through, in, on, under, and over the apparatus. Explosive power, a form of strength, is a definite asset for tumbling and vaulting. Strength is needed on the uneven bars as well as the beam—an individual must have sufficient strength to put and control her body through the many skills. Development of strength occurs when you increase resistance or increase the number of repititions with the same amount of resistance.

1. *Push-ups.* Keep body completely straight in both the push-up from a prone position and in a handstand position. (Fig. C-6)

Figure C-6

2. *Pull-ups.* With hands in a forward grip (back of hand toward face), pull total body up above bar. Start with five, increase to fifteen. If assistance is needed in the beginning, have partner lift with hands on legs above the knees. (Fig. C-7)

3. *Sit-ups.* With slow sit-ups, roll the body up; do not jerk the body forward; knees should be bent with feet flat on the floor. A partner may hold the feet stationary if necessary. In sit-ups to a V seat, try to move the upper and lower body simultaneously and the same distance. (Fig. C-8)

Figure C-7

Figure C-8

4. *Leg lifts.* Hanging from a bar, lift the legs to a position parallel to the floor, hold two counts, then lower to hanging position. On the next lift, raise the legs so the feet go above the head, hold two counts, then lower to hang. Repeat each sequence, starting with five and increasing to fifteen. Wearing heavy tennis shoes would add resistance and repetitions could be decreased. (Fig. C-9)

Figure C-9

14

5. *Leg tucks and extensions.* From a long hang position, bring the legs to a tuck position, then extend them forward to a horizontal position. Bring back to the tucked position, then extend to long hang position. Start with five, work up to twenty. (Fig. C-10)

Figure C-10

6. *Tuck jumps.* As rapidly as possible spring vertically and bring knees to the chest and extend before landing. Start with ten and work up to twenty-five. (Fig. C-11)

Figure C-11

7. *Leg pushes with partner.* Partner A stands with feet to side of Partner B's head. Partner B is on floor on back with legs vertical. Partner A forces partner's legs downward. Partner B tries to bring legs to vertical as quickly as possible and tries not to allow them to touch the floor. (Fig. C-12)

Figure C-12

15

8. *Single-leg squats.* Hold the ankle of one leg and slowly lower body until knee of bent leg contacts the floor. Repeat five times, then do with other leg. Until this can be done without support, grasp some object such as a chair, barre, or beam to assist with balance. (Fig. C-13)

Figure C-13

GROUP III <u>FLEXIBILITY</u>

Flexibility, the range of movement for a specific joint, is very important in gymnastics. When a gymnast can perform a split, she can execute a walkover with greater ease, since the weight can be displaced and redistributed past the center of gravity more quickly. Stretching carefully is the best way to achieve greater flexibility. Many times it is advantageous to have partners since they can produce more force or resistance, whichever is needed.

1. *Splits.* Start by standing in a lunge position with hips and shoulders directly perpendicular to legs (this is referred to as squaring the hips and shoulders). Slide the legs gently away from each other and hold at the point where some discomfort occurs. If needed, the hands can be placed to the side of the body to hold some of the weight. Repeat procedure on both sides, five times a warm-up session depending upon the present state of flexibility. If full splits have been attained, then the forward foot can be placed on a low bench or folded mat for added stretch. Reverse this procedure and have back foot resting on raised mat. (Fig. C-14)

Figure C-14

16

2. *Splits with partner and other variations.*

a) Stand with back against wall. Lift one leg parallel to floor and place in partner's hand. Push down on partner's hand for thirty seconds, then allow partner to lift leg above head. This method allows antagonistic muscles to rest, then work at maximum during the stretch. Repeat with other leg, then switch partners. (Fig. C-15)

Figure C-15

b) Stand with back to wall, lean forward, and place hands on floor. Lift one leg vertically and push body to split position. Repeat on other side. (Fig. C-16)

Figure C-16

c) Sit in straddle position facing partner with soles of feet together. Grasp wrists and rock forward and backward while applying pressure through the feet. As flexibility increases, grasp at elbows, then at shoulders. (Fig. C-17)

Figure C-17

17

3. *Lower back and shoulders.* Partner lies in prone position with arms by the head. While ankles are held, the partner lifts upward as high as possible, holding for three counts when she reaches the stress point. Eventually this exercise can be done with a twisting action upward. (Fig. C-18)

Figure C-18

4. *Lower back and shoulders.*
   a) Sit on rear of partner (not entire weight), grasp legs above the knees and lift. Lift only until hips begin to be pulled off the mat. (Fig. C-19)

Figure C-19

   b) Reverse sitting position and grasp partner's arms above armpits. Pull up and back gently until stress is felt, hold a few seconds and lower gently. Do not raise hips off the mat. (Fig. C-20)

Figure C-20

5. *Kneeling stretch.* For upper leg and hip flexibility and control of gluteals and lats. From an erect kneeling position, keep body tight and lean backward as far as possible, then return to upright position. Do five times with the knees together, then five times with the knees about twelve inches apart. (Fig. C-21)

Figure C-21

6. *Trunk stretch.* On stall bar, lowered beam, or barre, lean forward with the body in an open pike or 90° position while grasping the object. Apply pressure (stretch) through the shoulders or have partner press gently on upper back and shoulder area. Stretch three seconds, relax three seconds. Repeat five times. (Fig. C-22)

Figure C-22

7. *Backbends.* For shoulder, back, and trunk flexibility. Start in a lying position (face up). Place heels by hips and hands under shoulders as for a backward roll. Push with hands and hips simultaneously to push body into a backbend position. Rock back and forth, gently keeping the head between the arms (look at fingers). When a good backbend can be performed, then put the legs together and try to force the shoulders past the hand position. (Fig. C-23)

Figure C-23

8. *Knees to nose.* For flexibility in back of legs and lower back. Lie on floor on back with arms above head. Lift the legs upward and backward without bending legs and touch toes on floor behind the head. When this can be done without stress, flex the ankles, curl the toes under, and rock back and forth. (Fig. C-24)

Figure C-24

9. *Trunk stretch and rotation.* Stand with feet just outside shoulders. Stretch slowly to the right, return to stand, stretch to left, return to stand, stretch forward, return to stand, and then stretch backward and return to the standing position. Hold each position for three counts. Each time stretch to the stress point. (Fig. C-25)

Figure C-25

10. *Trunk stretch in straddle sitting position.* Sitting in a wide straddle position, twist the trunk forward, leading with the right shoulder and swinging the right arm across the chest and the left arm overhead. Hold three counts and repeat movement to the left side. (Fig. C-26)

Figure C-26

11. *Ankle stretch.* Kneel, then sit on heels. Place hands to side of the body beside knees. Lift the knees up toward the chest keeping weight on the ankles. Hold at stress point for five counts, then lower and repeat. (Fig. C-27)

Figure C-27

20

12. *Front-to-back stretch.* Stand with feet about eighteen inches apart. Bend forward to touch hands flat on floor in front of body, then stretch through the vertical and go backward to place the hands on the floor in a backbend position. Repeat five times. If student cannot get up from backbend alone, do with a partner and spot as if spotting for a limbre. (Fig. C-28)

Figure C-28

GROUP IV COORDINATION

Coordination is necessary to perform individual complex movements and series of movements in gymnastics. Coordination is the ability to put a body part in a certain position at the appropriate time. Actually, the best exercise to develop coordination is repetition of actual skills. Each skill has a specific rhythm; when this rhythm has been learned, the skill will be performed correctly. When the correct rhythm has been learned, coordination of the body parts has also occurred. In the process of repetition of exercises or specific skills, the mind and body are also learning concentration and dicipline.

1. *Jumping jacks—8 count.*
   1-2 Jump with feet apart, hands overhead, return to starting position.
   3-4 Jump, lift right leg, clap under leg, then behind back.
   5-6 Jump, lift left leg, clap under leg, then behind back.
   7-8 Same as 1-2.
   Jumping jacks aid in coordination, since they require concentration on putting the body parts in a specific position at a designated time. (Fig. C-29)

Figure C-29

2. *Jumping-jack variation—4 count.*
   1. Right foot forward, arms forward.
   2. Right foot sideward, arms sideward.
   3. Right foot forward, arms forward.
   4. Right foot beside left foot, arms at side.

   Repeat using left foot.

   Repeat having arms go in opposition. (Fig. C-30)

Figure C-30

3. *Walking in backbend position.* Push up into backbend position and walk twenty feet, hop twenty feet, and then run twenty feet. To begin, have partner at side to help student move in the proper direction. After they are comfortable with walking forward, then they should hop and run forward. Well coordinated and flexible girls should try walking, hopping, and running backward. (Fig. C-31)

   a) walking

   b) hopping

   c) running

Figure C-31

4. *Inside outs.* Begin in pike position with both hands and feet on floor. Lift arm and leg of same side, force hips upward, place hand and foot on floor in backbend position and rotate hand that is still on floor. From backbend position lift leg followed by hand to continue to original position. Try to cover twenty feet.

Figure C-32

22

5. *Swan exercise—8 count.* Lie on mat in prone position; arms by head.
    1. Lift arms and upper body, lower
    2. Lift legs together and straight, lower
    3. Lift right arm and left leg, lower
    4. Lift left arm and right leg, lower
    5. Lift total body, lower
    6. Lift right arm and right leg, lower
    7. Lift left arm and left leg, lower
    8. Lift total body, lower
    Repeat five times. (Fig. C-33)

Figure C-33

6. *Arm circles.* Start in standing position with arms at side. Start with the right arm and have the left arm follow one step behind. Repeat, leading with left arm. Four count.
    1. Right arm forward, left at side.
    2. Right arm vertical, left arm forward.
    3. Right arm to side parallel to floor, left arm vertical.
    4. Right arm to side of body, left arm to side parallel to floor.
    Repeat ten times. (Fig. C-34)

Figure C-34

GROUP V BALANCE

Good balance in gymnastics is a must for success. You must be able to balance in many positions—natural, inverted, horizontal forward (arabesque or scale), horizontal backward (back arabesques—beginning of back walkovers), and diagonal (various modern turns done on slant). Counterbalance is another factor one must be able to understand and perform for balance. Balance occurs only when body parts are equally distributed over the base of support, whether it be the feet, hands, seat, or other base. If one part extends past the base, moving the center of gravity, another part must counterbalance by extending in opposition; e.g., in an arabesque the chest moves forward and the leg lifts rearward.

1. *Leg lifts.* Stand without holding barre, beam, or other object. Lift foot forward parallel to the floor, move to the side, then move to the rear low arabesque, holding five counts in each position. Repeat with other leg. Perform four times on each side. (Fig. C-35)

Figure C-35

2. *Single-leg squat.* Stand on one leg with the other forward. Slowly lower to squat position and return to standing. Use a partner for support until you can do alone. Repeat using the other leg. (Fig. C-36)

Figure C-36

24

3. *V seat.* Sit on the floor, folded mat, or balance beam. Lift the legs forward to a V-seat position and hold for five counts. Arms can vary with each V seat; they may be vertical, forward, sideward, or crossed over the chest. (Fig. C-37)

Figure C-37

4. *Attitudes, arabesques, scales.* Assume any of the positions categorized here and hold for the count of ten. Vary the positions. (Fig. C-38)

Figure C-38

5. *Balanced handstand.* Stretch into a straight body handstand and hold for ten counts. To begin, have partner stand to side and spot legs just above knees to help with balance. (Fig. C-39)

Figure C-39

GROUP VI ENDURANCE

When a gymnast can finish routines without signs of exhaustion, she generally has developed a great deal of endurance. Endurance can be developed by running distances, jumping rope at least ten minutes a day, repeating entire routines daily, or circuit training of some sort. Circuit training is a combination of all types of exercises and skills performed in a relatively short period of time. At each station the individual must perform a specific number of repetitions or do the exercise for a specific length of time. Circuits can also be routines done on each event one after the other three times around. When circuits are interesting and there is stimulating background music, students will perform well and with fewer complaints. If circuits are used daily, the exercises should be changed to prevent boredom. Also, all the students should start at a different station each time.

Beginning Circuit

Station	Activity	Repetitions-time
1.	Run forward and backward 25 feet	10 times
2.	Run and jump off reuther board	10 times
3.	Kick to handstand against wall	2 times
4.	On bars jump to front support and cast	5 times
5.	Jump up and walk across beam, jump off	
6.	Push up to backbend	2 times
7.	Walking splits	20 feet
8.	Run, stepping on marks supplied	
9.	Push-ups	2 times
10.	Sit-ups	5
11.	Hold forward arabesque	30 seconds
12.	Leaps, chainés, jetés	5 each

Note: Circuits must contain only those skills the students are ready for. Those included here are only guides.

1

2

3

4

26

5

6

7

8

9

10

11

12

Intermediate Circuit

Station	Activity	Repetitions-time
1.	Run forward and backward 25 feet	15 times
2.	Squat vaults	5
3.	Pullover, back hip circle, underswing dismount	2
4.	Squat mount, chassé, toe turn, forward roll, step hop, round-off dismount	1
5.	Walk on hands for 6 feet	3 tries
6.	Walk in backbend 5 feet forward, 5 feet backward	1
7.	Walking splits 20 feet	1
8.	Slide hop, half turn, slide hop, forward and backward	5
9.	Walking splits 20 feet	1
10.	Push-ups	5
11.	Sit-ups	10
12.	Leaps, tour jeté, full turns	

28

Advanced Circuit

Station	Activity	Repetitions-time
1.	Run forward and backward 25 feet	20 times
2.	Squat handsprings	5
3.	Kip, catch high bar, straddle legs over low bar, kip to high, underswing dismount over low.	2
4.	Step on, run, kick turn, cartwheel, aerial dismount	2
5.	Walk on hands with legs in split	10 feet
6.	Run in backbend position, 10 feet forward and 10 feet backward	1
7.	Walking splits 20 feet	1
8.	Run in place for 16 counts, sit down, lie down, sit-up, stand	8
9.	Push-ups, clap hands between each	5
10.	Sit-ups to V seat	15
11.	Arabesque any position	1 minute
12.	Tour jetés, split leaps, cabrioles	5 each

Diet and Rest

You can exercise daily for hours and not develop the trim body necessary to excel in today's world of gymnastics. Exercise is only a part. Diet and proper rest in proportionate amounts are also essential to develop a body that can maneuver through the intricacies of gymnastic performances. A gymnast should not starve herself to skin and bones. When this occurs, so does loss of strength and other mental functions necessary for participation. One should decide in consultation with coach, parent, and doctor what the ideal weight should be for optimal performance of the particular body build. The weight level should be evaluated periodically as the body grows.

The body needs a regulated intake of food. Just as schools and buses function on a schedule, so should the body be able to rely on food at a given time. If individuals watch how much they eat, they should be able to eat three meals a day and have proportionate amounts of any kind of food.

As with food, the body needs a certain amount of rest daily. When muscles get tired they can't function at maximum. So the entire muscular, skeletal, and nervous systems need a chance to become revitalized through a process that occurs only when the body is at rest.

chapter three

LOCOMOTOR SKILLS

"WHY LOCOMOTOR SKILLS IN GYMNASTICS?"

We learn to walk when we are about a year old. We get a helping hand only when we fall, and as soon as we prove ourselves proficient, everyone seems to take it for granted that no more need be said about our locomotor skills. As we get more daring, we try our luck at running and begin to imitate older playmates as they hop, skip, and jump. Some individuals are fortunate enough to develop those locomotor skills during childhood; however, too often boys and girls go through twelve years of school without learning the basic locomotor skills essential to efficient movement.

Why do we need these skills in a gymnastics book? A gymnast, like any other athlete, can perform more gracefully and efficiently with a good background in basic movement, and for a gymnast, locomotor skills are an integral part of floor exercise and balance-beam routine composition. Learning to run well is a must for any individual who wishes to become a good vaulter because the efficiency and speed of the run greatly influence the execution of the vault. If proper technique of basic locomotor skills is taught, then gymnasts can execute skills more gracefully and efficiently.

The basic locomotor skills include walking, running, hopping, skipping, jumping, leaping, sliding, and galloping. The proper techniques of these skills and variations used specifically for gymnastics will be described.

Note: Refer to dance section of chapter 5 for description of ballet arm and leg positions

WALKS

Walking in gymnastic exercises is different from general everyday walking. The "dance walk," which is performed with the legs turned slightly out from the hips and the toe rather than the heel leading, is used. Walks should be performed lightly and fluidly, with the entire body erect. The shoulders must be relaxed for aesthetic appearance and good body lines. The arms should hold a definite position, with the index finger an extension of the arm. Abdominal and gluteal muscles should be tense, never allowing the hips to protrude backward. Small steps are more appropriate for gymnastics.

Variations for Practice aid in developing confidence, balance control, and awareness of body positions in motion.

1. Arms out to sides, palms down. Walk on line on floor. Do not allow body to be rigid. Eyes spot stationary object at eye level in front of body.
2. Start with both arms out to sides of body and parallel to floor. As left foot moves forward, bring right arm to front of body (parallel to floor) leading with inside of wrist. As right foot moves forward, move right arm out to side position leading with back of wrist; slightly bend elbow. (Fig. L-1)
3. Repeat #2 moving left arm.
4. Arms out to sides; walk on balls of feet with very little knee bend. (Fig. L-2)
5. Arms out to sides and parallel to floor; step onto left foot bending left knee. Step onto right foot on ball of foot, then step onto ball of left foot (low, high, high). On the low steps, the foot should be turned slightly out with the heal turned in. (Fig. L-3)
6. Repeat #5 starting low step on right foot.

7. Arms out to side and make steps (high, low, low).
8. Walk backward; be careful not to lean forward.
9. Walk on a diagonal, keeping upper body forward. (Fig. L-2)
10. Walk to music.
11. Transfer walks to balance beam.

Figure L-1

Figure L-2

Figure L-3

Figure L-4 (Running in semicircle)

RUNS

Learning to run gracefully requires many hours of concentrated practice. The beginner must run low and slowly at first and gradually increase the height and speed.

The stride should be even, and the movement should be smooth and free. The arms should swing naturally in opposition to the legs; never allow them to cross in front or in back of the body. The shoulders should be in a forward position, and the head should be held in a natural position. Never let the upper body sag forward; the entire body should lean slightly forward.

Forward momentum is created by full leg, ankle, and hip extension. When the back leg extends and moves to become the forward leg, it lands with a bent knee; then the ball of the foot pushes down and back on the floor, resulting in full extension of that leg. The last part of the foot to leave the floor and the first part to contact the floor should be the ball. The heels should not come in complete contact with the floor.

Variations for Practice

1. Run in a straight line, first slow and then fast.
2. Run in a semicircle to the right. Lean slightly into the center of the semicircle mostly with shoulders and head. (Fig. L-4)
3. Repeat #2 running to the left; reverse arms.
4. Run to music.
5. Transfer running in a straight line to the balance beam.

HOPS

A hop is the removal of weight from one foot and its return to the same foot; it is usually preceded by another locomotor skill, such as a walk (step). On the hop, the right leg is lifted in front of the body with the knee bent and the upper part of the leg parallel to the floor. The knee should be turned out and the heel turned in (closer to the midline of the body than the knee, but forward of the knee). The left leg starts in the bent-knee position; the toes point toward the floor as the foot leaves the floor to push the entire body upward. For maximum height the head and chest must also be lifted. The arms may move in opposition to the legs, may be in third position, or may be held sideways. (Fig. L-5)

Figure L-5

Variations for Practice

1. Take a step. Lift one leg and extend it sideways. As the other leg pushes off the floor, the knee will turn outward and bend, allowing the foot to contact the buttocks. Hold arms sideways. (Fig. L-6)

32

Figure L-6

Figure L-7 side view

2. Perform #1 but extend one leg forward and upward rather than to the side. (Fig. L-7)
3. Hop to music.

Figure L-7 front view

SKIPS

The skip is a combination of the step and the hop. It has an uneven rhythm. The step and hop are executed on the same foot. Refer to description of the hop for details of arm and body positions. Precede hop with step for skip.

JUMPS

The jump is a spring from one or two feet and a landing on both feet. The main purpose of jumps is to gain height or distance. If height is the main objective, the movement must go up and down in the same vertical plane. If the main objective is distance, then the center of gravity must be displaced to afford forward momentum. Arm and body positions will vary with the different types of jumps. Jumps should be explosive movements.

Variations for Practice

1. *Squat jump* (Fig. L-8)
   Hold arms sideways, stand with feet close together with one foot slightly in front of the other. Bend knees (go into semiplié position) and immediately spring upward, lifting the heels to the buttocks. Lower the legs (extend) before landing, and make sure the landing is in a semiplié position for balance and to absorb shock. The head and chest should be lifted for added height. Try to make the jump and landing in the same vertical plane to avoid loss of balance.

Figure L-8

2. *Tuck jump* (Fig. L-9)
The same principles of movement involved in the squat jump are used on the tuck jump. The only difference is the position of the legs. Instead of being lifted to the buttocks as in Figure L-8, the knees are brought to the chest.

Figure L-9

3. *"C" or cheerleading jump* (Fig. L-10)
The "C" jump is performed in a vertical plane. Start in standing position; slightly bend knees and spring vertically. As the feet leave the floor, lift them back and up toward the head; at the same time, arch the back, tilt the head backward, and move the arms upward and backward. Return to original position upon landing.

Figure L-10

4. *Straddle jump* (Fig. L-11)
Keep upper body erect at all times. After springing upward from floor, lift legs sideways and upward in a wide straddle position. Move arms sideways to touch toes. Bring legs together before landing.

Upper body should be vertical

Figure L-11

5. *Arch jump* (Fig. L-12 and 13)
The arch jump is used mainly to achieve distance; however, it is sometimes used to gain height.

Distance
From a stand, go into a bent knee position and simultaneously move the arms to a backupward position (palms up). The hips are directly over the feet, and the shoulders are forward of the knees and feet. (Fig. L-12)

Figure L-12

34

Height

Arms move same as preceding. When the bent-knee position is attained, the shoulders should be directly over the feet; maintain that relationship throughout the jump. (Fig. L-13)

Practice Hints for Jumps

1. Start jumps low; then gradually increase height.
2. Make all jumps appear explosive.
3. Practice a couple of jumps in succession.
4. Make sure to use arms to assist in gaining height.
5. Transfer squat, arch, and tuck jumps to balance beam.
6. Other jumps can be incorporated in floor exercise.

Figure L-13

LEAPS

Leaps are slower than a run because they involve height and distance. As the transference of weight from one foot to the other is made, the body is completely suspended in air. Height and distance are attained as a result of a very strong downbackward push from the back leg, which starts in a bent-leg position. As the back leg extends and the front leg reaches forward and up, the head and chest are strongly lifted. Arms are held in opposition to the legs. The leap should be a very explosive movement.

Variations for Practice

1. Run, run, leap, run, run, leap. (l=left foot, r=right foot) l r l r l r
2. Practice over a low object such as a bench or beam; the object should be at least twelve inches off the floor. This technique will force the performer to get off the floor and to lift the back leg and delay lowering it.

Leap Variations

1. *Step-push leap—step sissone* (Fig. L-15)
   Step forward on right foot and slide left foot to meet right (feet almost in fifth position after step). Bend knees, push with back (left) foot upward. Land on forward foot. Keep arms in opposition or to side of body parallel to floor.

Figure L-14

2. *Stag leap* (Fig. L-15)

As the leap is initiated by the back (right) leg, the forward (left) leg extends foreupward. Immediately bend left knee and touch left toe to right knee. Land on left foot. Keep arms in opposition to legs or in second position (sideways). Lift the head and chest.

Figure L-15

3. *Split leap* (Fig. L-16)

After the back leg initiates the foreupward movement of the body, one leg reaches forward while the other leg reaches backward and upward to an even split position. Lift the head and chest and allow the back to arch slightly. Land on forward foot with slight knee bend. When left leg is forward, hold right arm obliquely forward and left arm in second position. (Fig. L-16)

Figure L-16

4. *Scissors leap (preceded by a run)* (Fig. L-17)

Take off on the left foot, extending the right leg forward. While suspended, switch legs so that the right leg becomes the back leg and lift head and chest. Land on left foot. Keep arms to side (second position).

Figure L-17

GALLOP (Chassé) (Fig. L-18)

A gallop is a step, close movement with uneven rhythm. The original forward foot is always in the lead. Height is gained as the push-off is made from the front foot.

Step forward onto bent leg and transfer weight to that foot. Draw the back foot behind the front foot while the front leg is extending (on toe). Quickly shift the weight to the back leg while lifting the front leg forward to prepare for the next step.

Always hold the upper body and head erect. The arms may be held sideways or obliquely backward.

Figure L-18

Variations for Practice

1. Step, close, step, hesitate and bring back leg forward and step, close, step.
   l   r   l   r   l   r
2. Practice to music.
3. Transfer to balance beam.

SLIDE

A slide is a step, close with uneven rhythm and is usually performed sideways or on a diagonal. The same principles of movement involved in the gallop are involved in the slide, but the body moves sideways. Hold arms sideward. The body is always slightly behind the lead foot.

Variations for Practice

1. Step, close, step, half hop, pivot turn, step, close, step. (Fig. L-19)
      l   r   l   l   r   l   r
2. Slide on a diagonal.
3. Slide to music.
4. Transfer movement to floor exercise routine and balance beam.

Figure L-19

TEACHING SUGGESTIONS

The atmosphere for introducing locomotor skills is very important. For many students it will be an extension of movement exploration they had in elementary school physical education class. For some it will be new. The unit could be called "exploring movement" or could be a part or an extension of a modern dance class.

Suggested Format

1. Have very low background music.
2. Have group spaced on floor (sitting while talking) to allow freedom of movement.
3. Discuss unit plan.
4. Describe first skill (usually the walk) and demonstrate (or have demonstrated).
5. Immediately involve the entire class in performing the skill (so they won't have too much time to think about becoming "wall flowers").
6. Compliment the group and review the skill, pointing out mistakes made but not directing comments to any individual. Sometimes it helps to mock the mistakes in an exaggerated form since students often like to see the teacher being one of the gang.
7. Have one quarter of the class perform at a time while the others watch.
8. Use music and play follow the leader, with you (the teacher) being the leader. Decide on a floor pattern before class or improvise.
   Example: Moving in a single file around the gym, make a diagram similar to the one below.

Variations can be incorporated, such as low and high walks and walking backward. Be prepared for a possible jam-up!

9. Review two more skills, such as the step hop and slide. Practice each a few times, then combine them in a simple manner, such as four walks, four step hops, and four slides. Perform in small groups to music. Have the groups work in a straight line, on a diagonal, or in a circle. Sometimes it helps to make a contest out of this activity, such as "Which group is the most synchronized?"

10. After all skills are covered, have students move the way they "feel" to the music, combining the skills and adding turns. Expect anything from an empty floor until a "brave soul" makes the first move to patterns involving only one skill such as walks or turns.

Note: Commercial records made especially for locomotor skills or dance moves can be purchased. If this is not possible, then music such as "Alley Cat" or any similar record with an even rhythm can be used for walks, runs, skips, and fast slides and gallops.

chapter four

TUMBLING AND ACROBATIC SKILLS

The values of tumbling in the physical education program are numerous. This type of activity challenges students to compete against themselves, as they do not have a teammate to help them maneuver their bodies through some of the intricate skills (except as a spotter). Tumbling and acrobatic skills, along with single and dual stunts, help coordination, flexibility, balance, strength, self-confidence, agility, kinesthetic perception, courage, and rhythm or timing.

If students are given a strong program in basic tumbling skills and are required to master those skills, their chances for success on apparatus will be greater because movements learned in tumbling can be transferred to other activities.

It is essential to have a definite skill progression for each group or individual and to have students master the fundamental skills before attempting more difficult ones. The following is a list of skills to be covered in this chapter. They are listed in a suggested progression sequence; however, other progressions may be used, depending on the ability and size of the group.

The suggested progression is as follows:

Tripod
Tip-up
Headstand
Forward roll with variations
Handstand kick-up
Backward roll with variations
Dive roll
Handstand forward roll
Handstand chest roll
Cartwheel with variations
Back roll extension
Mule kick (snap down)
Limbre
Back walkover with variations
Front walkover with variations
Valdez

Hurdle
Round-off
Kip
Headspring
Handspring
Front handspring with variations
Mounter
Tinsica
Back handspring with variations
Side aerial
Front aerial
Back sommie
Round-off back sommie
Round-off back layout
Round-off full twist

In order to coordinate the spotting techniques and variations, skills are not described in the exact order. Some of the skills are oriented to the left or right. To perform the skills to the other side, reverse the directions. The code used in descriptions of the skills is on page iv.

SPECIAL CONDITIONING EXERCISES

TUCK JUMPS IN SUCCESSION (See C-11, page 15)

Purpose: To develop explosive power in the legs.
Technique: Spring vertically; bring knees to chest. Grasp ankles or hold legs around knees while suspended. Extend legs before landing.

STRETCH IN STRADDLE POSITION (See C-17, page 17)

Purpose: To develop flexibility in hamstrings and lower back.

Technique: Sit in wide straddle position; tilt pelvic area forward. Bend forward over knee, leading with chest; keep head up and arms back. Hold or bounce over right leg for eight counts. Hold or bounce between legs for eight counts. Hold or bounce over left leg for eight counts.

Variations: 1. Do not tilt pelvis; have arms overhead; round the back and reach forward, trying to touch the head to the knees.

2. With partner: Face each other sitting in a wide straddle position with soles of feet together; push and pull each other, trying to place upper body flat on floor when going forward and when going backward.

KNEES TO NOSE ON BACK (See C-24, page 19)

Purpose: To stretch hamstrings and Achilles tendon.

Technique: From supine position, lift legs (straight and together) and hips overhead to touch toes on mat behind head. Rest arms on floor at sides of body. Maintain straight knees, flex and extend ankles.

Variation: Grasp toes and pull legs closer to body.

PUSH-UPS (See C-6, page 14)

Purpose: To develop strength in triceps, rhomboids, and flexors and extensors in the forearm.

Technique: In a prone position place hands just under shoulders with fingers pointing forward. Curl toes under feet and extend arms, keeping entire body straight. Do not allow the hips to sag or to extend upward. Bend elbows, lowering body and allow chin to touch floor; extend arms so that body is pushed to the original position.

BACKBEND (bridge) (See C-23, page 19)

Purpose: ; To develop flexibility in the shoulders and lower back.

Technique: From a supine position on the mat, place the heels as close to the hips as possible. Place hands on mat at each side of neck (under shoulders) with fingers pointing toward feet. Extend arms and legs (look at fingers) and push body into arched position. It is very important to keep the arms straight. Rock backward and forward trying to force the shoulders forward of the hands.

Hint: Work with partner to learn. Partner assists performer in getting to arched position and aids with rocking motion. Partner should stand in front of performer (between legs) with one foot in front of the other. Place hands on lower back and upper hip area.

Variations: 1. Walk in backbend position.

2. Extend legs alternately to 90° while walking in backbend.

3. Go into backbend from standing position; hop from hands to feet.

4. Keep legs together and straight with feet flat on mat and push shoulders forward.

5. Touch toes, then go to backbend position from stand.

SPLITS (do both sides) (See C-14, page 16)

Purpose: To develop flexibility of the hamstrings and inner thigh muscles and to develop good split positions.

Technique: Standing on mat, step forward on right foot and turn left foot toward left side of body (similar to lunge position). Turn upper body toward forward foot and slide left foot back as far as possible. To learn, use the hands by placing them on the mat to the side of the body and force the body a little closer to the mat on each attempt.

Hint:	Sometimes it is better to do this exercise on the floor to enable feet to slide freely. Keep hips and shoulders square at all times.
Variations:	1. Stand with back to wall or some other flat surface. Bend forward and extend one leg up the wall. Force body as close to wall as possible with legs in split position.
	2. Stand with back to wall, heel of one foot touching wall. Have partner pick up other leg and try to lift it gradually to touch wall behind shoulder.

RUNNING (In place or laps around the gym)

Purpose:	To develop or strengthen flexors and extensors of legs; to stimulate circulatory system; to develop endurance.

LEG LIFTS

Purpose:	To develop strength in abdominals, hip flexors, and lower back muscles.
Technique:	Lie on mat in supine position, keeping small of back on mat. Lift legs (straight and together) about five inches off the mat, and move them into a wide straddle position; then return to starting position and lower to the mat. Repeat without resting.

SAFETY HINTS

1. Never allow students to tumble unless supervised.
2. Always tumble on mats.
3. Performers in a group should always work in the same direction to avoid collisions.
4. While others are performing, stay clear of the mats unless you are acting as a spotter.
5. Remove all jewelry before tumbling.
6. Keep mats clean and in good condition. Avoid tumbling on mats with tears or mats covered with any type of dust.
7. Use safety devices when necessary, e.g., spotting belts.
8. If mats are to be used in succession, they should be secured with tape, rope, or some other material that will keep them from slipping apart.
9. It is advisable to have student assistants if possible. Those girls should be given special instruction (before or after school) on correct spotting techniques.
10. Remind students that they should complete the skill being attempted and not "chicken out" in the middle of the skill.
11. Students should not be allowed to "goof off" at any time.
12. Advise students to keep eyes open at all times to develop kinesthetic awareness and to help prevent accidents.
13. Students should not tumble when fatigued.
14. Have a definite skill progression.

TUMBLING—TEACHING SUGGESTIONS

A piece of uncooked spaghetti can be maneuvered through space more easily than a piece of cooked spaghetti. Students can understand and relate to this as they experiment with tight and relaxed bodies in a standing position.

The following hints should become an integral part of your teaching patterns and vocabulary.

1. The head in almost all skills remains between the shoulders.
2. The arms are generally in three places.
   a) "up"—overhead, covering ears.

b) close to the body during twists.

c) close to the ankle area during sommies.

3. Moving into handstands, walkovers, etc., the forward leg acts as a fulcrum of a seesaw and the extended and rest of body as the seesaw (which does not bend at the hip). (See T-17, second position, page 50)

4. Moving out of back walkovers and cartwheels, the first foot to touch again acts as the fulcrum with the seesaw (the straight leg to fingertips). When the body has landed, the lunge looks very much like an empty seesaw. (See T-41, seventh position, page 50)

5. When one body part is directly over the other, movement is more efficient and there is less stress on the joints. (See T-3, page 44, and T-16, page 49)

6. When in an inverted position off balance, try to roll directly forward to avoid weight or stress being placed on one particular joint. (See T-17, page 50)

7. Teach students the fundamental principles of movements. Let them experiment in the basic skills with a small and large base for a headstand and discover why these analyses are necessary.

8. *Students should learn tumbling skills from a step or step hurdle. Many of these skills may be later transferred to the beam. Also by doing skills from just a step, more explosive leg power is developed.*

9. Just as it is easier to perform more efficiently as an uncooked piece of spaghetti, it is easier to manipulate or spot the person whose body is tight.

10. If students are taught correctly from the beginning and are ready for the next skill, chances are they need little spotting. Some of today's finest coaches spot very little, because they provide a good foundation and safe environment for learning.

LEAD-UP SKILLS

Before learning tumbling and acrobatic skills there are certain skills a student should master. These skills will help develop a better body awareness in space; they are skills that almost everyone can do with little effort.

TRIPOD (Fig. T-1)

PT From kneeling position place hands on mat at least shoulder width apart. Bend elbows and spread fingers apart. Place head on mat forward of the hands to form a triangular base. Lift hips upward by extending the legs and place one knee at a time on the elbows. Point toes toward ceiling. Hold for three seconds, and then come down one leg at a time.

SP Place one hand on back of neck and the other hand on the legs.

CE 1. Triangle (base) too small or too large.

2. Top of head rather than area of hairline on mat.

3. Elbows not stable while inverted. (Think about forcing them toward each other.

4. Trying to jump into position rather than controlling the leg lift.

Figure T-1

TIP-UP (Fig. T-2)

PT From squat position with knees apart, place hands on mat between legs (fingers spread apart). Press knees forcefully against elbows, which are slightly bent, and shift body weight to hands. Keep head up. Hold for three seconds and then return to squat position.

SP Kneel beside performer and assist by supporting shoulder and back of thigh.

CE 1. Arms not slightly bent.
2. Knees too far apart or too close.
3. Failure to keep head up.
4. Failure to elevate hips before tipping forward..
5. Failure to squeeze knees against elbows forcefully.

Figure T-2 side view

Figure T-2 front view

HEADSTAND (Fig. T-3)

PT From tripod, slightly arch back and bring knees together. Extend legs slowly to an inverted position while slowly shifting hips forward so the body will have a slight arch. Hold for three seconds, reverse procedure, and return to tripod.

SP For all variations of headstand: Stand to side of performer and assist with balance by grasping legs just above the knee or at the ankle.

CE 1. Top of head rather than hairline area on mat.
2. Not allowing back to slightly arch.
3. Not keeping calf and thigh muscles tense.
4. Allowing arms to collapse or wobble
5. Insufficient base of support (triangle).

Figure T-3

PT From prone position (Fig. T-4), lift hips to allow hands and head to form triangle on mat. Draw (or walk) hips to an overhead position. When hips are overhead, lift both legs (together and straight) to an inverted position while slightly arching the back. Keep calf and thigh muscles taut.

CE 1. Same as 1-4 from tripod position.
2. Failure to lift hips to an overhead position before extending legs vertically.

44

Figure T-4

KICK-UP (Fig. T-5)

PT From squat or lunge position, form a triangle with the head and hands. Draw one leg close to the chest, extend other leg to the rear. Lift the extended leg to an inverted position while pushing with the bent leg. Bring both legs together in the inverted position; extend body with a slight arch in the back. Hold three seconds and return to the mat, one leg at a time.

CE 1. Same as 1-4 of tripod technique.
2. Insufficient lift of first leg and push with the second leg.

Figure T-5

TUMBLING AND ACROBATIC SKILLS

FORWARD ROLL (Fig. T-6)

SL Beginner

PT From a deep squat position with the knees together, place hands on mat approximately eighteen inches in front of the toes. Push down backward with the feet to extend legs and lift hips upward. Bend arms and lower upper shoulder area to mat (head tucks at the last possible second before shoulder contact). Keeping legs extended, continue rolling, and as soon as hips have contacted the mat, tuck the legs and come to a squat position reaching forward with the hands. Eyes spot stationary object after returning to a squat position to assist in maintaining balance and to help prevent dizziness when doing several in a row.

45

Figure T-6

Hints: a) There should be a continuous motion from the squat position throughout the roll. If the performer stops or pauses in any one phase, it will be more difficult to complete the roll successfully.

b) The reason for keeping the legs extended while on the back in the inverted pike position and then forcefully tucking them as the hips contact the mat is to develop extra momentum to return to the squat position.

c) Having students learn to use their feet for pushing from the very beginning will enable them to catch onto other skills such as the dive roll more rapidly.

d) Have small youngsters or weak or overweight students roll down an inclined plane covered with a mat. This plane should be no more than a foot high. A reuther board or some homemade plank (both covered with a mat) could be used for this purpose.

SP Kneel to side of performer. Place hand on back of head and neck to keep her from placing her head on the mat. If the performer has difficulty returning to a squat position after rolling, place hand on back and push to assist her in returning to the squat position.

CE 1. Incorrect hand placement on mat. Hands should not be placed to side of knees.
2. Failure to push with feet to develop momentum.
3. Failure to bend arms, tuck head, and place shoulders on the mat.
4. Tucking head too soon (results in back flopping to mat).
5. Failure to keep legs extended while rolling and then to tuck them forcefully as hips contact mat.
6. Placing hands on mat to assist body to squat position after rolling.

MO 1. Continuous forward rolls.
2. Forward rolls to single leg squat and pose.
3. Forward roll to knee and pose.
4. Forward roll to V sit.
5. Forward roll straddle to split.

VA 1. *Remain in tuck position throughout* (Fig. T-7)

Figure T-7

2. *From stand to single-leg squat* (Fig. T-8)

Figure T-8

3. *Forward roll to knee pose.* (Fig. T-9)

Figure T-9

4. *From stand to knee to splits.* (Fig. T-10)

Figure T-10

5. *From stoop position to stand.* (Fig. T-11)

Figure T-11

6. *From straddle stand to straddle stand.* (Fig. T-12) As hips contact floor, place hands between legs (as close to body as possible) with fingers pointing forward to assist in pushing to straddle stand.

Figure T-12

7. *Without hands* (Fig. T-13). From deep lunge position tuck head and roll onto upper back and shoulder area, allowing back of hand and arm to contact mat (out to side of body). End in any of the above variations.

Figure T-13

DIVE ROLL (Fig. T-14)

SL Beginner

PT Assume semisquat position with shoulders forward of the feet and arms obliquely backward. Force arms forward and upward while simultaneously pushing with feet to extend legs and lift hips, causing the body to leave the mat and be suspended in air above the mat momentarily. Place hands on mat and support body weight. Bend arms with control, tuck head and lower upper shoulder area to mat and continue rolling.

Figure T-14

Hints: a) Start from a deep squat position and gradually raise the body as confidence is gained. Eventually the skill should be executed from a standing position, then a run.
b) On all rolls forward, it is essential to keep the head up until the last possible second. However, if this is mentioned in the beginning phases of learning, some students tend to collapse and fall on their heads, especially those with weak arms. If your class is fairly strong, I would recommend emphasizing this point from the beginning.

SP Stand in front and to the side of the performer. Place hand behind head and neck and assist in lowering body to mat without head touching the mat.

CE 1. Failure to push with feet and lift hips.
2. Failure to gain height as well as distance (not allowing the body to be momentarily suspended).
3. Failure to tuck head after arms start to bend and just before placing shoulders on the mat.

MO 1. Any of those skills mentioned for the forward roll.
2. Dive roll, headspring combination.
3. Dive roll, spring immediately into some type of jump.

VA 1. Dive over people or rolled up mats.
2. Dive through legs of person doing headstand with legs in straddle position.
3. Continuous dive rolls.
4. Dive through hula hoops.
5. Layout dive roll.

48

HANDSTAND

A good handstand position is a very important skill to master because the body passes through this position in performing many skills. It is advisable to learn where the body is and how or what it feels like partially upside down before attempting the handstand balanced position. One lead-up to the handstand should be a kick-up to near handstand position, switch legs and come to a stand.

Handstand kick-up (Fig. T-15)

SL Beginner

PT Lift arms overhead while simultaneously lifting right leg. Step forward onto right foot (as if making a small lunge) and bend right knee. Place hands on mat in front of shoulders. Swing left leg (straight) backward and upward. Immediately follow with a strong push from foot of right leg. Eyes spot hands. As soon as the body is almost inverted, switch legs and come to a stand on the left foot.

Figure T-15

SP 1. Grasp above knee with both hands on one leg, stretch body to fullest.
2. Stand to side and forward of performer. Place inside arm across abdomen (palm up) grasping waist and outside hand (palm up) under shoulder to keep performer from collapsing.

CE 1. Failure to maintain straight arms.
2. Allowing shoulders to move forward of the hand position.
3. Not keeping the head in line with the body.
4. Keeping the head too high.
5. Placing hands too far away from or too close to the feet.
6. Insufficient kick, push, or both.

Balanced handstand (Fig. T-16)

SL Beginner

PT In order to achieve the handstand or straight body position, many muscles in the body must work simultaneously. For a test of body tightness, stand in an erect position with the feet together and try the following:

1. Inhale to feel chest lift.
2. Pull in abdominal muscles.
3. Squeeze gluteal muscles (rear end).
4. Squeeze knees and ankles together.
5. Extend ankles to raise on toes.
6. Arms overhead, elbows by ears.
7. Do 1-6 all at the same time.

Figure T-16

49

8. From a relaxed position jump vertically to a relaxed body position.
9. From a relaxed position jump vertically to an extended body position (note difference between 8 and 9). N.B.: #9 is very similar to hitting the board for vaulting and springing vertically in a tight position.
10. Kick to handstand, relax, then tighten. This tight position is what should be hit immediately upon reaching the handstand. There should be absolutely no sags.

Checkpoints for balance

Shoulders over hands.
Hips over shoulders.
Heels over head.
Head in line with shoulders.

Hint: Use fingers (spread apart) to assist in balance by flexing them to feel as if they are trying to grasp the mat.

SP Stand to side but forward of performer. Grasp the leg (swing leg) above the knee as it reaches the inverted position. After student can almost balance herself, place arm (extended) toward back of her legs in case she should overbalance.

CE 1. Same as 1-5 in handstand kickup.
2. Failure to extend shoulders and hips (body should be straight with slight arch in back).
3. Allowing back to sag (body overarched).

MO 1. *Handstand forward roll* (Fig. T-17)

Figure T-17

SL Beginner

PT Slightly overbalance handstand, bend arms slowly; flex hips and go into pike position. Tuck head and place shoulders on mat and continue to roll.

CE Beginners have a tendency to keep arms straight too long, or tuck head too soon.

VA 1. Handstand forward roll with straight arms to pike.
2. *Handstand pirouette (quarter or half turn) into limbre or walkover.* (Fig. T-18)

SL Beginner

PT Shift weight to the hand that is in the direction to the turn. Quickly make turn, with eyes looking in the direction of the turn. Push off with, then lift opposite hand. After completing turn, go into limbre or walkover. Keep hips over shoulders throughout handstand position.

50

Figure T-18

3. *Handstand snap down (mule kick)* (Fig. T-19)

SL Beginner

PT Allow hips to lead body downward, flex knees slightly. Push forcefully from hands and lift chest while simultaneously thrusting from bent leg to extended leg position and land on mat.

CE Most common errors are not pushing with the hands and not coordinating the hand push, leg thrust, and slight hip flexion.

Figure T-19

4. *Handstand snap down, back handspring step out* (Fig. T-20)

Figure T-20

5. *Handstand to splits* (Fig. T-21)

SL Advanced Beginner

PT Slightly overbalance handstand position. As body is beginning the downward movement, split the legs and force the leading leg downward and through arms as the shoulders extend, hands push from mat, and hips are raised. Finish in deep split position.

CE Most common error is not keeping the hips overhead when the leading leg begins to move downward. When this occurs, there is not enough room to maintain straight leg position through the arms.

Figure T-21

6. *Handstand chest roll* (Fig. T-22)

SL Advanced Beginner

PT While in the handstand position, force head up and back as far as possible and maintain a very arched position. As the arms bend, lower the body to the mat, chest first, then roll until the toes contact the mat. Keep elbows close to the body when lowering the body to the mat. Finish in knee pose or roll on floor.

Figure T-22

VA *Yogi handstand* (Fig. T-23)

SL Intermediate

PT From handstand balanced position, flex the hips forcefully and allow legs to move into forward piked position. Simultaneously extend shoulders and bring head between arms to look at knees.

Figure T-23

BACKWARD ROLL (Fig. T-24)

SL Beginner

PT Assume a deep squat position with knees together (hands in front of body on mat partially supporting weight). Tuck head (chin to chest), push body backward off fingertips, and immediately transfer hands (palms up) to side of neck at shoulders. As hips contact mat, push downward on mat with feet and extend legs. Maintain straight legs until hands have contacted mat (palms down, fingertips toward hips). Place toes on mat overhead and simultaneously tuck legs.

52

As hips go overhead, keep elbows close to head and neck area, extend arms (push with hands), and come to squat position.

SP Kneel to side of performer; as hips are brought to overhead position, grasp waist of performer and assist in lifting hips overhead to squat position.

CE 1. Not keeping back rounded on roll.
2. Incorrect placement of hands at shoulders. (Fingertips should point toward hips.)
3. Failure to push with hands (extend arms) as hips pass overhead.
4. Pushing with one hand more than the other (results in a crooked roll).
5. Allowing the head to turn to the side.
6. Allowing knees to contact the mat instead of the toes.
7. Failure to eye spot when reaching squat position to assist in balance and prevent dizziness.

Figure T-24

MO 1. Back roll to standing position.
2. Back roll to squat, then execute some type of jump.
3. Continuous backward rolls.
4. Back roll, back roll extension.

VA 1. *Back roll to knee scale* (Fig. T-25)

Figure T-25

2. *Back roll to straddle stand.* (Fig. T-26)

Figure T-26

53

3. Back roll from straddle position to end in straddle position (Fig. T-27)

Figure T-27

Figure T-28

4. Back roll from stoop position (Fig. T-28)

SL Beginner

PT Shift hips backward, allowing shoulders to come forward. Keep arms straight and extended downbackward and upward as if to reach for mat. Slowly lose balance, keeping legs straight, causing body to go into deep pike position. Place hands on mat and immediately lower buttocks to mat and continue to roll.

BACK SHOULDER ROLL *(over right shoulder)* (Fig. T-29)

SL Beginner

PT From a squat or sitting position, lower back to floor and lift legs upward straight and together. Have arms at side of body on the floor. Continue moving legs over body until toes touch floor over right shoulder. Head should be turned with eyes looking toward knees. At this point bend knees; keep looking at knees; left arm will come off the floor. Then transfer remainder of the body weight onto knees in a sitting position.

CE 1. Stopping in the middle of the skill, thus losing momentum needed to get hips over shoulders.
2. Not placing knees on floor close to shoulders.

MO 1. Toe rise.
2. Knee spin.
3. Forward roll.

Figure T-29

BACK ROLL EXTENSION (Fig. T-30)

SL Beginner

PT Go through backward roll procedures to placing hands on mat under shoulders. As hips begin to pass over chest, thrust the legs by extending upward while simultaneously pushing with the hands (extend arms) against the mat. Come to a momentary handstand position. Snap down to standing position or lower one leg at a time.

Hint: Have spotter assist in performing this skill slowly, so the performer will know at what point in the roll to extend and what extending arms in an inverted position feels like.

SP Stand to the side and in front of the performer. As the legs begin to thrust vertically, grasp the legs above the knee and assist in lifting body to handstand position.

54

CE 1. Thrusting the legs too soon or too late.
2. Failure to thrust the legs vertically and push with the hands simultaneously.
3. Insufficient thrust of legs, insufficient push with hands, or both.
4. Failure to lift up back and arch back when arms extend.
5. Failure to attain handstand position before returning to mat.

MO 1. Snap down, back handspring.
2. Back extension, back roll.
3. Back extension to split (covered in handstand variations).
4. Back extension straddle down (covered in handstand variations).
5. Back extension stoop through.

Body here
should be vertical

Figure T-30

VA *Back roll extension, step out* (Fig. T-31)

SL Advanced Beginner

PT Performed the same as the back roll extension, except when the body reaches the handstand position, one leg is lowered to the mat before the other.

SP Same as the back roll extension.

Figure T-31

CARTWHEEL (left) (Fig. T-32)

SL Beginner

PT Facing forward, lift arms overhead while lifting left leg. Step forward onto left foot (bend knee) while shifting weight to that foot. Place left hand on mat with fingers pointing to left side of body (hand placement is to be directly in front of the body). Forcefully swing the right leg upward and immediately follow with a strong push from the foot of the left leg. (The legs maintain a straddle position throughout entire skill.) As the body executes a 90° turn, the right hand is placed on the mat about fourteen to eighteen inches directly in line with (and forward of) left hand. Push off the mat (about twenty inches or more from left hand) with slightly bent knee. As the left foot contacts the mat, the right leg is already in motion with a backupward swing. Right leg extends and the upper body is raised. The entire body ends up facing 90° (quarter turn) right of starting position. The eyes spot the hands as they are placed on the mat.

Hint: This is a four-count skill: hand, hand, foot, foot.

Figure T-32

SP For left cartwheel: Stand to left side and slightly forward of performer. As performer places hands on mat, grasp waist. Assist in keeping hips over hands. If the performer has difficulty with the second leg (left), slide the right hand to thigh and force the leg upward.

CE 1. Placing hands on mat simultaneously.
2. Placing the hands to the left of the body rather than directly forward in front of body.
3. Placing left hand too close to or too far from left foot.
4. Insufficient swing from right leg, insufficient push from left foot, or both.
5. Allowing shoulders and upper body to turn before hands are placed on the mat. This skill should be done in a straight line.
6. Allowing legs to close while inverted.
7. Failure to maintain straight arms and legs.
8. Allowing right foot to contact mat before left hand leaves.
9. Allowing hip to flex while inverted.
10. Failure to eye-spot hands as they are placed on the mat.
11. Failure to land with right leg slightly bent and to raise the body as the right leg is extending.
12. Failure to keep arms by head throughout skill.

MO 1. Quarter turn and a second cartwheel.
2. Quarter turn and stop in a handstand.
3. Quarter turn to any locomotor skill.
4. Quarter turn and cartwheel to opposite side.

VA 1. *Cartwheel quarter turn* (Fig. T-33)

Figure T-33

2. *One-handed cartwheel near arm* (Fig. T-34)

Figure T-34

3. *One-handed cartwheel far arm* (Fig. T-35)

Figure T-35

4. *Dive cartwheel* (Fig. T-36)

SL   Beginner

PT   Usually preceded by a hurdle. Same preparation as for cartwheel. Begin kicking and very strong pushing action, lifting the head and chest; reach forward and upward before placing the hands on mat. There will be a stronger push from the hands, and they will contact the mat almost simultaneously.

Stronger
lift with chest

Stronger push
with forward
foot

Figure T-36

LIMBRE (Fig. T-37)

SL Beginner

PT Kick to momentary handstand with eyes looking at fingers. Extend shoulders behind hand placement. As balance is lost, legs will move in an arc; arch back and place feet on mat so that body is in momentary backbend position. As soon as feet are flat on mat, push with hands and force hips forward over feet to allow the legs to extend (straighten knees). Arms are kept up by head until standing position is achieved.

   Hint: Head position is very important. The head must be kept in a normal position with arms stretched by the head at all times. If the head and arms are brought forward, the body will collapse into a sitting position. It is also very important to fully extend shoulders to cause the body to overbalance in order to go into the backbend position.

SP Stand to side of performer. As performer places hands on mat, grasp upper arm (with palm up and thumb to outside of arm) with inside hand. As the body arches, place the outside hand on the small of the back. As feet contact the mat, the outside hand forces the hips forward so legs can extend and the hand on the arm assists in bringing the body to an erect position.

CE 1. Not keeping head between shoulders in normal position through entire skill.
   2. Not keeping arms straight through entire skill.
   3. Failure to extend in shoulders after inverting.
   4. Allowing feet to "flop" to mat rather than placing them on mat.
   5. Failure to push with hands and to thrust hips forward in order to come to stand.

MO 1. Turns of any kind.
   2. Any locomotor skill.
   3. Walkover.
   4. Handstand or handstand forward roll with variations.

Figure T-37

FRONT WALKOVER (Fig. T-38)

SL Advanced Beginner

PT Lift arms over head while simultaneously lifting right leg. Step forward onto right foot (small lunge) shifting weight to right foot. Place hands on mat, shoulder width apart, and immediately swing left leg upward to invert the body, immediately push with the right foot (extend leg). Extend in the shoulders so that they go behind the heel of the hands. Keeping the legs in a wide stride position, allow the back to arch and place the left foot on the mat (close to the midline of the body). Push with hands and thrust hips forward and straighten left knee. Come to an erect position on the left foot keeping head, arms, and shoulders back until a controlled erect position is achieved. Right leg should be kept up high so it can be placed down on mat. Keep right foot extended in front.

Hint: Think of stepping over a hurdle with the right foot in order to keep it extended until the erect position has been achieved.

SP Same as for limbre.

CE 1. Not keeping arms straight throughout.
2. Not keeping arms by head throughout.
3. Failure to extend shoulders behind the hands.
4. Not arching lower back.
5. Failure to place foot on mat.
6. Allowing legs to go over crooked (to side of body rather than in vertical plane).
7. Not pushing with hands and thrusting hips forward.
8. Allowing second leg to catch up to first leg and be placed on the mat.

MO 1. Any locomotor skill.
2. Continuous walkovers.
3. Handstand.

Figure T-38

VA 1. *Switch legs while inverted* (Fig. T-39)

Figure T-39

2. Scissors leg while inverted (Fig. T-40)

Figure T-40

BACK WALKOVER (Fig. T-41)

SL Beginner

PT Stand on left foot with the toes of right foot on the mat and about eight to fourteen inches in front of the left. Lift arms foreupward, stretch (extend) vertically in the shoulders, head between arms, and allow the back to arch. (Keep hips over left foot until last possible moment. This will stretch the shoulders more.) As the hands contact the mat (about shoulder width apart), the right leg lifts vigorously upward and overhead. The left foot immediately pushes off the mat to allow the body to be inverted with legs in a wide stride (split) position. As the right foot contacts the mat with a slight knee bend, the hands push off the mat, and the body is raised to an erect position with left leg extended to the rear. After skill is learned, start with forward leg parallel to floor or higher.

SP Stand to side of performer. Place inside hand on lower back and outside hand on back of upper thigh of front leg. Assist by supporting lower back and helping to lift forward leg as hands contact mat.

CE 1. Failure to start with weight on one foot.
2. Failure to extend shoulders as well as to arch the back.
3. Allowing the hips to move forward of the feet while going into backbend position.
4. Not maintaining straight arms.
5. Not lifting forward leg vigorously as hands contact mat.
6. Failure to push off with hands and lift upper body as first foot contacts mat.
7. Failure to keep legs in a wide stride position.
8. Allowing legs to go out to side of body rather than moving in a vertical plane.

Figure T-41

MO 1. Any locomotor skill.
　2. Consecutive back walkovers.
　3. Back walkover, back handspring. Bring second leg to mat beside first foot and immediately spring into back handspring.

VA 1. *Back walkover to splits.*

From inverted position with legs in wide stride position, slightly overbalance and extend shoulders. Lift chest and forcefully thrust lead leg (leg in rear) between arms. Refer to Fig. T-21.

2. *Back walkover to handstand straddle down* (Fig. T-42)

Gain balance in handstand position from walkover. Allow shoulders to move slightly forward of the hand position as the legs move to a wide straddle position. Flex hips and allow shoulders to move backward of hand position. Lower hips to floor with legs in wide straddle position.

Figure T-42

KIP (Fig. T-43)

SL Advanced Beginner

PT From supine position on mat, lift legs and flex hips (together and straight) overhead, touching toes on mat behind head. Place hands under shoulders with fingertips pointing toward hips. Lower hips slightly; then simultaneously thrust legs forward, upward, and outward, and push forcefully with hands. Keeping arms straight and head up and back, come to stand with body fully extended (slight knee bend to absorb shock).

Figure T-43

　Hint: Learn to thrust legs first by extending hips vigorously. Then practice thrusting legs and pushing with arms to get into backbend (bridge) position.

SP Kneel (one knee) to side of performer. Place inside hand on upper arm and outside hand on small of back as leg thrust begins.

CE 1. Failure to lower hips before thrusting legs and pushing with hands.
　2. Insufficient thrust with legs, insufficient push with hands, or both.
　3. Leg thrust and hand push not simultaneous.
　4. Failure to keep head up and back until standing.
　5. Failure to keep arms back overhead until standing.

HEADSPRING (Fig. T-44)

SL Advanced Beginner

PT From squat position, place head and hands on mat forming a triangle. Place toes on mat with slight knee bend. Push through toes, extending legs and forcing hips to an overhead position. Keep the body in a pike position; as the hips continue past head position and loss of balance occurs, force (heels first) the legs foreupward (extending hips) and simultaneously push forcefully with the hands. Body is fully extended with arms over head as feet contact mat (with slight knee bend).

Hint: Sometimes it is advantageous to learn this on a rolled up mat.

SP Kneel (on one knee) beside performer. Inside hand grasps upper arm and outside hand supports lower back.

CE 1. Failure to allow hips to pass head position before thrusting legs and pushing with hands.
2. Failure to keep in tight pike as hips are going to overhead position.
3. Same as 2-5 in the kip.

MO 1. Any locomotor skill.
2. Another tumbling skill such as dive roll.

Figure T-44

VALDEZ (Fig. T-45)

SL Advanced Beginner

PT Sit on floor with left knee to chest (foot flat on floor), right leg extended. Put left hand on floor behind hips with arm straight and right arm forward horizontal. Thrust the right arm overhead while simultaneously extending the left leg and kicking with the right leg to push the body to an inverted position. As the body is reaching the inverted position, place the right hand on the floor next to the left (shoulder width apart) and rotate the left hand around so that both hands are pointing forward. Lower one leg at a time as in a back walkover.

SP Kneel at left side and place inside hand on lower back and outside hand on back of upper thigh. Assist in lifting to inverted position.

CE 1. Insufficient kick, push, or both.
2. Allowing arms to bend.
3. Not thrusting hips upward with leg push.

VA Some people prefer to have the forward arm on the same side as the bent leg.

Leg should be straight here

Figure T-45

HURDLE (Fig. T-46)

A hurdle is a step hop preceded by one or two running steps. It is used to transfer forward momentum up, then forward again with added force from the takeoff foot (push leg).

To practice: Step right, step left, hop left while keeping right leg behind and lifting arms overhead. Step onto right foot (bent leg) and immediately push from mat (extend leg) and lift the body vertically. Left leg is now behind and ready to kick backupward.

When coordination is learned, add one or two running steps. Allow each student to use the side that feels most comfortable to her for performing the hurdle.

European hurdle   **Figure T-46**   American hurdle

FRONT HANDSPRING (Fig. T-47)

Note: Basic tumbling skills such as front handspring, round-off, and round-off back handspring should be learned from a step without a hurdle. This forces the student to make maximum use of explosive power.

SL Beginner

PT Execute hurdle. Step onto right foot, bending knee. Place hands on mat in front of right foot (about eighteen inches) while simultaneously swinging left leg backupward. Immediately execute a very strong push with the right leg (which is bent under body) so that the legs will meet as the body passes through the handstand position. Extend shoulders and as balance is lost (when the legs and hips pass over hands), push the body away from the mat with the hands and shoulders. The body is momentarily suspended in air in a fully extended position. Reach for the mat with the toes. Body should be slightly arched upon landing, with head in a normal position, arms overhead, and a slight knee bend.

Hint: On the front handspring, front handspring step out, and tinsica, the legs are mainly responsible for inverting and rotating the body. The kick-push action of the legs should be emphasized along with the fact that, if the pushing action starts slightly before the hands contact the mat, the body will invert faster. If the kick-push action is quick and strong, the hands will support the entire body weight for a very short duration. Also, overbalancing from the inverted position can occur much faster so that the arms and hands do not push "dead weight."

SP Same as for front limbre.

CE 1. Uncoordinated hurdle and step.
2. Placing hands on mat before initial kick is made.
3. Placing the hands too close or too far away from the feet.
4. Insufficient thrust of right leg (extended leg); insufficient push from left bent leg.

5. Failure to extend shoulders, keep body stretched, and maintain arms overhead until feet make contact with the mat (knees slightly bent to absorb shock and assist in maintaining balance).

Note: When head and arms come forward after the hands leave the mat, this usually causes the hips to flex and the body to fall backward or finish the skill in a squat position.

MO 1. Step into any locomotor skill.
2. Front handspring, handstand forward roll.
3. Front handspring, walkover.
4. Front handspring, squat jump, back roll extension.
5. Front handspring to straddle seat. (See T-50, page 65)

Figure T-47

VA 1. *Front handspring step out* (Fig. T-48)

SL   Beginner

PT   Execute on the same principles of the handspring, but keep legs in a wide stride position throughout (as in a walkover). There must be a very strong kick and push with the foot of the second leg and with the hands so that the body will return to the mat with the lead leg almost straight and the hips forward of the foot that contacts the mat first. Keep head in normal position at all times.

CE 1. Same as 1-5 in handspring.
2. Failure to keep legs in a wide stride position throughout.
3. Failure to land on lead foot with hips forward of that foot.

Notice total body lift

Figure T-48

64

MO 1. Any locomotor skill.
2. Consecutive handspring step outs.
3. Round-off.
4. Aerial cartwheel or aerial walkover (front and side aerials).

VA 2. *Front handspring step out switching legs* (Fig. T-49)

SL Intermediate

PT Use same principles as for the handspring step out except that, while in the inverted position, reverse leg positions so that the back leg becomes the forward leg.

CE Most common error is switching legs too soon or too late, or allowing either leg to be directed sideways rather than straight forward.

SP Same as for front handspring.

Hips should be more forward over left foot.

Figure T-49

VA 3. *Front handspring to straddle seat* (Fig. T-50)

Figure T-50

FRONT HANDSPRING, FRONT SOMMIE (Fig. T-51)

SL Intermediate

PT From a well-executed front handspring, "punch" the mat with the feet, keeping arms in the vertical position. Spring upward; then whip the arms down and tuck chin to chest, as hips flex and knees bend to chest. Rotate three-quarters of a full spin; then extend legs, hips, and upper body to a stand.

SP As soon as the feet are ready to land from the front handspring, place the near arm (hand) across the abdomen with the palm up. As the performer is springing vertically, lift far arm upward to grasp her back and rotate body.

CE 1. Stopping after front handspring.
2. Tucking head and lowering arms before vertical lift.
3. Poor "punch" from mat, creating inadequate vertical lift.
4. Opening tuck too soon or too late.

Note: Whenever two skills are put together, e.g., front handspring, front sommie, round-off back handspring, etc., performer must execute first skill well and anticipate landing so explosive punch can occur for second skill.

MO 1. Round-off back handspring.
2. Forward roll back handspring.
3. Any kind of dance turn.

VA Front handspring, front sommie with a step out (front handspring front aerial step out).

Figure T-51

TINSICA (Fig. T-52)

SL Intermediate

PT Execute this skill as if you were going to do a handspring step out. The major difference is the hand placement on the mat. After the hurdle, step onto the right foot, bending the knee; simultaneously swing left leg upward, and immediately start the pushing action of the right foot. Place the right hand on the mat about eighteen inches in front of the right foot, and then place the left hand in front of the right hand (approximately ten to sixteen inches). Eyes spot hands as they are placed on the mat. The head remains up and back throughout the skill. As the body overbalances (hips falling toward mat), vigorously push with the hands and extend the shoulders. Maintain the legs in a stride position and land on the left foot, push the hips forward, and immediately step into the right foot (Fig. T-52).

SP Same as for front handspring.

CE In general, they are the same as for the handspring step out, plus failure to place the hands on the mat one after the other (in a straight line) and failure to allow the second foot to contact the mat after the first foot makes contact.

MO 1. Into any locomotor skill.
2. Consecutive tinsicas.
3. Tinsica, dive cartwheel.
4. Tinsica into round-off.

Figure T-52

MOUNTER (Fig. T-53)

SL Intermediate

PT Can be performed from a run and two-foot takeoff, a handspring, or a tinsica. From a two-foot takeoff, spring vertically, driving the hips upward to invert the body through a tucked or piked position. The hands can be placed approximately eighteen to thirty-six inches from point of takeoff. Push from the hands and shoulders to assist in the lift of the body upward, to the feet. Landing is the same as for a handspring step out.

SP Stand to side of performer. Place near hand on abdominal area and lift hips upward, then switch to arm. With far hand, lift at hip area as in handspring.

CE 1. Insufficient lift at hip area to invert body.
2. Failure to split legs as hands hit mat.

MO Any tumbling or dance skill.

Figure T-53

ROUND-OFF (Fig. T-54)

The primary purpose of the round-off is to change forward momentum into rearward movement.

SL Beginner

PT From a hurdle, step onto left foot, bending knee. Swing right foot forcefully backupward, and begin pushing action with the left foot as the left hand contacts the mat in a direct line of the body, with the fingers pointing to the left side of the body. Immediately place the right hand on the mat (about five inches in front of the left) with fingers facing to the left of the body. As the body passes through a handstand position, it will complete a 180° (half) turn. Force legs together while inverted (before the turn), and as the body is overbalanced, push hard with the hands and shoulders. Flex hips, force feet close to hand placement, lift the upper body. As feet contact mat, immediately punch and lift vertical.

Hint: Go through the skill in slow motion without a hurdle to get the feeling of bringing the legs together and turning before snapping the legs down. Have students jump (spring up) immediately upon landing as if rebounding. This forces them to push with their hands and raise their heads and chests as their feet snap to the mat.

SP When going through the skill in slow motion, spot as if spotting for a cartwheel. When performing from a hurdle, stand to the nonturning side and grasp hip area.

CE 1. Not placing hands on mat in direct line with body.
2. Insufficient kick, push, or both.
3. Failure to bring legs together and pass through vertical before completing the half (180°) turn.
4. Failure to push with the hands and lift the head and chest after feet have passed handstand position.
5. Failure to keep legs straight and together (slight knee bend when landing).
6. Failure to rebound vertically upon landing.

MO 1. Back roll extension.
2. Back handspring.
3. Back handspring series.
4. Back handspring, back sommie.
5. Back sommie.
6. Back aerial layout.

Figure T-54

BACK HANDSPRING (Fig. T-55)

SL Advanced Beginner

PT Stand with feet parallel and together. Keep arms at front of body and parallel to floor. Flex knees and hips, keeping shoulders over hips and begin to move backward as if to sit in a chair. As the sitting movement begins, the arms move downbackward. When balance is lost push vigorously with the legs and simultaneously force the arms foreupward and overhead. Extend in shoulders, and reach for the mat with the hands. The body is suspended in air momentarily before the hands contact the mat (shoulder width apart and approximately three feet from foot placement on the mat). Just after the hands contact the mat and the body passes through a handstand position, flex the hips and force (snap) the legs and feet to the mat while simultaneously pushing from the mat with the hands and lifting the head and upper body. Keep head in normal body alignment to prevent undercutting.

SP Stand to side of performer. Place inside hand on back of upper thigh and outside hand on small of back. Use outside hand to assist performer to maintain an arched position and to keep her from falling on her head (if she should bend her arms). Inside hand assists with leg thrust and snap down to stand.

> Hint: Some people find it helpful to start from a squat position, rock forward, then continue with above procedures from the squat position. Spotter on one knee with hands in same position as above.

CE 1. Failure to maintain shoulders over hips when sitting backward to lose balance.
2. Insufficient thrust of arms backward.
3. Allowing arms to bend when hands contact the mat.
4. Failure to keep legs together after takeoff.
5. Pushing with the feet too soon or too late.
6. Insufficient push with the feet and picking feet up from mat instead of allowing upper body to pull legs over.
7. Flexing hips too soon or too late (not allowing the body to pass through a handstand position).
8. Not extending the shoulders, pushing away from the mat with the hands, and not lifting the head and chest as the feet are about to contact the mat.
9. Allowing the feet to flop to the mat rather than being forced down.

MO 1. Continuous back handspring.
2. Back sommie.
3. Back aerial layout.
4. Jump, then to any other locomotor skill.
5. Split.

Figure T-55

VA *Back handspring step out* (Fig. T-56)

> **SL** Advanced Beginner
>
> **PT** Same beginning procedures as for the back handspring. As the body is passing through the handstand position, allow the body to slightly overarch, maintain one leg inverted, allow the other foot to be placed on the mat. Place the second foot on the mat. Foot placement on the mat is the same as for back walkover.
>
> **SP** Same as for back handspring.

Figure T-56

ROUND-OFF BACK HANDSPRING (Fig. T-57)

SL Intermediate

PT It is one thing to do the back handspring alone and the round-off as a single skill, but it is difficult to get a student to do them together for the first time. Some fear is involved as a change of direction is required while upside down. Go through the first couple in slow motion, but do not attempt to put the skills together until both are learned well. As the feet are coming down in the round-off, they should drive toward the hands. (This is to get the body into position so that it can go immediately backward.) As the feet contact the mat the knees are slightly bent with head and chest forward. The arms and upper body immediately extend upward and backward, and the legs extend explosively to complete the back handspring.

CE 1. Inadequate leg thrust on the round-off causing loss of momentum.
2. Not driving the legs under the body enough in the round-off.
3. Stopping between the two skills.

SP Have a designated spot for the performer to start and for her to place her hands on the round-off. Stand about two feet beyond hand placement area. As soon as the performer is coming down out of the round-off, place your outside hand on small of back and inside hand on back of upper thigh. Follow through as if you were spotting a standing back handspring.

Hint: In the learning process if the student fears this skill, have her do a handstand, snap down, then back handspring. This technique helps develop a bit more confidence.

MO 1. Series of back handsprings.
2. Round-off back handspring, back sommie.
3. Round-off back handspring, back layout or full twist.

Figure T-57

70

TIMERS FOR BACK SOMMIES, LAYOUTS, AND TWISTS (Fig. T-58)

PT Punch out of round-off, directly vertical and make the total body as rigid as possible. Stay in this position until momentum has stopped and spotter assists in lowering.

SP As performer punches out of round-off, place near hand on rump and back of thighs and other hand on shoulder. Direct total body upward, then lower as momentum slows down. Make sure to use the legs to assist with the lift.

Figure T-58

BACK SOMMIE (from standing position) (Fig. T-59)

SL Intermediate

PT Bend knees slightly and spring vertically, swinging the arms vigorously foreupward to assist in gaining height. As maximum height is attained, drive the knees to the chest, and rotate rearward in a tuck position. As eyes contact spotting point, extend the legs, keep raising upper body, and land on mat with knees slightly bent. Keep head between shoulders throughout.

Note: Before performer begins back sommie, she should pick out an object at eye level to keep looking for during rotation.

SP 1. Use spotting belts.
   2. One spotter to each side of the performer. Place inside hand on small of back (grasp garment if necessary) and lift or support throughout the skill. The outside hand is placed on the back of the thigh as soon as possible after tuck position is attained and assists in rotating the body. Never lose contact with the performer.

Poor body position. Lift should be vertical rather than backward.

Figure T-59

CE 1. Throwing head back any time during skill.
2. Failure to spring vertically.
3. Failure to gain sufficient height on jump.
4. Failure to force knees to chest and stay in tight tuck until ready to open.
5. Opening tuck position too soon or too late.

VA 1. *Round-off back sommie* (Fig. T-60)

    SL Intermediate

    PT When performing the back sommie or back layout out of a round-off, the feet do not drive in toward the hands as much as they do for the back handspring because on the sommie or layout the entire body must go directly upward before rotating. As the feet contact the mat from the round-off, the arms lift vertically as if jumping to reach the ceiling, with the head in normal position. The feet in essence "punch" the mat so the lift can be rapid and high. When reaching the peak of the lift, the knees thrust toward the chest, the head is in normal position, and the body starts rotation. When three-fourths of the sommie has been completed, extend hips and legs and lift upper body and head.

    SP Same as for round-off back handspring. Make sure contact is made on the round-off.

    CE 1. Stopping after the round-off—move must be continuous.
2. Not punching the mat out of the round-off to make the vertical lift.
3. Throwing the head and arms back immediately out of the round-off.
4. Not tucking enough.
5. Opening tuck position too soon or too late.

Figure T-60

    2. *Round-off back handspring, back flip*

ROUND-OFF BACK LAYOUT (Fig. T-61A)

SL Intermediate

PT From the round-off or round-off back handspring, "punch" the mat with the feet and immediately spring upward while lifting arms overhead. Squeeze the hips as tight as possible and lift with the chest. When maximum height is almost reached, tilt head slightly backward and keep lifting chest and squeezing hips. If body is kept completely tight, it will rotate around the head position. At this point arms may be kept at the side of the body.

    Hint: Learn layout on trampoline first.

SP As soon as performer lands from the round-off or back handspring, place hands on small of back and hip area. If the individual has learned this skill well enough on the trampoline first, all the spotter should have to do is assist with the lift. (T-61B)

72

CE 1. Throwing head and arms back immediately—should go UP.
2. Failure to lift with chest.
3. Failure to keep hips and legs tight and together.

VA Layout step out. When body is inverted in layout position, split legs and keep them split; then land on one foot followed by the other in a lunge position.

Body too
relaxed in hip area

Figure T-61A

Figure T-61B

TUMBLING

Learning fulls without a spot (Fig. T-62A, T-62B, and T-62C)

Using a twelve-inch landing mat, a port-a-pit, or a tumbling pit, gymnasts perform the following sequences. Insist that the body remain tight throughout each step and do not proceed to second phase until first is mastered.

A. Jump through a layout position to a front drop (prone position) on the mat. Both arms up by head. (Fig. T-62A)

B. Jump through a layout position making half turn to back drop. Keep arm to turning side up by head, look at armpit, and pull other arm across body in direction of turn. (Fig. T-62B)

C. Jump through a layout position making full turn to front drop. Keep arm to turning side up by head, look at armpit, pull other arm across body forcefully then to vertical position. (Fig. T-62C)

Figure T-62A

Figure T-62B

Figure T-62C

FULL TWIST (Fig. T-63A)

SL Advanced

PT (Must learn good back layout first, then learn the twist on the trampoline or on mats as suggested in T-62A, B, C.) From back handspring or round-off, "punch" the mat and lift vertically as if to do a back layout. As body starts backward motion, turn the head over left shoulder and look for left hip area. Left arm can rest on chest at this point and right remains up. Keep looking for hip and, as body rotates, pull right arm across chest and left arm lifts up. As one-half of the spin is completed, both arms will be in front of the body, usually crossed. Eyes focus on mat at this time and remain focused here until skill is completed. As feet pass head position, the hips will slightly flex before landing. Both hands will lift to forward-upward position. Body must stay tight throughout skill.

74

SP 1. Hand spot (T-63B).
2. Learn on trampoline using twisting belt.
3. Use twisting belt on floor until adjusted to twisting on mats.

Figure T-63A

Figure T-63B

CARTWHEEL AERIAL (to the left) (Fig. T-64)

SL Intermediate

Lead-ups:

1. Cartwheel from lunge to lunge inward.
2. Dive cartwheel, then dive cartwheel with one hand.
3. Use reuther board to get extra spring.

PT From hurdle, step forward, keeping the head and chest high and not allowing the chest to go forward of the foot position, and forcefully swing the right leg backupward; then immediately push very strongly with the left foot. Put arms up on the hurdle, and as the swing-push leg action is started, swing them down to the side of the body. The arms may keep moving with the body or may be brought to the side of the body and bend and remain in this position throughout. As right foot lands on mat, followed by left foot, lift the head and chest.

Figure T-64

SP 1. Place inside hand palm up on abdomen. Place outside hand on shoulder with fingers pointed toward floor. As performer rotates, support body with hand on shoulder and lift waist area forcefully up and over with hand that is on waist area.

2. Stand to nonturning side of body; place both hands in hip and thigh area and lift (Fig. T-65).

Figure T-65

3. Stand to nonturning side of the performer. As the body is turning to inverted position, grasp waist and assist by lifting the entire body as with regular cartwheel (Fig. T-66).

Figure T-66

CE 1. Uncoordinated hurdle.

2. Allowing the shoulders and head to drop too far forward or move forward of the feet.

3. Insufficient swing, push of the legs, or both.

4. Not allowing the body to make quarter (90°) turn as push foot leaves mat.

5. Failure to place leading foot under body as much as possible.

6. Failure to continue lifting head and chest upon landing.

Note: The body when finishing should be facing more the direction of the skill when started rather than directly sideways.

VA Glide aerial. (Chassé aerial)

76

FRONT AERIAL (Fig. T-67)

SL Low Intermediate

PT From hurdle, lean slightly forward keeping head and chest high. Do not allow shoulders to go forward of the feet. Vigorously swing backupward with the back foot; then immediately push with the forward foot. Bring arms from overhead position to sides of the body or allow them to continue backward. Arch the back and maintain legs in a wide split position. Land on swing leg first. When foot contacts mat, keep head back and chest up.

Hint: Learn from standing position. One spotter to each side of the performer. Grasp hand and as performer is inverting, place other hand on shoulder to assist in lifting throughout skill.

Figure T-67

SP 1. Stand to side of performer. Place inside hand on abdomen as skill is started. Lift and support about halfway through. Put outside hand on small of back; lift and support through the last half of the skill (Fig. T-68).

Figure T-68

2. Stand to side of performer, and as shoulders move forward, place inside hand on abdomen and outside hand under shoulder and assist in lifting throughout rotation. This method is also used for side aerial.

CE 1. Same as 1-3 in aerial cartwheel.
2. Failure to keep the legs in a wide split position throughout.
3. Failure to continue keeping chest and head up after landing on first foot.

TUMBLING ROUTINES FOR CLASS, Beginning to Advanced

Tumbling routines for class will depend on the ability level of the students involved. Each class should be given routines that they can perform with little difficulty but that will be challenging. Performers should start and end routines at attention or some other static position.

Suggested routines:

Forward roll, dive, forward roll, step out, cartwheel. (Fig. T-69)

Figure T-69

Handstand, forward roll, limbre, cartwheel. (Fig. T-70)

Figure T-70

Cartwheel, quarter turn, cartwheel, quarter turn, handstand, forward roll. (Fig. T-71)

Figure T-71

Right cartwheel, left cartwheel. (Fig. T-72)

Figure T-72

Back roll, back straddle roll, back roll extension. (Fig. T-73)

Figure T-73

Back roll extension, back walkover. (Fig. T-74)

Figure T-74

Front walkover, turn, back walkover. (Fig. T-75)

Figure T-75

Fast cartwheels. (Fig. T-76)

Figure T-76

Front walkover, cartwheel, quarter turn inward, back walkover. (Fig. T-77)

Figure T-77

Front limbre, front handspring. (Fig. T-78)

Figure T-78

Front handspring step-out series. (Fig. T-79)

Figure T-79

80

Round-off, back handspring. (Fig. T-80)

Figure T-80

Cartwheel, back handspring. (Fig. T-81)

Figure T-81

Back walkover, back handspring. (Fig. T-82)

Figure T-82

Front handspring step out, round-off, back handspring. (Fig. T-83)

Figure T-83

Back handspring series. (Fig. T-84)

Figure T-84

Side aerial series. (Fig. T-85)

Figure T-85

Front aerial, side aerial. (Fig. T-86)

Figure T-86

82

Front aerial, back handspring. (Fig. T-87)

Figure T-87

Front handspring, front sommie. (Fig. T-88)

Figure T-88

Round-off, back handspring, whip back, back handspring. (Fig. T-89)

Figure T-89

Round-off, back handspring, back sommie. (Fig. T-90)

Figure T-90

83

Round-off, back handspring, half-turn, front sommie. (Fig. T-91)

Figure T-91

Front handspring step out, front handspring, front sommie. (Fig. T-92)

Figure T-92

Front handspring, front sommie, round-off, back handspring, back sommie. (Fig. T-93)

Figure T-93

84

Cartwheel, side aerial, round-off back sommie. (Fig. T-94)

Figure T-94

Round-off, back handspring, full twist. (Fig. T-95)

Figure T-95

chapter five

FLOOR EXERCISE

Floor exercise is the most beautiful event in women's gymnastics. To perform well in this event, a gymnast must be an "actress on the floor," able to convey a feeling or create an atmosphere that will stimulate and impress the audience and judges.

In competition, the exercise is performed in a 12 X 12 meter area. The gymnast must cover the entire area within the sixty-to-ninety-second time limit.

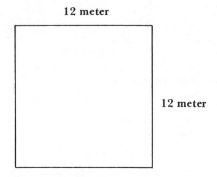

12 meter

12 meter

COMPONENTS OF A FLOOR-EXERCISE ROUTINE

1. *Tumbling and acrobatic skills.* These must be incorporated with smooth transitions into and out of moves.
2. *Dance.* Ballet, modern, and jazz dance skills are used mainly as connecting moves or as static and semistatic position. They are also used to vary the tempo and for change of direction.
3. *Locomotor skills.* Skills such as leaps, hops, and jumps add variety to a routine. They are used to vary the tempo and level and to give the routine a more dynamic and explosive appearance.
4. *Static positions.* Poses and holds are included in a routine for variations in tempo and level so that the routine will not be monotonous. Poses are held only long enough to show control in that particular position or to gain a desired effect.
5. *Variations in level.* A routine should be composed of skills on the floor (e.g., splits) and in the air (e.g., leaps) and positions that could be considered a middle level (e.g., arabesque).
6. *Changes in direction.* Changes should be fluid and varied (e.g., battement tourney, chainé turn, round-off, reversed stag leap).
7. *Variations in tempo.* A good routine is not monotonous since some of the movements included are fast, slow, percussive, sustained, etc. These movements or sequences should fit and express the tempo of the music used.
8. *Floor pattern.* A floor design that meets the requirement of covering the entire area and allows the gymnast to move with grace and continuity is of utmost importance. Skills should not always be performed in a straight line but should vary in different patterns that will add to the beauty of the routine.

9. *Dynamic opening and ending.* Whether slow or fast, the opening of a routine should set the stage for the remainder of the exercise. The ending should also be dynamic and should convey a happy feeling.

10. *Difficulty.* A competitive routine must contain seven elements of difficulty, three superior difficulties and four medium. These can be tumbling, dance, or locomotor skills, or combinations of these skills. A list of these difficulties can be found in the F.I.G. code of points.

11. *Use of entire body.* The entire body must be used in a routine. Body lines are important for aesthetic beauty and can be varied to meet this requirement. Moves of flexibility and agility must be shown, but moves of strength must be avoided.

12. *Music.* The music, which must be played by a single instrument, should fit the routine. It must be dynamic when the skill combinations are dynamic, light when the skill combinations are light, etc.

COMPOSITION

A gymnast has almost unlimited freedom when composing a routine because she must conform only to the basic rules of time, difficulty, space to be covered, and form. Creating or putting together combinations of tumbling and acrobatic skills, ballet, modern dance, and jazz moves, and locomotor skills in an original and exciting manner is not an easy task. Most gymnasts change sequences in a routine many times before the entire routine is fluid, enlightening, and completely harmonious throughout.

If a girl is strong in tumbling, she should include many tumbling sequences, along with meeting the other requirements of composition. If a girl is proficient in dance, many dance combinations should be included as long as they do not dominate the routine.

Change of direction and passes should not be repetitious; they should be fluid, elegant, and express the creative ability of the performer. *Be original.*

DANCE FOR THE GYMNAST

One does not have to spend years training in ballet technique to become proficient and graceful in performing dance skills in the floor-exercise event. It is always advantageous, though, to have some type of training or exposure to dance to learn proper body carriage and skill techniques.

The following skills have been selected for description since they are adaptable to movement in floor exercise or are excellent exercises to develop leg strength and proper body positions. The skills will be divided into two categories: (1) ballet and (2) modern dance and jazz.

Ballet

Fundamental Positions for the Arms and Feet

In all positions you should be concerned with correct body alignment. Abdomen is taut, shoulders relaxed, and hips pulled under the body, causing the back to be more straight than curved. head should be up at all times.

FIRST POSITION (Fig. F-1)

Arms: Held in a circular pattern in front of and away from the body. The elbows are slightly bent so that the hands are just below waist level. It is helpful to think that you are holding a very large ball. Palms face inward.

Feet: Heels together with toes pointing outward. Force the little toe onto the floor to maintain correct arch in the foot.

SECOND POSITION (Fig. F-2)

Arms: Held sideways with a very slight bend in the elbow to give a soft rather than a rigid appearance. Make sure that the arms are slightly forward of the body and the thumb is under the second finger (as if holding a small ball with the thumb and finger). Palms face down. First finger is the extension of the arm. It is now acceptable to have the palms face forward and upward depending on the move being performed.

Feet: In same position as for first position but about twelve inches apart.

Figure F-1

Figure F-2

FOURTH POSITION (Fig. F-3)

Arms: One is in first position, the other in high fifth (which is curved overhead and slightly in front of the body).

Feet: One foot is approximately twelve inches in front of the other with the heel of the forward foot in line with the arch of the back foot.

FIFTH POSITION (Fig. F-4)

Arms: Both arms curved overhead and slightly in front of the head.

Feet: Heel of right foot against toe of left foot. Toe of right foot against heel of left foot. May be reversed with left in front.

Figure F-3

Figure F-4

Many girls look awkward, clumsy, or unpolished in floor exercise simply because they do not know what to do with their arms. Arms are very important in creating proper body lines. This part of the body should not be neglected when training for the floor-exercise event.

The arms should hold a definite position and move smoothly from one skill to another, avoiding very jerky or wavering movements (unless for a specific effect). Always think of the arms as coming from the middle of the back rather than from the shoulder joint.

Exercises for Developing Proper Flexibility and Body Positions for Dance Moves

DEMI-PLIÉ (may be done in any position) (Fig. F-5)

PT Keeping upper body erect, bend the knees and return to original position. Heels must remain in constant contact with the floor.

Note: Pliés are very important for developing flexibility in the legs and for upper body control. They are used when taking off and landing in locomotor, tumbling, and dance skills. Pliés should be done daily as a part of conditioning. It is suggested that they be done in all positions, both at a barre and away from a barre. If a barre is not available, a chair will suffice.

CE 1. Allowing shoulders to move forward of the hips.
  2. Allowing back to curve greatly with the hips protruding in the rear rather than keeping them under the shoulders.
  3. Allowing the heels to come off of the floor.
  4. Allowing the knees to stay to the medial line of the body rather than come outward directly in line with the toes.

BATTEMENT TENDU (Fig. F-6)

PT Starting position: Arms in second, feet in fifth. Lift the heel of the forward foot and slide the foot as far out as possible. Place the heel down and snap back to fifth position with the heel leading.

CE 1. Poor body alignment.
  2. Allowing back leg to bend.
  3. Allowing supporting hip to relax (sag).
  4. Allowing forward leg to bend when returning to the original position.

BATTEMENT DÉGAGÉ (Fig. F-7)

PT Starting position is same as for battement tendu. The movement is the same as for the battement tendu, but the foot is lifted one inch off the floor and the entire movement is done faster.

Figure F-5   Figure F-6   Figure F-7

GRAND BATTEMENT (may be done forward, backward, or sideward) (Fig. F-8)

PT Starting position: Arms in second, feet in fifth (right in front). Slide right foot forward, then lift as high as possible and return to original position. The toe touches the floor first, then the heel touches. The heel pulls the leg back to the original position.

CE 1. Poor body alignment, especially at the hip area.
  2. Failure to rotate forward leg outward from the hip.

Figure F-8

ROND DE JAMBE A TERRE (en dehors) (Fig. F-9)

PT Starting position: Arms in second, feet in first. Begin with plié. Move right foot forward; lift heel and keep toe on floor. Move foot in circular pattern forward and around; then return to original position. Perform eight circles front, then eight circles back, then switch legs.

CE 1. Allowing working knee to relax.
2. Not enough outward hip rotation.

GRAND ROND DE JAMBE EN L'AIR (en dehors) (Fig. F-10)

PT Starting position: Arms in second, feet in fifth (right in front). Grand battement with right leg, carry to side, then to the rear. When returning to the original position go through first to a grand battement in front.

CE 1. Poor body alignment.
2. Allowing either leg to bend.
3. Allowing shoulders to move forward or back as the leg circles.

Figure F-9

Figure F-10

GRAND ROND DE JAMBE EN L'AIR (en dedans) (Fig. F-11)

Same as en dehors except that back leg will be lifted to the rear, then forward.

PASSÉ POSITION (Fig. F-12)

PT Start in fifth position. With forward foot, draw toe to ankle and up the inside of the leg to the knee. Shift to the back of the knee and slide down the back of the leg to the ankle.

Figure F-11

Figure F-12

DEVELOPPE FORWARD (Fig. F-13)

PT Starting position: Arms in second, feet in fifth with right in front. Bring right foot up to knee (to passé position); then extend forward at least 90°. Lower toe to floor and slide back to fifth position.

CE 1. Failure to keep knee of bent leg rotated outward.
2. Extension of forward leg not high enough.
3. Allowing supporting leg (knee) to bend while lifting leg.
4. Allowing supporting hip to relax (sag).

DEVELOPPÉ SIDEWARD (Fig. F-14)

Same procedures for developpé forward except that the leg lift is sideways.

Figure F-13

Figure F-14

ÉCHAPPÉS (Fig. F-15)

PT Starting position: Arms in second, feet in fifth, with right in front. Demi-plié, jump to second in demi-plié, return to fifth with same type of jump.

CE 1. Allowing hips to protrude rearward.
2. Failure to keep knees turned outward.

Figure F-15

ASSEMBLÉ (Fig. F-16)

PT Starting position: Arms in second, legs in fifth with right in front. Demi-plié, and slide left foot out to second on the floor. Hop on right foot extending toes, and land in fifth position with left foot in front. Arms move to second position on hop.

Figure F-16

Ballet Moves That Can Be Used in Floor Exercise or Beam Routines

The body positions and skills are sometimes varied for use in a gymnastic routine. If the skill starts and ends in the same position, gymnasts, due to the nature of their exercise, will complete only the first half of a skill or will make additional movements.

ATTITUDE (Fig. F-17)

PT Start on both feet with body erect. Shift weight to right foot, lift left foot rearward bending the knee outward. Keep upper body erect at all times. The left arm is in fifth position, and the right arm is a little below second. For gymnastics, the arm positions will vary.

ARABESQUE (Fig. F-18)

PT Start with weight on both feet and body erect. Shift weight to the right foot, and lift left leg (straight) rearward turned out from the hip. As the left leg is lifted as high as possible, the upper body will have a slight forward lean. Arms may be in second; in opposition; left arm to side of the left leg, right arm forward; or both arms forward, one slightly lower than the other.

CE 1. Allowing the upper body to bend while leg is being lifted in rear.

Figure F-17

Figure F-18

CHANGEMENT (Fig. F-19)

PT Starting position: Arms are in first or second position; the feet are in fifth with the right in front. Plié, then spring upward, and land in fifth position with left foot in front.

Figure F-19

JETÉ (Fig. F-20)

PT Starting position: Arms in second position, legs in fifth position facing forward. Demi-plié, leap forward, slide left foot to second position with straight knees, spring to left foot from the right foot, Sur le coup de pied in back. Alternate from side to side moving forward.

92

Figure F-20

BALANCÉ (Fig. F-21)

PT Starting position: Arms start in first position and move to second, then back to the first; legs are in fifth position. From the fifth position, the right foot in front, step on a diagonal and step left foot forward to close to fifth position behind the right. Step right in place. May be done forward or back.

Figure F-21

GLISSADE (Fig. F-22)

PT Starting position: Arms in second, feet in fifth. Slide back foot to second position and close front foot to fifth. Movement is very similar to that of slide when stepping and shifting weight.

Figure F-22

PAS DE CHAT (sideward) (Fig. F-23)

PT Starting position: Arms in second, feet in fifth, left in front. Lift forward foot through passé position (heel in, knee out). Spring onto left foot, and allow the right leg to pass through the bent leg position before landing in back of the left in fifth.

CE 1. Failure to keep knees turned out as far as possible.
2. Failure to keep upper body erect.
3. Failure to go through passé position.

Figure F-23

PAS DE CHAT (forward) (cat leap) (Fig. F-24)

This is used more in gymnastics than the regular pas de chat. Usually preceded by a step.

PT Starting position: Feet together (arms in second). Step onto right foot; bend left leg lifting knee (through developpé position). Spring onto left foot while lifting and bending right leg. Arms go to first position while body is suspended and return to second as foot contacts floor. Step onto right foot.

CE 1. Insufficient knee bend.
2. Allowing body to lean forward or backward.
3. Failure to keep heels inward of knees.

Figure F-24

CABRIOLE (forward) (sometimes called a hitch kick) (Fig. F-25)

PT Starting position: Feet in fifth (left in front), arms in second. Step forward on left foot, demi-plié. Thrust right leg to 90° angle upward. Bring left leg up to right leg, and have calf of right contact shin of left leg. Lower left foot to floor and return right foot upward to at least a 90° angle. The upper body leans slightly backward as the legs make contact. Reverse movement for back cabriole.

Figure F-25

94

CE 1. Allowing right (top) foot to be lowered to contact left (bottom).
    2. Failure to keep legs straight while suspended.

SISSONE (back closed) (Fig. F-26)

PT Starting position: Right arm forward and left in second. Legs in fifth with left foot in front. Plié on both knees and spring diagonally backward on right foot while left foot is raised in front. Land on right foot and drop left to front fifth position in a plié.

Figure F-26

SISSONE (forward closed) (Fig. F-17)

Reverse the movements for the back sissone in closed position. This skill is the same as a push leap.

Figure F-27

CHASSÉ (Fig. F-28)

PT Starting position: Arms in second, feet in fifth with right in front. Demi-plié on left foot as right foot steps forward. Demi-plié on right, springing off the floor and bringing the left leg to contact the back of the right leg. Land on the left foot. (Same movement principles as for slide and gallop, only performed forward.)

CE Allowing the rear foot to pass the forward foot.

Figure F-28

CHAINÉ (small turns done in a straight line or on a diagonal) (Fig. F-29)

PT In moving left, step left and start turning; step right beside the left foot and finish one full (360°) turn. The arms move to second on the step and slightly close to low fifth (slightly below waist curved in front of body) on the completion of the turn. Eyes should spot an object to the left and maintain that focus as long as possible. Chainés should be practiced on the half toe.

Figure F-29

PIQUÉ BACK (Fig. F-30)

PT   Stand on the right foot with the left raised on the back of the right calf. Step back on the left foot. Turn 360° to the left with right foot on calf of left leg.

Figure F-30

PIROUETTE (Fig. F-31)

PT   Start from fifth position with the left foot in front. Step on the left, inward rond de jambe on right, and throw left arm outward for speed. Do one or more spins on the left. Just before completion of the turn, drop the right foot in front of the left and pivot as the turn is finished. Keep arms close to first during turn.

Figure F-31

TOUR JETÉ (from glissade forward) (Fig. F-32)

Refer to balance beam chapter for descriptions. (Fig. B-24, page 132)

Figure F-32

TOUR JETÉ (from glissade backward) (Fig. F-33)

Figure F-33

Modern Dance and Jazz Moves

A gymnast can show her creative ability by using the modern dance and jazz moves for connecting sequences in her floor-exercise routine. These moves are usually in the form of locomotor skill variations and static positions. However, it is suggested that these forms of dance not dominate the routine.

Locomotor Skill Variations (For other variations refer to Chapter III.)

SCISSORS KICK (preceded by a step) (sometimes called a hitch kick) (Fig. F-34)

PT Step onto the left foot and kick the right leg up as high as possible. As right leg begins downward motion, force the left leg upward. Land on the right foot. Keep arms in second position throughout the skill.

CE 1. Failure to keep upper body erect.
2. Failure to switch legs in air.

Figure F-34

CABRIOLE FORWARD WITH BENT LEGS (Fig. F-35)

PT Step onto right foot and kick the left foot up as high as possible. Lift the right foot up to touch the left. At this point both legs bend with knees turned out, and contact is made with the toes. Lean upper body slightly backward as the toes contact. As the right foot returns to floor, straighten left leg and return upward. Arms are in second position throughout the skill.

CE 1. Insufficient thrust of first foot.
2. Failure to allow upper body to lean slightly backward when toes contact.

CANCAN KICK BACKWARD FROM KNEES (Fig. F-36)

PT Keeping upper body straight or with very slight forward lean, bend right leg and kick backupward. As the right leg is returning to the floor, bend the left knee and kick backupward. *Keep knees together on kicks.* Keep arms in second position.

Figure F-35

Figure F-36

STEP SLIDE

A. *Leg forward* (Fig. F-37)

PT From a chassé or other locomotor skill, step onto right foot (bending knee) and kick left leg forward and upward as high as possible. As left leg is kicking, allow the upper body to lean backward, and extend right leg to allow body to be lifted so that only the toes of the right foot remain on the floor for the sliding action. When momentum is lost, come down on sliding foot, and allow upper body to move forward and go into another skill.

Figure F-37

B. *Leg sideward* (Fig. F-38)

PT Same principles as leg forward except that the forward leg kicks to the side.

98

Figure F-38

C. *Both legs bent* (Fig. F-39)

PT Same principles as above. Body is in croisé position or the step-hop position (as described in Chapter 1) with both legs bent.

CE (For F-37, 38, 39)
1. Insufficient kick with the forward leg.
2. Failure to extend the back leg to lift the body weight up so that the toe of the front foot can slide freely.
3. Failure to lean body backward on slide.

Figure F-39

HOP, STEP HOP (Fig. F-40)

PT Step onto the left foot, lift the right knee to the chest, curl the upper body forward over the knee and hop on the left foot. Arms are obliquely backward. Step forward on the right foot (directly from tucked position), lift the upper body, bring arms forward and up to a forward oblique position, and hop on the right foot, keeping the left leg extended in the rear and off the floor.

Figure F-40

JUMP WITH BENT LEGS REARWARD
(Fig. F-41)

PT Spring vertically,, keeping the upper body (from knees up) in a straight line. Bend the legs as the feet leave the floor and lift the arms to a forward horizontal position.

CE Allowing the hips to flex.

VA During the jump, execute 180° or 360° turn.

Figure F-41

SIDE STEP AND KICK (Fig. F-42)

PT Moving sideways, step with the left foot to the left; step behind the left foot with the right; quickly step left with the left foot; then step in front of the left with the right. Swing the left leg sideways and upward as the right arm stays in second and the left arm moves down to the side of the body in front of the left leg.
Count: 1-2 and 3-4
      1 step, 2 step back, and step, 3 step front, 4 kick.
       l   r   l   r   l

Figure F-42

STEP HOP KICK TO A SEMISQUAT POSE (Fig. F-43)

PT Step on a diagonal with the right foot; kick the left leg upward as a hop is executed forward and upward on the right foot. While in the air, the body is leaning slightly backward. Land with feet together, knees and hips slightly flexed, and upper body directly over the feet. On the jump, keep arms in second position; on landing, move them alongside the body (natural hanging position), with the wrists flexed and fingers pointing outward.

Figure F-43

SCHOTTISCHE STEP (Fig. F-44)

PT Run right, run left, run right, and hop right.

Figure F-44

POLKA STEP (Fig. F-45)

PT Hop on left, step forward on right, step beside the right with the left foot, and step forward with the right.

Note: The schottische and polka step may be used for variations of movement into a tumbling sequence.

Figure F-45

Moves and Static Positions (Refer to Chapter 6, page 135, for other static positions.)

BODY WAVE (Fig. F-46)

PT Assume a squat position on the floor with the arms horizontally forward, palms up. Slightly flex the elbows and move the arms downward and backward to an oblique position. Bring arms forward overhead as the body comes to an erect position. Force the knees forward, straighten the legs pushing the hips forward, arch the back (keeping the shoulders back), and then hunch the shoulders slightly forward as the legs straighten completely.

Note: Arms move with body movement upward.

Figure F-46

ROLL TO BODY ARCH FROM PRONE POSITION (Fig. F-47)

PT From a prone position on the floor with the arms bent and hands just outside the shoulder, lift the left leg from the knee (upper part of leg remaining on floor), roll over on the right side, extending the left arm and place the left foot on the floor by the right knee. Use the right hand to push the upper body to a sitting position, and slide the right hand close to the hip. When the body reaches the sitting position, move left arm to a forward horizontal position. Extend the hips so that the body is arched and supported on the right hand and the right and left feet. Move left arm to an overhead position. Return to a sitting position, and go into a seat spin, into a backward roll, or execute a valdez.

Figure F-47

STEP HOP' KICK TO KNEE POSITION ON THE FLOOR (Fig. F-48)

PT Step onto the right foot and hop on the right while lifting the left leg forward and upward. As the right foot contacts the floor from the hop, bend the left leg, and move it past the right leg to a kneeling position on the floor.

102

Bend right knee as left leg is placed on the floor. Keep arms in second position or in opposition to the legs.

Figure F-48

KNEE SPIN (Fig. F-49)

PT Kneel on right knee with left leg bent (at right angles to foot and floor). Turn toward the right. As the body has completed a quarter turn (90°), place the left knee on the floor, and lift right knee and foot from the floor (keeping knee bent). Spin 270° right on the left knee to complete the full 360° turn. Upon completion of the turn, place the right foot on the floor with the knee bent at right angles to the body. *Do not allow the hips to flex on any part of the turn.*

Arms: To begin, bring the right arm (parallel to floor) across the body to the left side. As the turn begins, force the right arm to the right to assist with the spin. The left arm remains in second position and slightly to the front of the body.

Figure F-49

SEAT SPIN (Fig. F-50)

PT Sitting on the floor, bring the knees to the chest and lean toward the direction of the turn, allowing the hands to initiate the spin. Turn the head and shoulders in the direction of the spin. Turn 180° or 360°.

VA May have one leg extended (as in V seat) and the other leg bent (Fig. F-50).

Figure F-50

103

BACK SPIN WITH LEG CIRCLING FROM SPLIT POSITION *(right leg in back)* (Fig. F-51)

PT From a deep split position swing the right leg forward to an inverted position as the body rolls onto the back. Keeping the legs as wide apart as possible, make a large circle. As the left leg goes to an inverted position, bend the right leg, and come to a kneeling position; then stand or execute another skill from this position.

Figure F-51

STATIC POSITIONS (Fig. F-52)

Just changing the arm or leg positions in many of the standard poses may create a different effect. Instead of having palms down or wrists extended, try turning the palms up on some poses and flexing the wrists on others.

Remember that not everyone looks good performing the same pose because of various body types.

Use a full-length mirror and try to find the static positions that are most becoming to you as an individual and ones that will achieve the desired effect. Be original.

Figure F-52

104

TRANSITIONAL MOVES AND COMBINATIONS

Beginnings

1. Fig. F-53

Start in corner 1, facing corner 3. Forcefully extend right leg to rear while lifting body to left toe. Have arms from fifth position to an overhead oblique position. Hesitate momentarily; then run, hurdle, and execute a fast tumbling pass toward corner 3.

Music: Fast, dynamic, and continual.

Figure F-53

2. Fig. F-54

Stand in corner 1, facing corner 1. As music begins, shift weight on left forward leg, right leg extended to rear with toe on floor. Right arm obliquely forupward and left arm forward horizontal. Bend left knee and then extend it as the body makes half (180°) turn. (Saute or supersole.) Arms pass through downsideward position to original position on turn. Step, push, leap, step, pivot turn 180° on left bringing right foot to left, and execute back handspring step-out to a lunge.

Music: Mazurka portion from "Coppelia."

Figure F-54

3. Fig. F-55

Start in middle of area facing between corners 3 and 4. After music begins, jump and land sitting on heels with upper body leaning forward over the knees, arms obliquely back. Forcefully lift upper body and place right foot (toe) on floor to the right, body weight supported by left leg; right arm overhead and left arm forward. Make 90° turn to left while lowering right knee to floor and raising left knee (left toe still on floor). Reverse arm position by going through second position. Perform forward roll without hands with right arm leading under left leg.

Come to squat, make 180° turn right, and perform a split jump. Land in semi-squat position, twist body from left to right, take three running steps, and slide forward with other leg forward and upward.

Music: *Asia Minor.*

Figure F-55

4. Fig. F-56)

Stand about ten feet in from corner 2 facing corner 3; place arms at sides and feet together. Perform a C jump; step into lunge; then execute forward roll without hands to the knee, then to split. Make 180° turn in seat spin, pause momentarily, and perform valdez.

Figure F-56

5. Fig. F-57

Stand in middle of floor exercise area. Step and execute jump turn 360° on right while lifting left leg at 90° angle from hip (parallel to floor). Land on both feet. Immediately perform back handspring to split. Lift upper body over back knee, stand, step into piqué turn and pose. Run, run, leap, step, two chaîné turns, and pose.

106

Figure F-57

Note: The five above sequences have been described from various positions on the floor so that the readers will realize that not all floor exercises must start from any particular part of the 12 X 12 meter area. The suggested music is only for those movements described and is just an example of the types of music that can be used. It is highly recommended that the desired music be improvised and that students not use one song or piece of music in its entirety because they were not written for this purpose. The above sequences may also be used as passés within a routine rather than as openings.

Sequences for Routines

1. Fig. F-58

Chassé, step, step push leap, chainé turn 360°, step, cat walk, grand battement, forward roll without hands to stand.

Figure F-58

107

2. Fig. F-59

Run, run, leap, step, semisquat turn (feet together) 180°, grand battement front walkover.

Figure F-59

3. Fig. F-60

Run in a circle (four runs), back cancan kick from the knees, step push leap, step hop, cartwheel.

Figure F-60

4. Fig. F-61

Kick turn, arabesque, forward roll, stand, pose, step, front cabriole, run, run, stag leap.

Figure F-61

5. Fig. F-62

Back walkover, glissade backward, step, tour jeté, open toe turn (360°) run, front handspring.

Figure F-62

6. Fig. F-63

Forward roll without hands to the knee, then into splits. Back roll to squat stand, arch jump, step, battement tourney, step, scissors kick, step, pose.

Figure F-63

7. Fig. F-64

Round-off back handspring, back handspring step out, lunge pose, arabesque, glissade, step, tour jeté.

Figure F-64

8. Fig. F-65

Hop, step hop, run, front handspring step out, forward roll without hands to single-leg squat, stand, step, cat walk.

Figure F-65

9. Fig. F-66

Chassé, step, step, turn, back roll from stoop position to knee scale, 90° turn toward extended leg in rear, stand, glissade, step, tour jeté, toe rise with feet together and forward, arms over head, run, front handspring step out.

Figure F-66

10. Fig. F-67

Back walkover to arabesque, toe rise with feet together and forward—arms down and obliquely down and back; three runs in a semicircle to jeté forward, step, open toe turn, step, front cabriole with bent legs.

Figure F-67

11. Fig. F-68

Chainé, turn, piqué, turn, run, run, leap, step, semisquat turn (feet together), run backward with the upper body curved forward, toe rise, round-off back handspring.

Figure F-68

12. Fig. F-69

Saute, step, back cabriole, step, cartwheel with quarter turn, walkover, step, pose.

Figure F-69

13. Fig. F-70

Kick turn (battement tourney), step, back cabriole, step, cat walk, grand battement, front walkover (scissor legs), illusion splits to splits.

Figure F-70

14. Fig. F-71

Pose, cartwheel with quarter turn, chassé, step, cabriole with bent legs, handstand forward roll to knee, knee spin, stand, pose.

Figure F-71

15. Fig. F-72

Forward roll to squat position, body wave, step hop, step hop, front limbre, step, pas de chat sideways.

Figure F-72

114

16. Fig. F-73

Side step and kick, 90° turn toward lifted leg, cartwheel with quarter turn, run, run, hurdle, round-off back handspring step out.

Figure F-73

17. Fig. F-74

Back handspring to splits, seat spin to back roll, come out in pose, extend leg back, arms up, glissade, step, tour jeté with half pivot turn immediately upon landing, run, run, step slide.

Figure F-74

18. Fig. F-75

Polka step, hurdle front aerial, front walkover, step hop kick to kneeling position on the floor, half turn on knee, cartwheel with quarter turn, step, step hop, and jump to a semisquat pose.

Figure F-75

19. Fig. F-76

Balancé right, balancé left, step right on right and execute piqué (360°) turn right, grand battement with left foot upon completion of the turn, chassé, step, cat walk, front limbre (or walkover).

Figure F-76

20. Fig. F-77

Front handspring to straddle seat, seat spin 360°, valdez, half turn, run, run, run, step slide, step push leap.

Figure F-77

ROUTINE COMPOSITION FOR CLASS

Mass floor exercise seems to be the answer to involving large classes in the floor-exercise event. With limited space in most schools, the floor pattern and duration of the exercise will probably have to be altered from that of competitive requirements.

Mass floor exercise should involve more dance and locomotor skills than tumbling moves if the routine will be performed on the floor without a regulation mat.

This type of activity assists in developing grace, poise, and rhythm as well as introducing dance and locomotor skills. The students will also gain an appreciation for and understanding of the event when performed by an advanced gymnast in competition.

These routines can be created in advance or can be a class project. If your background in dance is limited, take advantage of those students in your classes who have had training in dance. Students enjoy the opportunity to assist in composition. Also, some of the compulsory routines could be used even if, by modification, a few of the tumbling skills were omitted. Compulsory routines can be found in the DGWS Gymnastic Guide, or USGF Handbook.

chapter six

BALANCE BEAM

The scope of imagination and creative capacity that enhances balance-beam performance is unlimited. This four-inch-wide, sixteen-foot-long piece of apparatus presents a challenge to the student because much body control and courage must be exhibited to manuever the body through the intricacies of the skills and routines performed on the beam. A few years ago one would not believe that girls would even think of performing aerial cartwheels on the beam, but conquering this and similar skills are now a must for a gymnast with international competitive desires.

It is advisable that students practice all skills on the floor (preferably on a line) first to develop proper technique. The skills should next be practiced on a low beam to develop confidence, then finally on a beam of regulation height. In a class situation where you have so many body types and levels of ability, it is suggested that students work and be graded on a *low* beam. This will eliminate a great deal of fear, and students with lesser abilities will find more success. The low beam is also safer and will require less teacher supervision. Skills on the beam will be divided into the following categories:

> Mounts
> Locomotor skills
> Turns and pirouettes
> Static positions
> Tumbling and acrobatic moves
> Dismounts

GENERAL SAFETY HINTS

1. Students should not be allowed on the equipment unless supervised.
2. Surround the beam with mats.
3. Check before each class period to make sure beam is secure in its supports.
4. Use safety aids, such as beam training pads, for certain skills if possible.
5. Spotters should be alert at all times to avoid accidents. Whenever possible, arrange to have certain students informed in advance of spotting techniques.
6. Avoid mounting the beam around the supports (exceptions being when mounts are performed from the end of the beam).
7. Tell students to get off the beam when fatigued in order to avoid accidents.
8. If the reuther board is used to mount the beam, it should be removed as soon as the performer is on the beam and out of the way. If the students are just practicing mounts, the board does not have to be moved each time. Many times in competition the board is not moved.
9. Wear nonrestrictive clothing and proper footwear.
10. Have a definite skill progression designed for each class.

Note: In the following skills, where certain parts of the body have been designated, such as "the right foot," it has been done only for ease of clarification.

TEACHING SUGGESTIONS

Since working on the beam requires a balance adjustment, the following suggestions are offered.

1. Make the beam(s) as low as possible. Use benches or bleachers. Have students stand on beam and attain a straight body position. Ask them to move right or left shoulder out of line, then try to correct imbalance. Try with other body parts until students have feeling of the importance of a straight body.

2. Mark areas on walls for students to look at while working on turns. Eye spot is important for balance.

3. Turns are generally done on toe. Body should be in correct alignment and total body should lift at time of turn.

4. Concentration is a must; distractions must not be allowed.

5. Students with adequate training should mount the beam and walk the beam slowly—then hop, run and leap. Never perform skills without first orienting self to space.

6. One end of the beam can be used for mounts while the other is being used for dismounts.

7. Several students can practice turns at the same time.

MOUNTS

FRONT SUPPORT TO STRADDLE SEAT
(Fig. B-1)

PT Stand facing beam (toward middle); place both hands across the beam with fingertips facing away from the body. Jump to a front support with straight arms, upper thighs resting on beam. As the right leg is lifted sideways, up and across the beam to a straddle position, shift the weight to the right hand

Figure B-1

119

and turn the left hand across the beam so that the heels of the hands are together. Then lift left leg to complete the straddle position on the beam.

Hint: To learn, allow the legs to lower to the side of the beam and move directly into the straddle sitting position. When more abdominal strength is developed and confidence is gained, maintain legs in wide straddle position as above.

SP Stand on opposite side of the beam; hold upper arms while in a front support to help support and control the performer.

CE 1. Failure to allow shoulders to move forward of the hand position on the beam.
2. Failure to maintain straight arm and leg position throughout mount.
3. Failure to shift weight to one hand when going into straddle position.

MO 1. V seat: Place both hands on beam behind the body and lift the legs forward and upward. Do not allow the head and shoulders to slump.
2. To squat position: While leaning forward and shifting weight to hands, swing legs downbackward, then upward to a squat position on the beam with one foot slightly in front of the other. Eyes spot end of beam throughout movement.

CE 1. Failure to keep arms straight on backswing of legs before feet are placed on the beam in a squat position.
2. Failure to lean forward (shoulders over hands) throughout backswing.
3. Failure to lift the heels higher than the hips on the backswing before the squat position.

KNEE-SCALE MOUNT (Fig. B-2)

SL Beginner

PT Stand facing the beam; place both hands across the beam. Jump to a straight arm support while simultaneously placing the right knee (not shin) on the beam. Left leg is extended to the rear. When springing upward to straight arm support, allow the shoulders to be forward of the hand position. For full extension of the knee scale, change the hands to the opposite grip (fingers pointing toward feet), keep shoulders and head up, and fully extend the left leg to the rear.

Figure B-2

SP Stand to opposite side of beam. Support upper arm and hip area.

CE 1. Failure to use spring from legs for getting into knee position on the beam.
2. Failure to allow shoulders to lean forward of the hands on the jump to the straight-arm support.
3. Failure to maintain straight arms in a knee-scale position.
4. Failure to keep head and shoulders up.

MO Quarter (90°) turn right or left on knee to knee scale parallel to length of beam; pose, then stand.

VA Use reuther board placed perpendicular to the beam. Take a running approach into the knee-scale mount.

SQUAT MOUNT (Fig. B-3)

SL Beginner

120

PT Stand facing beam with hands across the top of the beam. Jump to straight-arm support allowing the shoulders to move slightly forward of the hand position. Lift knees to chest, then land on beam with both feet between hands in a deep squat position. Head should be held up at all times.

SP Stand on opposite side of beam and support upper arms, or stand to side of performer and grasp upper arm with inside hand and back of upper leg during the squatting action.

CE 1. Failure to maintain straight-arm position.
2. Jumping into rather than up and onto the beam.
3. Failure to keep hips low when squatting.

MO 1. Quarter (90°) right or left into pose.
2. Quarter (90°) turn right or left into forward roll.
3. Stand, quarter (90°) turn right or left into a pose or other locomotor skill.

VA Single-leg squat mount.

Figure B-3

WOLF MOUNT (Fig. B-4)

SL Beginner

PT Stand facing the beam with hands across the beam. Jump to straight-arm support while lifting one knee to chest; then put foot on beam between hands and lift the other leg (straight) to the side of the body and parallel to the beam. Keep the hips low and the shoulders slightly forward and up. The head should be forward and up at all times.

Figure B-4

SP Stand on opposite side of beam and support upper arms of the performer, or spot one arm and squatting leg.

CE 1. Failure to maintain straight arms.
2. Failure to allow shoulders to move slightly forward of the hand position when jumping onto the beam.
3. Failure to tuck one leg and extend the other leg to the side simultaneously.
4. Failure to keep the extended leg straight.

MO 1. Right leg bent. Quarter (90°) turn right into deep lunge, then stand or perform forward roll.
2. Right leg bent. Quarter (90°) turn left to pose, then stand and continue.

121

STRADDLE MOUNT (Fig. B-5)

SL Beginner

PT Jump to straight-arm support, allowing shoulders to move slightly forward of the hand position while simultaneously extending the legs sideways in a wide straddle position. Head should be held up and forward.

SP Stand on opposite side of the beam and support the upper arms.

CE 1. Failure to keep arms straight.
2. Failure to allow the shoulders to lean forward of the hand position.
3. Failure to lift the hips high enough to allow the legs to remain straight and for placement on the beam.

MO Quarter (90°) turn right or left into a lunge position; then stand or go into a forward roll.

VA 1. Use reuther board placed perpendicular to the beam.
2. *Free aerial straddle* (Fig. B-6)

    SL Advanced beginner

    PT Same general procedures as for the straddle mount except that the feet do not touch the beam; instead, allow them to pass over the beam and maintain a straddle position across it.

    SP One spotter on opposite side of beam to support upper arms. Second spotter steps in from behind performer to make sure she does not fall backward as her legs straddle.

    MO Quarter (90°) turn maintaining straddle position; sit, go into V seat, then into backward roll, or swing the legs downbackward and upward to a squat position on the beam.

Figure B-5

Figure B-6

SINGLE-LEG SHOOT THROUGH TO STRIDE LEG POSITION (Fig. B-7)

SL Beginner

PT Place hands across beam. Jump to straight-arm support while simultaneously lifting the hips high enough to allow one leg to bend; bring knee to the chest; then extend leg forward across the beam. Other leg remains straight at all times. Keep the head and shoulders forward and up.

SP Stand beside performer's shoot-through leg, grasp upper arm, and support throughout skill.

CE 1. Failure to maintain straight arms.
2. Failure to allow shoulders to move forward of the hand position.
3. Failure to elevate the hips high enough to allow one leg to bend and pass over the beam.
4. Failure to follow through with shoot leg (extend knee and thrust leg forward).
5. Allowing shoot-through knee to turn outward rather than lifting it directly toward the chest.

MO 1. Rest on beam in stride position, quarter (90°) turn to a V seat.
2. Rest on beam, quarter (90°) turn, backward roll.
3. Rest on beam, quarter (90°) turn, swing legs downbackward and upward to squat position on beam.

122

Figure B-7

FORWARD-ROLL MOUNT (usually done with reuther board placed at end of beam) (Fig. B-8)

SL Beginner

PT At the end of the beam place both hands on the beam with the heels of the hands facing each other. While springing from feet, extend arms; elevate hips high enough to be able to tuck head and to place the back of the neck and upper back on the beam. When neck and upper back have contacted the beam, immediately shift the hands to the bottom of the beam. Keep the elbows close to the head and pull with the hands to maintain balance, Keep body in piked position and lower body to beam as if trying to make each vertebra contact the beam, one after the other.

SP One spotter on each side of the beam. One standing beside performer to keep her in the inverted position by lifting her thighs to get hips overhead. Second spotter helps lower body to beam by grasping performer's waist. Second spotter stands to back of performer as she is rolling.

CE 1. Failure to maintain straight-arm support and to allow the hips to get high enough to tuck the head.
2. Not tucking the head soon enough.
3. Failure to transfer hands to bottom of beam and to pull to help maintain balance.
4. Failure to remain in pike position while lowering body to beam.

MO 1. To V-seat position.
2. Roll to squat stand; immediately stand.
3. Roll to crotch (straddle) seat position; swing legs downbackward and upward to a squat stand on beam.
4. Roll to squat stand, pose, then stand.

Hips not up high enough

Figure B-8

123

VA 1. *Forward roll to lever* (Fig. B-9)

    SL   Beginner

    PT   Same preparation as for regular forward-roll mount; after tucking head and lowering back of neck and upper shoulders to beam, extend body (hips foreupward and legs foreupward and down) to lever position, then continue to roll.

Figure B-9

2. *Swing-forward roll* (Fig. B-10)

    SL   Advanced Beginner

    PT   Jump to front rest support on end of beam (hands across beam with heel of hands toward each other). Immediately swing legs forward and upward to a straddle position. Allow shoulders to move forward of the hand position as the legs forcefully swing downbackward and upward. Lift hips; tuck head, lowering upper shoulders to beam; shift hands to bottom of beam; then continue to roll.

    SP   Spot same as for forward-roll mount on beam.

Hips should be higher

Figure B-10

STEP-ON MOUNT (usually done obliquely to or at end of beam) (Fig. B-11)

SL   Beginner

PT   After approaching the beam from an angle, swing the inside leg foreupward onto the beam, followed by the outside leg. (Leg action is very similar to the scissors kick in the high jump.) Put second foot on the beam slightly in front of the first. Extend legs when kicking but immediately tuck in order to land in a squat position. Upper body must be slightly forward to allow momentum to carry the body up onto the beam. Keep eyes focused forward and upward.

    Hint: To learn this, use the hand closest to the beam until in a squat position. Eventually the hand should not come in contact with the beam.

SP   1. Hold outside hand of performer and run with her, giving assistance on the jump.
      2. Stand on the opposite side of the beam and reach across the beam to grasp the performer's inside hand and upper arms.

124

CE 1. Failure to use one-foot takeoff..
2. Failure to swing the inside leg vigorously foreupward.
3. Failure to keep momentum going forward by slightly leaning into the jump.
4. Trying to stand too soon on the beam after reaching the squat position.

MO 1. Immediately stand after balance is attained in the squat position.
2. Pose, then stand.
3. Forward roll.
4. High squat jump.

Figure B-11

VA *At end of beam* (Fig. B-12)

SL Beginner

PT From a running approach and one-foot takeoff, spring vertically and step onto the end of the beam. The foot that makes first contact with the beam is the foot that did not make contact with the reuther board. The second foot doesn't usually touch the beam until a static position has been shown.

Figure B-12

HALF-TURN STRADDLE MOUNT ON END OF BEAM (Fig. B-13)

SL Beginner

PT Learn on lower beam, then raise beam and use reuther board. With a two-foot takeoff, grasp end of beam with both hands, arms extended. Immediately make a half turn left while removing left hand from beam. As body comes to sitting position on beam, right hand may be placed on beam in front of body for support.

SP Grasp waist area and assist in the lift and turn.

CE 1. Not jumping high enough before turning.
2. Removing left hand too late.

MO 1. Backward roll.
2. V seat; then swing legs downward and upward to squat stand.

Figure B-13

SHOULDER STAND (Fig. B-14)

SL Intermediate

PT Approach the beam from an oblique run. Grasp the top of the beam (thumbs on top, fingers down the side). With a two-foot takeoff, lift the hips forcefully so they arrive just above the shoulders as they are placed on the beam. (Approach from the right, place left shoulder on beam and vice versa.) When the hips are vertical, the legs can be split or stag. At this point some girls find it necessary to slide the hand on the balancing shoulder side to grasp under beam.

SP Stand facing performer. As hips rise, lift and support waist and hip area.

CE Not lifting hips high enough.

MO 1. Shift hands, forward roll.

Figure B-14

126

HANDSTAND MOUNT (using reuther board perpendicular to beam) (Fig. B-15)

SL Advanced Intermediate

PT Run and place hands across beam. Jump to straight-arm support while simultaneously raising hips overhead (inverted position). Keep arms and shoulders extended at all times. When hips are over hands, shoulders will be slightly forward of hands. At this time extend harder in shoulders, pulling them back. Continue lifting legs to handstand position.

SP Stand in front of performer on opposite side of beam. Grasp hips and help them overhead. (May have to stand on something to be high enough; or keep beam very low.)

CE 1. Failure to maintain straight-arm support.
2. Failure to spring enough to attain inverted position.
3. Failure to keep hips overhead while lifting legs overhead.

MO 1. Stoop down to beam, quarter turn, pose.
2. Straddle down to beam and use any suggestion given for movement out of straddle mount.
3. Quarter turn to English handstand and forward roll.
4. Quarter turn to English handstand and swing down or chest roll.
5. Stoop through to V sit crossways on beam, quarter turn and backward roll.

Hint: Should master a press handstand on floor before attempting this skill on beam.

Figure B-15

HANDSTAND MOUNT ON END OF BEAM (Fig. B-16)

SL Advanced Intermediate

PT From run and two-foot takeoff on reuther board, punch board as if vaulting and place hands on end of beam. Drive hips upward keeping arms straight with head up (eyes looking in front of hands), legs staying close to the body in a straddle position. When hips are over hands, extend legs upward to a completely stretched handstand position. At all times keep shoulders over hands and do not allow back to arch.

SP Two spotters in the beginning. Stand on floor beside board and beam. As performer takes off board, grasp upper arm with near hand and hip area with far hand. Steady arm and assist with lift in hip area. One spotter could stand on a solid object at side of beam and grasp waist area as hips are coming over shoulder position.

MO 1. Forward roll.
     2. Walkover.
     3. Pirouette.

Figure B-16

CARTWHEEL MOUNT (Fig. B-17)

SL   Advanced

PT   Place reuther board about one foot from end of beam. From a two-foot takeoff on the board, lift the total body vertically as the first hand grasps the end of the beam. Quickly split the legs to the second lift upward. As the second hand contacts the beam, the hips may be slightly toward end of beam, not directly over shoulders. Momentum will bring body weight forward and first leg will begin to lower to beam, followed by second to end in lunge.

SP   Stand to back of gymnast at end of beam on stack of mats or spotting box. Grasp waist and hip area and guide through cartwheel to lunge.

CE   1. Insufficient total body lift from the board.
     2. Not passing through the vertical plane.

MO   1. Any movement from a lunge position, e.g., turn, leap, or back walkover.

Figure B-17

AERIAL MOUNT (Fig. B-18)

SL   Intermediate

PT   From the side of the beam, with or without a board, step approximately one foot from the beam to a lunge. Drop head and shoulders below beam as arms reach backupward toward

128

beam. Simultaneously, forcefully drive the back leg upward while pushing vigorously off the forward leg (as in an aerial on floor). Hands contact beam and hips basically roll over beam to sitting position.

SP On lowered beam:

1. Stand to side of performer. Have her bend over, grasp the beam, then kick up and over. Spot shoulder and help lift hip.
2. Spot shoulders at side of beam.

CE 1. Insufficient kick and push of legs.
2. Lifting head and chest too soon when coming up.

Figure B-18

LOCOMOTOR SKILLS

Locomotor skills are a major part of balance-beam performance; however, they are mainly used as transitional and contrasting moves. These skills must be practiced individually, but when a routine is being composed, there must be continuity from one skill to the next. The following skills should be practiced on the floor first, then transferred to the beam. Since most of the skills have been previously discussed in Chapter 3, only information pertinent to the balance beam will be mentioned.

Spotting for most locomotor skills is usually done to the side of the beam. The spotter walks along with or stands by the performer and offers an outstretched hand at all times, so that she may assist in maintaining balance or preventing a fall. It is very important for the spotter to know what skills are being performed and to be alert at all times.

Walks

FORWARD WALK

SL Beginner

PT Stand with body erect, abdominals tense, hips tucked under body. Lead with the toe, leg slightly turned out from hip. Arms hold definite position. Take small rather than large steps. Eyes spot end of beam (never look at feet) or stationary object at eye level.

CE 1. Walking flat footed.
2. Body posture incorrect.
3. Taking too large or too small a step.
4. Body too tense.
5. Allowing arms to dangle.

MO Usually not more than one or two walking steps are made at one time in a beam routine, so almost any of the tumbling skills, poses, and other locomotor skills can be done out of the walks.

VA 1. Walk high and low with various combinations.
2. Walk backward, allowing the foot to extend to the side of the beam as it is moving to the beam in back of the body.
3. Increase speed of walk and gradually develop into a run.

Hops, Leaps, and Jumps

These locomotor skills should be learned on the floor first because they require the body be momentarily lifted above the beam. Toes leave the beam last when taking off and contact the beam first when landing. These skills are always started in a demi-plié (slight knee bend with heel off of beam) position and ended in a demi-plié or some other position that allows for flexion of the knees to absorb shock, allows for smooth landing, and assists in maintaining balance. The upper body is almost always held erect except in skills used to convey certain body lines. The arms should be soft and flowing and also used to assist in gaining or giving the impression of attained height. When the leg goes backward in a certain skill, it is turned out from the hips rather than extended directly backward.

It is very important that hops, leaps, and jumps be explosive and show maximum height and full body extension. If the skills are to be used for height, the movement must start and end in the same vertical plane; if they are to be used for distance, then loss of balance forward should occur before movement is taken forward and upward.

When spotting, stand to side of beam and offer outstretched hand to performer at all times.

Suggested combinations of locomotor skills (foot and arm positions should be reversed so performer will not become one-sided):

1. Step, step hop, run, run, jump into deep squat.
      l   l   r   l   slightly in front of l
2. Grand battement forward, changement, slide, step, cat walk.
      r   r in front   l   l   start with r
3. Run, run, regular leap, run, run, stag leap.
      l r   l   r   l   r
4. Step, cat walk, step hop, extend forward leg, two steps backward, squat jump.
      r   start l   r   l   l,r

TURNS AND PIROUETTES

Turns are used on the balance beam to change direction and add variety to a routine. They should be done high on the balls of the feet except in variations. The body should be held erect, with the head up, shoulders relaxed. Turns should convey a feeling of lightness and continual motion. For balance, the center of gravity must always be over the base of support (feet). Turns should generally be executed using small steps. Arms should hold a definite position and help lift the body to the balls of the feet when turning. When the leg is lifted in a turn, such as the kick turn, it should be lifted at least parallel to the beam. Eye spotting is very important in turning for balance and to prevent dizziness.

Spotting for turns: Stand at side of beam and assist with outstretched hand.

SQUAT TURN (Fig. B-19)

SL Beginner

PT Assume deep squat position on balls of feet with one foot slightly in front of the other and hips directly above feet. Keep shoulders and head up with slight arch in back. Hold arms out at sides. Lift body very slightly and pivot a half turn (180°) on balls of feet. Eye spot other end of beam after turning.

130

CE 1. Failure to squat with the hips over the heels and maintain this position throughout the turn.
2. Failure to keep the shoulders directly over the hips.
3. Allowing the head to tilt forward and down.
4. Failure to eye spot.

MO 1. Pose, then stand.
2. Forward roll.
3. Squat jump.
4. Immediately stand.

VA *Semisquat turn* (Fig. B-20)

    SL Beginner

    PT Be careful that upper body does not sag forward. Be conscious of body lines in this position.

Figure B-19

Figure B-20

PIVOT TURN ON TOES (Fig. B-21)

SL Beginner

PT Stand with one foot slightly in front of the other on the balls of the feet. Keep body erect, head up, and shoulders relaxed. Initiate the turn with the hips and shoulders and squeeze the inner thighs or knees together for balance. Pivot, making half (180°) turn, and end facing the opposite direction. Arms may be held sideways throughout turn, or have one arm forward in opposition to the front foot and the other arm sideways. Eyes spot other end of beam or some object at eye level after turn.

CE 1. Failure to maintain body erect throughout turn (if body leans forward, backward, or sideward, loss of balance will occur).
2. Failure to eye spot.
3. Allowing feet to be too far apart on turn.

MO 1. Go into any of the locomotor skills.
2. Pose.
3. Step, kick into English handstand, execute a cartwheel or another tumbling skill.
4. Go into deep squat position and perform an arch jump (for distance).

Figure B-21

BATTEMENT TOURNEY *(kick turn)* (Fig. B-22)

SL Beginner

PT Kick right leg forward and upward; twist the body to the left and pivot on ball of left foot making half (180°) turn. As the turn is completed, the right leg should be carried up high behind the body. Keep shoulders directly over the left foot throughout the turn for balance; during the twisting action the back must arch to allow the shoulders to remain over the foot. End in a low arabesque, high arabesque, or go directly into another locomotor skill or some other move such as the forward roll. Arms may be in second position or go from a natural hanging position to fifth position as the body twists. Eyes spot stationary object or end of beam.

Figure B-22

Note: This turn is usually preceded by a step, chassé, or glissade.

CE 1. Allowing shoulders to move backward on the kick forward and upward.
2. Allowing the shoulders to drop forward after the turn is completed.
3. Failure to lift body and turn on the toes.

VA *Kick hop turn* (Fig. B-23)

    SL Intermediate

    PT Perform in the same manner as the kick turn, but have left foot completely leave the beam during the turn.

Figure B-23

TOUR JETÉ (Fig. B-24)

SL Advanced

PT Step on right foot; kick left leg forward and upward. Quickly twist the body a half turn (180°) and land on the left foot, swinging right leg to the rear. Shoulders should not lean forward or backward during the turn. Take arms overhead when the left leg swings forward. Eyes spot end of beam or stationary object after turn.

Figure B-24

132

CE 1. Allowing the shoulders to move backward as right leg swings forward.
    2. Allowing shoulders to move forward after turn and landing on right foot.
    3. Failure to flex right knee slightly upon landing on right foot.

VA Precede tour jeté with a chassé or a glissade.

CHAINÉ TURN (Fig. B-25)

SL Beginner

PT Step onto left foot; pivot a half turn (180°). Step onto right foot and pivot a half turn (180°) to complete the full turn. Steps are very small and are made on the half toe. Arms usually open to second position on the step and close (not completely) on the completion of the turn. Eye spotting is very important in this turn. When stepping to the left, turn the head to the left and hold this focus as long as possible. As you step on the right foot, turn head at the last second.

CE 1. Leaning into the turns or allowing the shoulders to move backward of the foot.
    2. Poor eye spotting.

Note: When these turns are performed on the beam, usually only one is performed; however, when performed on the floor in floor exercise, they are done in a series. When performed in a series, the same eye focus should be used.

Figure B-25

PIROUETTE (Fig. B-26)

SL Intermediate

PT On the beam, the pirouette is usually preceded by a step. It is a fast vertical spin of the body on one foot (tip-toe). The second foot (or free foot) can be held at the ankle, in attitude, or in arabesque position. Allow the body to lean very slightly forward on the turn in order to get up on toes. Arm positions will depend on the position of the second foot.

CE 1. Failure to step into and then lift body vertically onto toes.
    2. Leaning too far forward into the turn and letting the shoulders move too far backward at any time during the turn.

Figure B-26

LUNGE TURN–JAPANESE TURN–WOLF TURN (Fig. B-27)

SL Intermediate

PT With one leg squat under body, other leg extended sideways, arms to side, extend leg in opposite direction of turn. Lift body slightly as arms and leg swing in the direction of the turn. Arms will vary here depending on body build. Most people, however, will find success if arms go to curved overhead position. Others need them to be to the sides of the body. The hips and shoulders must remain balanced over the turning foot. To end, place extended leg on beam to side or end in a squat position.

CE 1. Allowing shoulders to move forward, backward, or sideward of the turning foot.
2. Not lifting body slightly in initial turn action.

VA 1. Full turn, one and a half turn.
2. Turn to squat position, three-quarter turn and stand.
3. Turn to split.

Figure B-27

BACK SPIN (Fig. B-28)

SL Intermediate

PT Get into a piked position on the back on the beam. Lift the hips off the beam and the head forward to lessen turning area. If turning to the right, put the right hand across the beam under the hip area and the left hand across the beam near the head (reverse hands for left). Maintaining a tight pike position, push against the beam with both hands, compress just a bit more and spin on the upper portion of the back, keeping eye contact on the knees.

SP Stand to side of performer and help rotate hips during spin.

CE 1. Pushing with one hand more than the other.
2. Dropping the hips or head during the spin.

MO 1. Back roll or back-roll extension.
2. Swing forward roll.
3. Swing to squat position and any skill from that position.

Hint: Practice spin on floor before attempting on beam.

Figure B-28

STATIC POSITIONS (Fig. B-29)

Poses are held only long enough to show that balance has been achieved in that position.

The following are just a few of the many static positions; but the performer will receive more credit for her routine if she can create something original or even vary some of the following.

Figure B-29

TUMBLING AND ACROBATIC MOVES

FORWARD ROLL (Fig. B-30)

SL Beginner

PT With one foot slightly in front of the other, stretch forward and place both hands across the beam (thumb and heel of hand on top of beam, fingers down side of beam). Shift the weight to the hands while lifting the hips above the head. Keeping the hips forward and upward, start bending elbows, tuck the head, and lower to beam in order to place back of neck and upper shoulder on beam. *Head must go between arms.* As the neck and upper shoulder area contact the beam, immediately shift the hands to the bottom of the beam and squeeze the elbows together (pulling with hands to keep body on beam). Continue rolling forward slowly, maintaining a pike position as long as possible (should feel as if each vertebra contacts the beam one after the other). Once learned, the hands need not grasp the bottom of the beam.

    Hint: Some people find success starting from the knees on the beam and then going directly into the roll.

SP Stand at side of beam and face performer. As arms are bending and head is tucked, grasp the hips and waist area and help lower the back and hips to the beam.

CE 1. Failure to lift hips high enough to allow head to be tucked and placed between arms on the beam.
    2. Failure to keep elbows close together and to pull on bottom of beam after shoulders have been placed on beam and hands switched to the bottom of the beam.
    3. Failure to maintain pike position when rolling on the back.
    4. Rolling too fast.

MO 1. Straddle beam and swing legs downbackward and upward to squat position, or land in a knee scale and go into pose.
    2. To V seat.
    3. To single-leg squat, pose, then stand.
    4. To squat position, pose, then stand.

Figure B-30

136

VA 1. *Forward roll from stoop position* (Fig. B-31)

SL Beginner

In general, requires better than average flexibility.

Figure B-31

2. *Swing-forward roll* (Fig. B-32)

SL Intermediate

PT From straddle position, thrust hips upward, simultaneously swinging legs (heel leading) downbackward and upward while shifting weight to hands. Allow hips to become high enough to successfully tuck head and continue rolling.

Figure B-32

3. *Forward roll without hands* (Fig. B-33)

SL Advanced

PT Go into deep lunge, arms out at sides of body and parallel to floor. Lower shoulders and back of neck to beam (constantly look at other end of beam until body is on beam) and continue to roll. Arms remain to side of body throughout skill or extended vertically by head.

Figure B-33

BACKWARD ROLL TO SQUAT (Fig. B-34)

SL Beginner

PT Maintain balance in supine position. Place thumbs on top of beam under neck, with fingers on side of beam. Some people prefer both hands on the bottom of the beam in front of the head; some prefer one hand on top and the other hand on the bottom of the beam. Lift legs in a tuck or pike position (should be straight knees eventually) to an overhead position. As the hips pass overhead, extend the arms (push with thumbs and grasp beam with fingers); place foot or feet on the beam and finish in a squat position, or immediately stand. As soon as the head can be lifted, the performer should eye spot the end of the beam.

SP Two spotters at first, one on each side of the beam. Assist the performer by grasping at the waist or hips as the hips are passing over the head. May also assist placement of the foot or knee on the beam before the roll is completed.

CE 1. Failure to maintain tuck or pike position when rolling.
2. Failure to push with hands as hips pass over head.
3. Failure to eye spot end of beam to assist in maintaining balance.

MO 1. End in squat position, pose.
2. End in squat position, half (180°) turn and pose.
3. End in knee scale, sit back on heel, then stand.
4. End in single-leg squat position, pose.

Figure B-34

5. *End in knee-scale position, pose, then stand* (Fig. B-35)

Figure B-35

VA 1. Two backward rolls in succession.
2. Backward roll to needle scale.
3. Backward roll to head stand.
4. Backward roll to English handstand.

138

BACK SHOULDER ROLL (head to left of beam, rolling over right shoulder) (Fig. B-36)

SL Beginner

PT From a supine position, place head to side of the beam so that right shoulder is on the beam; adjust balance. Place left hand on top of beam (fingers to side of beam, thumb on top), left arm across neck, and right hand on bottom of beam. Some people prefer to have both hands on the top of the beam. Lift legs to chest in a tuck or pike position and continue rolling over shoulder until head and torso can be lifted upward. The right knee should contact the beam, and the right hand should be shifted to the top of the beam. *Eyes spot end of beam toward shoulder when rolling,* and shift to other end of beam as roll is completed.

SP Same as for backward roll.

CE 1. Failure to stay in a tuck or pike position while rolling backward.
2. Failure to use hands in a push-and-pull fashion to maintain body on beam (bottom hand pulls, top hand pushes).
3. Failure to constantly eye spot.

MO Same as backward roll.

Figure B-36

ENGLISH HANDSTAND (Fig. B-37)

SL Beginner

PT Lift arms overhead while lifting left leg parallel to (or above) the beam. Step forward onto the left foot, bending the knee slightly and supporting the majority of the body, weight. Place the hands on the beam (heel of hands together, fingers to side of beam) about eighteen inches in front of the left foot. Shift weight to hands, swing the right leg up immediately followed by a push from the second leg. When body reaches inverted position, the legs are together and straight, shoulders and hips are fully extended. Eyes spot hands.

Figure B-37

SP Spotters on each side of the beam. One spotter supports upper arms, and the other grasps the hips to support and control the performer. If the handstand is not attained the performer should be told to keep arms straight and shift body weight slightly to one side of the beam and allow feet to be lowered to the floor by the spotter.

CE 1. Failure to maintain straight-arm support.
2. Failure to squeeze the beam with the hands.
3. Too much arch in back.
4. Insufficient swing with first leg, insufficient push with second leg, or both.
5. Failure to extend body fully in inverted position.

MO 1. Forward roll.
2. *Swing down* (Fig. B-38)

SL Low Intermediate

PT Shift weight forward over hands, making sure elbows do not bend. Leading with pelvis, lower legs to beam (one to each side) with inside of thighs making contact. As soon as the legs have contacted the beam, the shoulders and head should be lifted up and back while slightly arching the back. As the pelvis is leading downward, the heels must be forced upward.

Elbows bent too soon

Figure B-38

HANDSTAND FORWARD ROLL (Fig. B-39)

SL Advanced Beginner

PT After attaining full body extension and balance in the English handstand, shift hips and shoulders backward as if beginning to pike. Control elbow bend and lower body to beam; tuck head and place back of neck and upper shoulder area on the beam between arms. As soon as upper shoulder area contacts the beam, transfer hands to the bottom of the beam. Maintain a pike position and continue to roll.

SP Grasp the hips to support and maintain control while performer lowers to beam and rolls.

CE 1. Failure to shift hips and shoulders slightly backward when beginning to lower body to beam.
2. Failure to lower body to beam in the same vertical plane that the handstand was in (shoulders should not move forward of the hands).
3. Failure to keep legs well behind head (tight pike) momentarily after upper back contacts the beam.
4. Failure to control the elbow bend (either too fast or too slow).

MO Same as for forward roll.

140

Figure B-39

CARTWHEEL (left) (Fig. B-40)

SL Advanced Beginner

PT Lift arms overhead while simultaneously lifting the left leg at least parallel to beam. Step forward onto left foot, bending the knee slightly and shifting the body weight to that leg. Begin swinging the right leg up and immediately place the left hand across the beam (heel of hand toward the center of the beam). Push off the beam with the left leg. Just before the body reaches the inverted position, place the right hand on the beam shoulder width apart from the left. The right foot should contact the beam closer to the right hand than in a regular cartwheel on the floor. The right leg should bend slightly upon landing. The left hand should push off the beam slightly before the right foot lands on the beam. Left leg continues as the right leg extends (straighten knee) and the right hand is removed from the beam. After completion of the skill, the entire body should be facing toward the end of the beam. Eyes spot hands on the beam when inverting and look at the end of the beam or stationary object at eye level as the body is raised.

SP Stand beside beam and support second arm placed on beam and waist. If performer is off balance, she should do a round-off dismount to the side of the beam. Spot as if spotting a cartwheel on the floor.

CE 1. Placing hands on beam before beginning kicking action.
2. Failure to kick legs through vertical plane (many tend to pike).
3. Failure to step forward and shift the weight to bend forward leg after preparatory leg and arm lift.
4. Failure to place hands fairly close together (when learning).

Figure B-40

5. Failure to straighten up immediately after first foot contacts beam. (Students tend to feel that they can maintain balance by staying low and delaying hand releases from the beam; however, their center of gravity is too high to maintain balance, so it is more advantageous to raise upper body as soon as possible.)

MO
1. Go into lunge position.
2. Bring back leg forward and continue walking; or pose; or turn on toes.
3. Go into pose.

VA
1. *One-handed cartwheel (near arm)* (Fig. B-41)

Figure B-41

2. *One-handed cartwheel (far arm)* (Fig. B-42)

Figure B-42

FRONT WALKOVER (Fig. B-43)

SL Intermediate

PT For detailed description, refer to Chapter 4, since movement is identical to that on floor, except the hand placement. Hands are placed on beam so that fingers are on side of beam pointing downward and heels of hands toward each other (same as for English handstand). Master on line on floor before attempting on beam.

Hint: Sometimes it helps to perform the walkover on a low bench (about 8 to 10 inches) before going directly to a low beam or to a beam of regulation height. The wider base will also help minimize fear of height.

142

SP Stand facing the performer. With the inside hand (palm up) grasp the upper arm as the performer places her hands on the beam. Outside hand is placed on lower back giving support throughout skill. Spotter should also watch performer's placement of foot on the beam and control if necessary.

CE Refer to tumbling.

MO 1. Into pose.
2. Into lunge.
3. Step forward and go into a high pivot turn on both feet.

Figure B-43

BACK WALKOVER (Fig. B-44)

SL Low intermediate

PT For details refer to tumbling section. Master on floor first. The back walkover seems to be easier to learn than the front walkover because the eyes can spot beam and performer can see where she is going.

SP Stand with back to performer's back. With palms up, grasp hip area with thumbs pointing toward each other and fingers grasping outer hip area. As hands contact beam and hips are passing over hands, force wrists in opposite direction to assist in shifting weight past her hands.

Figure B-44

VA 1. *Back walkover to splits (refer to tumbling)* (Fig. B-45)

Figure B-45

2. *Back walkover, stop in English handstand, then swing down* (Fig. B-46)

Figure B-46

SIDE HANDSTAND TO STOOP THROUGH (Fig. B-47)

SL Advanced Intermediate

PT Kick up to side handstand. Start to stoop legs down, let hips move outward from beam to counteract weight distribution. Shoulders just slightly move past beam at this point. As the feet come closer to the beam, the hips move back to be directly above beam, and the shoulders are more forward on the beam. As the feet pass over the beam between the arms, the hips are lowered and shoulders forced directly over the beam. Finish in a high V-seat position.

SP Stand to side and back of performer on stack of mats. Grasp waist and hip area in handstand and guide forward and then backward during stoop through.

CE 1. Allowing hips or shoulders to ride too far across beam or not far enough on stoop down.
2. Not keeping head up throughout.

MO 1. V seat on beam, quarter turn, then back roll or stand.
2. Lie backward across beam, then up to straddle beam, another skill.
3. Press back to handstand.

Figure B-47

144

Tumbling Skills on the Beam

BACK HANDSPRING (Fig. B-48)

Figure B-48

SIDE AERIAL (Fig. B-49)

Figure B-49

FRONT AERIAL (Fig. B-50)

Figure B-50

145

BACK SOMMIE (Fig. B-51)

Figure B-51

FRONT SOMMIE (Fig. B-52)

Figure B-52

Once the back handspring, side aerial, front aerial, back sommie, and front sommie are mastered on the floor, the gymnast should then master the skills on a low beam without a spot before attempting to perform them on the high beam. The element of risk is reduced greatly when the gymnast goes from a successful performance on the low beam without a spot to the high beam. At this point, only a light spot is necessary to help build confidence and success.

All skills should be learned thoroughly on the floor before going to the low, then high beams. This method eliminates a lot of heavy spotting on the high beams and encourages good execution and most of all, readiness. Start with:

1. Line on floor.
2. Eight-inch stable bench.
3. Low beam.

DISMOUNTS

Landing on all dismounts should be with slight knee bend to absorb shock and to help maintain balance. For safety reasons, it is advisable to have two spotters when first learning most of the dismounts. Make sure there are sufficient mats beside or at the end of the beam where the dismounts will be performed. For the more difficult dismounts use a landing mat.

ARCH JUMP DISMOUNT (Fig. B-53)

SL Beginner

PT Stand sideways on the beam. Bend knees and spring up and forward. While suspended, keep upper body erect. Keep head up and eye spot stationary object at eye level throughout skill.

SP Stand beside beam and performer. Have outstretched hands ready to push performer forward if she should come too close to the beam. Another spotter could stand in front and to the side of the performer to prevent her from falling forward.

CE 1. Failure to keep upper body erect.
2. Failure to push off balls of feet in order to gain maximum elevation.
3. Jumping out too far or not far enough.

Figure B-53

ENGLISH HANDSTAND DISMOUNT (Fig. B-54)

SL Beginner

PT Kick up into English handstand balance as shown in Fig. B-37. Slightly shift weight to right side of the beam, slightly flex and then extend hips, and thrust legs and feet to the mat (similar to snap down). As feet are coming to right of beam, lift upper body and remove right hand from beam and lift it sideways. Eyes spot beam in front of hands until feet have been forced downward. Shoulders and head are then lifted, and eyes spot stationary object (eye level) or end of beam.

Figure B-54

147

Hint: To learn, go from a deep lunge position and only kick legs upward to a 45° angle. Action is very similar to front or face vault action.

SP Stand across beam to performer's left, directly in line with performer's hand placement. Place inside hand on upper arm and outside hand on abdomen or left thigh to make sure performer clears the beam. This method enables the spotter to maintain complete control of the performer throughout the entire skill.

CE 1. Not achieving full handstand position before descending.
2. Failure to maintain straight arms throughout dismount.
3. Failure to lift upper body and remove one hand to side as legs make downward movement.
4. Failure to shift body weight to right side of beam so as to land on the mat.

ROUND-OFF (end of beam) (Fig. B-55)

SL Beginner

PT Stand about two and one-half feet from the end of the beam, facing the end. Lift left leg upward as arms go overhead. Step onto left foot, shifting weight to that foot, and begin swinging right leg backupward. Place both hands together on the beam with fingers (of both hands) going down right side of beam. Push with left foot and bring both legs together in the inverted position. Make a half turn with entire body and pike at hips to allow feet to land on the floor. Push off end of beam with hands after feet have passed the inverted position. Eyes spot hand placement on the beam. When feet have contacted the mat and head and shoulders are lifted, eyes spot a stationary object at eye level.

SP Stand to nonturning side of performer, grasp upper arms as they are placed on beam and maintain contact until feet are on mat.

CE 1. Failure to maintain straight arms throughout skill.
2. Not achieving a handstand position before turning.
3. Failure to push off the beam with the hands and eye spot correctly.

Figure B-55

VA *Round-off to side of beam* (Fig. B-56)

    SL Beginner

    PT If performing on same side as above, student should land on the mat to the right side of the beam. You do not cross the beam on this dismount.

Figure B-56

CARTWHEEL QUARTER-TURN DISMOUNT (Fig. B-57)

SL Beginner

PT Stand approximately three feet from end of beam. Lift arms and right leg. Lunge forward on right bent leg, and place hands on beam to right side (close together) while kicking left leg. Immediately push with right leg to get body to handstand position. When body is sideways and vertical, bring legs together. As the body continues past the vertical plane, push and release the right hand, turn head to right, and push off with the left hand, keeping both arms overhead. Land with back to beam, bending knees and hips slightly to absorb shock.

SP Stand to back of performer and grasp under armpits after body is on down flight to help keep upper body from falling forward.

CE 1. Too much momentum developed from leg kick and push action, causing lack of control and falling forward on landing.
    2. Failure to pass through the vertical position, causing landing to be off to the side of the beam.
    3. Allowing head and upper body to drop forward on landing.

Figure B-57

HANDSTAND QUARTER TURN SQUAT THROUGH (Fig. B-58)

SL Intermediate

PT Kick up into side handstand position as if to perform cartwheel. Place hands on the beam with fingertips on the side of the beam and heels of hands on top. After handstand position is achieved, slightly overbalance, maintaining shoulders over hands. (It is very important not to allow the shoulders to move forward of the hands.) As balance is lost, flex hips and knees while simultaneously forcing (lifting) head and chest upward. Extend legs before landing.

    Hint: Lead-ups. 1. Handstand quarter turn, hold.
                           2. Snap down on floor.

SP Two spotters. One stands on performer's pivot side and supports arm with outside hand; as the performer begins to squat, spotter places inside hand on abdomen. Second spotter stands on nonpivot side of performer. As handstand position is attained, she places outside hand on upper arm and inside hand on abdomen. When performer can achieve handstand position alone, spotters can stand on each side and grasp forearm with outside hand and upper arm with inside hand and help pull performer through squat position and off beam.

CE 1. Failure to achieve proper handstand position (slight overbalance).
    2. Failure to maintain straight arms.
    3. Allowing shoulders to move forward of the hands.
    4. Not following through completely on the squat as it is executed.
    5. Failure to push with hands as squat is executed.
    6. Failure to keep head up.

150

Figure B-58

VA 1. *Handstand stoop through* (Fig. B-59)

Figure B-59

2. *Handstand straddle off* (Fig. B-60)

Figure B-60

151

WINDY (Fig. B-61)

SL   Advanced Intermediate

PT   Arm and leg lift the same as for handstand position. Place left hand on beam, with fingers at left side of beam and heel of hand on beam. Kick up into a one-arm handstand position, keeping the left shoulder over the left hand. Lean body in the direction of the pivot. Make half (180°) turn and allow feet to move toward the mat, keeping body fully extended. As legs are lowering to mat, lift head and upper body forcefully. Eyes spot supporting hand while inverted and end of beam as head and upper body are lifted. Hand remains in contact with the beam until feet contact the mat. Right arm should swing vigorously down, back, and overhead as the skill is initiated.

SP   Stand at pivot side of performer. Support upper arm with inside hand and abdomen with outside hand.

CE   1. Failure to achieve handstand position on one arm.
2. Failure to keep supporting arm straight.
3. Failure to lean body into the direction of the pivot.
4. Failure to keep shoulder over supporting hand.
5. Failure to execute forceful swing and push from the legs.
6. Failure to use left arm.

Hint: Learn with both hands on the beam.

Figure B-61

FRONT HANDSPRING (Fig. B-62)

SL   Low Intermediate

PT   Approximately from middle of beam, take a step, lift other leg, step into lunge; place hands on end of beam. Kick push with legs to inverted position; then as feet pass hand position, give push with hands. Maintain straight-body position throughout. As landing occurs, slightly bend knees and hips to absorb shock. Keep arms overhead.

SP   Stand to side of beam. Have near arm on wrist or upper arm and help keep it in position. Have far arm on rear to keep weight going forward to over feet when landing.

CE   1. Insufficient kick push to give rise to total body.
2. Over rotation usually caused by too much kick-and-push action, or by allowing arms and shoulders to move forward on landing.

152

Figure B-62

FRONT AERIAL (end of beam) (Fig. B-63)

SL Intermediate

PT Same technique as for skill on floor (refer to tumbling section for details). Legs are brought together in the inverted position; then toes reach for the mat to allow body to "float" to the mat in a wide arc. Be careful not to allow legs to undercut (pass under) body before the landing.

SP 1. To learn, use inside hand on shoulder and outside hand on wrist. Standing at end of beam, move with performer to prevent undercutting.
2. Inside hand on abdomen, outside hand on small of back.

Figure B-63

SIDE AERIAL DISMOUNT (Fig. B-64)

SL Intermediate

PT Lift arms over head and leg up in preparation for step into aerial. Step forward onto bent right foot with toes near end of beam. Keeping head and shoulders erect over right knee, immediately kick the left foot as a push is made with the right foot. As the body moves forward and upward, drop the right shoulder so that it is in line with the beam and bring legs together in vertical position. Land with left side to beam, arms overhead, then down, and hips and knees slightly flexed to absorb shock. Eyes focus on object at eye level.

SP 1. Stand to back of performer, place near hand on right side of waist and far hand on left. Same as spotting cartwheel on floor.
2. Place both hands on pelvic area, and lift and assist with rotation when leg thrust is made.

CE 1. Dropping head and chest too far forward when stepping into kick-push action.
2. Too much leg action—can cause overspin.
3. Failure to bring legs together when inverted.

Figure B-64

BARANI (Fig. B-65)

SL Intermediate

PT The barani is often confused with the cartwheel aerial. The movement is the same as a round-off without hands or the barani on the trampoline. Actually a quarter turn is made with the upper body on initial takeoff and a quarter turn after passing the vertical position. After preparatory arm and leg lift, step forward on bent right leg. Keeping head and chest up, immediately kick left leg upward while pushing with right. Eyes spot area on dismount mat; right shoulder rotates a quarter turn on takeoff; legs are brought together; then a quarter turn is initiated with right shoulder and hips. As legs pass head position, lift chest and focus eyes on end of beam. Land facing end of beam, arms obliquely forward and upward.

SP Same as for cartwheel aerial dismount.

154

Figure B-65

CE 1. Lowering head and chest too far past knees during takeoff.
2. Allowing quarter turn to be made to the side of the body rather than directly in front.
3. Not bringing legs together in vertical position.
4. Allowing the legs to move around the vertical position rather than passing through it.

BACK SOMMIE DISMOUNT (Fig. B-66)

SL Intermediate

PT Gain balance on balls of feet on end of beam with arms out to side of body. As knees and hips flex slightly, bring arms down, forward, and upward. Lean back very slightly to lose balance and forcefully spring off feet, bringing knees to chest. Head should remain in a normal position. A slight tilt of the head backward would be okay but, if the head is thrown back, the body will rotate downward rather than up and back. After back is parallel to ceiling, lift chest, extend hips and legs, and look for end of beam. Land with knees and hips slightly flexed and arms overhead or at the side.

SP Stand at end of beam to the side of the performer. Place inside hand on back of upper thigh and outside hand on buttocks. Rotate with hands on thighs, and lift with hands on buttocks or lower back.

CE 1. Throwing head back.
2. Inadequate push from feet or lift with the arms.
3. Turning head to one side causing body to rotate on an angle rather than in a straight line.

VA Back sommie in piked position.

Figure B-66

LAYOUT DISMOUNT (Fig. B-67)

SL Advanced Intermediate

PT With one foot slightly in front of the other, slightly flex hips and knees and bring arms to side of body. Lean back very slightly to lose balance, then immediately spring upward from both feet while lifting arms overhead. Keep body totally tight and force hips upward. As the mat comes in sight keep squeezing hips and lift chest until feet are on mat.

SP Same as Fig. B-66

CE 1. Throwing head back.
2. Body not tight.
3. Pushing off feet backward rather than upward.

VA Layout full twist

    SL Advanced

    PT As body leaves beam keep arm up in direction of turn, pull across body with other arm. Keep body tight throughout.

Hips too
relaxed here

Figure B-67

156

FRONT SOMMIE (Fig. B-68)

SL Advanced Intermediate

PT With one foot slightly in front of the other, punch off the end of the beam, lift vertically, then bring hands to lower legs as hips lift and shoulders drive forward to tuck position. When three quarters rotated, extend body, leading with feet to landing with arms overhead, knees and hips slightly flexed.

SP Stand to side of performer. With near hand, lift in hip area. With far hand, rotate back. Both hands grasp abdomen and back upon landing.

CE 1. Throwing body down rather than lifting up before tucking.
2. Opening too soon—generally resulting in a fall backward.
3. Opening too late—generally resulting in a fall forward.
4. Relaxing the upper body and dropping arms forward upon landing.

VA 1. Do from run.
2. Do from side of beam.
3. Piked front sommie.

Figure B-68

CARTWHEEL QUARTER-TURNOUT FRONT SOMMIE (Fig. B-69)

SL Advanced

PT Land the cartwheel with the feet together on end of beam. Turn shoulders toward end of beam with arms up, push off, and complete quarter turn, lifting up into front sommie.

SP Same as Fig. B-68, front sommie.

CE 1. Loss of balance in cartwheel.
2. Same as those for front sommie.

VA 1. Cartwheel quarter-turn front pike.
2. Cartwheel quarter-turn sommie in middle of beam.

157

Figure B-69

GAINER DISMOUNT (Fig. B-70)

SL Advanced

PT Stand approximately two feet from the end of the beam. Step forward on the right foot, immediately swing left leg forcefully forward and up, and push off the beam with right foot to join left in tucked position. Arms come from side position to overhead; then they can touch knees in tuck position. Tilt head back only slightly after the body has rotated in a three-quarter spin, extend hips and legs, and lift chest to come to stand.

SP Stand to side and end of beam. As push leg leaves beam, place near hand on back to help lift and far hand on hips to spin body.

CE 1. Inadequate kick push or arm lift.
2. Not tucking tight enough (the tighter the tuck the faster the spin).
3. Forcing the head back on takeoff. This only causes the body to drop.

Hint: Work gainer on trampoline or into pit before using beam.

Figure B-70

Combination Dismounts

The dismounts B-71 to B-78 are just a combination of skills. Each skill should be mastered individually before being combined. All dismount combinations are in the advanced skill level.

CARTWHEEL, SIDE AERIAL (Fig. B-71)

Figure B-71

FRONT WALKOVER, FRONT AERIAL (Fig. B-72)

Figure B-72

FRONT WALKOVER, FRONT SOMMIE (Fig. B-73)

Figure B-73

ROUND-OFF, BACK SOMMIE (Fig. B-74)

Figure B-74

160

BACK HANDSPRING, BACK SOMMIE (Fig. B-75)

Figure B-75

VALDEZ, BACK LAYOUT (Fig. B-76)

Figure B-76

BACK WALKOVER, FULL TWIST (Fig. B-77)

Figure B-77

BACK HANDSPRING, HALF TURN, FRONT SOMMIE (Fig. B-78)

Figure B-78

ROUTINE COMPOSITION FOR CLASS

Routines on the balance beam for classes should be short and easy but challenging and should contain all aspects of beam composition. The routine should contain a mount, locomotor skills, static positions, a tumbling skill, and a dismount. It is often not feasible to incorporate a tumbling skill in a class routine due to the level of ability of the students and the time needed for learning them well enough to perform.

For a beginning class it is best to have all students perform the same routine. If the students have had previous experience and training on the beam, they might enjoy creating their own routines.

There are many compulsory routines that could be used in a beginning class. Some may be found in the DGWS Gymnastic Guide and the USGF Handbook.

162

Suggested Beginning Routine (for class) (Fig. B-79)

Figure B-79

Squat mount on left end of beam, quarter (90°) right with arms in second position. Single-leg squat pose, stand, step left, step hop right, arms in second position. Step left, draw right foot to left, squat turn to right with arms obliquely backward. Forward roll (may omit) to straddle sitting position. Swing legs downbackward and upward to squat position on the beam with right foot in front of left. Stand, make half turn (180°) left on toes, and shift weight to right rear foot. Run left, run right, run left. Draw right foot to left, pose. Step forward on right foot chassé, half turn left on both feet (flat pivot), ending with left foot in front. Step right, slide left foot to right foot, changement, ending with left foot in front. Step left and kick right leg high while making quarter turn left. Arch jump dismount. (Make own arm movements.)

Intermediate Routine (for class)

Step on mount. Pivot toe turn, squat jump, chassé, step push leap, kick turn to lunge position. Forward roll to single-leg squat, stand, two steps back, pose, step, catwalk, step, semisquat turn to pose. Run, run, leap, step, squat, then perform back roll to knee scale. Stand, quarter turn left, two slides sideways, quarter turn, grand battement, cartwheel quarter-turn dismount. (Make own arm movements.)

ROUTINES FOR COMPETITION

The time limit for competitive routines on the balance beam is from one minute fifteen seconds to one minute thirty-five seconds. The watch starts as soon as the feet leave the mat or reuther board and stops when the dismount has been completed.

Movement on the beam should flow from one skill to the next with creative sequences. The routine should include locomotor skills, tumbling and acrobatic skills, turns, and static positions and must bring into action all parts of the body.

Static positions should be held only long enough to show control in that position.

There must be seven elements of difficulty, three being of superior difficulty. For difficulty rating, refer to the FIG Code of Points Book.

A performer should vary the tempo (fast and slow) and the level (high, low, medium positions) of the skills in a routine to avoid monotony and to give an overall impression of lightness.

The performer should convey a feeling of confidence. Leaps should be as high as possible. Toe turns should not be performed flat footed. The entire beam routine should be lively and exciting to watch.

Routines

1. Swing forward roll mount to single-leg squat (legs very close), half turn in squat position, immediately execute squat jump. Stand, step into single-leg pivot turn, grand battement forward, two cartwheels, step, catwalk backward, pose.

   Chainé, step, chassé, step back, cancan kick, step kick turn to handstand forward roll to single-leg squat. Quarter turn into full wolf turn to splits. Backward roll to squat position, body wave, one and one-half pirouette turn, back walkover, back walkover to lunge, step, catwalk, step, split leap, step toe turn to arabesque. Step, front walkover, front walkover, front aerial dismount.

2. Handstand mount on end of beam into front walkover. Step, pose, step, split leap, jump turn, far arm cartwheel, step slide. Handstand forward roll, pirouette, two poses. English handstand, pirouette, chest roll down to backward roll, pose. Stand, step, tour jeté, step, jazz turn, two back handsprings, back full twisting dismount.

3. *Advanced Routine* (Fig. B-80)

Figure B-80

165

chapter seven

UNEVEN PARALLEL BARS

The uneven parallel bar event is most exciting to watch. As girls display their skill at releasing the low bar to grasp the high bar and then circle the low bar, there are many "ohs" and "ahs" from spectators.

To perform well in this spectacular event girls must first have interest, and we cannot overlook the strength factor involved. If you can support or suspend your own body weight for at least ten seconds, you are on your way.

Skills will be described in the following classifications:

> Mounts
> Moves on one bar
> Moves from one bar to the other
> Releases
> Dismounts

Note: Some of the releases (such as seat circle, catch high bar) are described in the moves on one bar section as variations.

Since this event requires strength in the arms, shoulders, and abdominal and back areas, you must first strengthen those areas. The following exercises should be done daily.

SPECIAL CONDITIONING EXERCISES

PULL-UPS (See Fig. C-7, page 14)

Purpose: To develop strength in upper arm and shoulder.

Technique: Jump to long hang on high bar, ladder, or some other object to hang from. Grasp with forward grip (palms forward). Keeping body as straight as possible, bend arms, and pull body upward until chin reaches over top of bar.

Variation: Chin-up. Same technique with hands in reverse grip.

Hint: Have partner assist until pull-up can be done alone. Stand close to performer, grasp above knees, and use your legs to assist in lifting so as not to strain back.

LEG LIFTS (See Fig. C-9, page 14)

Purpose: To develop rectus abdominus and quadriceps. Also acts as isometric exercise for the upper arms and grip.

Technique: Hang from wall ladder or high bar; lift toes slowly to head (or to L position), then slowly lower them to starting position. Work up to ten.

SIT-UPS WITH TWIST (See Fig. C-8, page 14)

Purpose: To develop abdominal and lower back muscles.

Technique: Assume supine position with legs bent and together, hands on shoulders; tilt pelvis and curl up to an erect sitting position. Twist to right and touch left elbow to right knee. Return to original position and repeat to other side. Work up to at least fifteen.

SWAN EXERCISE (See Fig. C-33, page 23)

Purpose: To develop flexibility in upper abdomen and lower back. Assists in tightening gluteal muscles and strengthening lower back.

Technique: From prone position, arms overhead:
1. Lift arms, tilt head back, tense gluteal muscles, and arch back as far back and up as possible.
2. Keep upper body on floor, tense gluteal muscles, lift legs with heels together (legs straight) as far off the floor as possible.
3. Combine 1 and 2 simultaneously.

Variation: Have partner lift arms then legs. (This is for flexibility.)
1. Straddle body around chest area; grasp arms above elbows and lift body as far as possible, making sure hips do not leave the floor.
2. Sit on performer's buttocks and grasp legs above knees and lift legs as high as possible.

SHOULDER STRETCH (partner exercise) (See Fig. C-18, C-19, C-20, page 18)

Purpose: To develop flexibility in the shoulder area.

Technique: Sit on floor with legs together and straight and with back erect. Partner stands behind and places leg (not knee) against performer's back. Reach between arms, grasp above elbows, force arms and shoulders up and back while simultaneously forcing chest forward with legs. Switch partners and repeat. Stretch shoulder area a little further each time.

SAFETY HINTS

1. Check bars before each use to make sure they are secure in their supports.
2. Surround bars with mats, making sure that enough area is covered for mounts and dismounts.
3. If bars have a tendency to rock, they should be weighted with sand bags, other members of the class, or by some other method.
4. If a reuther board is used for mounting the bars, it should be removed as soon as the performer is on the bars and will not be hindered by the person moving the board.

167

5. Use chalk and/or hand grips to prevent palms of hands from being ripped.
6. Do not continue working on the bars when the hands feel hot and become red, because that is a sign that the hands should be given a rest so they won't rip.
7. Don't allow students on the bars unsupervised.
8. Have a definite skill progression for each class.

Hand Care

Chalk or magnesium can be used to help keep hands from slipping from the bar, Girls whose hands perspire a great deal (probably due to nervousness) will have to chalk up more frequently.

Hand guards can be purchased from gymnastic supply companies or made from two-inch adhesive tape. Whichever is used, they should fit tightly but allow freedom of movement. The tape can be put around any finger and then taped around the wrist. If calluses develop, they should be filed or shaved carefully. For rips, the skin should be cut off as close to the end of the rip as possible. The area should be washed, then covered with Vaseline. If the skin is allowed to become dry, it will crack and cause more discomfort. Keep it moist.

Hip Pads

Hip pads are very helpful in preventing bruises while learning certain skills. These can be half-inch foam cut to fit under the leotard, or a new snap-around body guard can be purchased from gymnastics supply houses. Rubber tubing to fit around the bar can be purchased at local plumbing supply companies. These can be slit and taped around the bar and easily removed.

GRIPS

FORWARD (over) (Fig. U-1)

The forward or overgrip is used for approximately 75 percent of all uneven parallel bar skills. The hands are placed on the bars with the back of the hand (knuckle) facing upward. The thumb may be either alongside the fingers or around the bar. This is a matter of preference since the size of individuals' hands vary.

REVERSE (under) (Fig. U-2)

The reverse or undergrip has the hands on the bar with the fingers facing upward and the thumb around the bar.

Figure U-1

Figure U-2

MIXED GRIP (Fig. U-3)

One hand in forward grip and the other hand in a reversed grip.

EAGLE GRIP (twist grip) (Fig. U-4)

This grip is used for just a few skills. The arms are lifted sideways and grasp the bar with backs of hands facing up and thumbs under bar.

Figure U-3

Figure U-4

SKILLS

In all skills it will be assumed that knees are straight and toes are pointed unless otherwise stated.

Mounts

JUMP TO FRONT SUPPORT (Fig. U-5)

SL Beginner

PT Stand between bars, close to and facing low bar. Grasp low bar with forward grip. Bend knees and spring vertically; extend arms and allow upper thighs to come to rest on the low bar. Keep head up, legs together and straight, slight arch in back. Keep shoulders forward of the bar.

SP Assist weak girls by lifting at waist.

CE 1. Failure to keep elbows straight (locked) when support position is achieved.
2. Failure to keep body taut and slightly arched.
3. Allowing shoulders to be shrugged (failure to extend in shoulders and keep head up).

MO 1. Single leg flank to stride support.
2. Back hip circle.
3. Front hip circle.
4. Single- or double-leg shoot through.
5. Squat stand.
6. Straddle stand.
7. Double-leg shoot through.
8. Stoop stand.
9. Underswing dismount.
10. Drop kip.
11. Free straddle support.

Figure U-5

BACK HIP PULLOVER TO FRONT SUPPORT ON LOW BAR (Fig. U-6)

SL Beginner

PT Stand between bars facing low bar; grasp bar with forward grip with body close to bar and elbows bent. Keep one foot slightly in front of the other with weight on back foot. Shift weight to forward foot and simultaneously swing back leg forward and upward to lift hips to the bar. As hips move under the bar, push off with forward foot and allow legs to come together as body is revolving around the bars. Keep elbows bent and pull hips to the bar. Rotate grip backward to allow wrists to finish over hands to help maintain support on hands. Finish in front support by lifting head and extending arms as the pullover is completed.

SP Stand beside performer outside low bar. Place inside hand on small of back and outside hand on back of upper thighs. Help keep hips close to bar by lifting legs if necessary.

CE 1. Allowing arms to extend (straighten). When this happens, the hips cannot be kept close to the bar and the performer's lower body will drop to the mat.
2. Failure to kick or swing vigorously with the back leg and push off with the forward foot.
3. Failure to rotate hand grip backward.
4. Failure to end in front support.

MO Same as for jump to front support.

Figure U-6

170

BEAT-SWING SQUAT OVER (from long hang on high bar) (Fig. U-7)

SL Beginner

PT Jump to long hang on high bar facing the low bar. Use forward grip. Keeping upper body as motionless as possible, force hips backward and lift legs forward and up, then hips forward and legs back. As hips start to move forward draw knees to chest and extend legs upward. As body moves forward, force hips upward (extend hips) and lower backs of upper thighs to the low bar. Extend upper body to finish in rear support.

SP Stand beside performer between bars. Place hands on waist to help keep upper body motionless. Then pull waist (and hips) back slightly as squat movement is initiated. Help to lift hips upward if necessary.

CE 1. Improper timing on swing.
2. Failure to lift knees to chest at start of second forward swing of legs.
3. Failure to lower backs of upper thigh onto bar with control.
4. Failure to make beat swing short and forceful.

MO 1. Stem rise to high bar.
2. Pull over to high bar.
3. Kip to high bar.
4. Release high bar, grasp lower bar, and perform front or back seat circle.

Figure U-7

VA 1. *Beat-swing stoop-over mount* (Fig. U-8)

Follow same procedures as for squat mount but keep legs straight at all times.

Figure U-8

171

2. *Beat-swing straddle mount* (Fig. U-9)

Follow same procedures as for squat mount but lift legs upward and sideward in a wide straddle before placing backs of upper thighs on bar; then finish in a rear seat support with hands on high bar.

Figure U-9

BACK HIP-CIRCLE MOUNT (using reuther board) (Fig. U-10)

SL Advanced Beginner

PT After a two-foot takeoff on reuther board, grasp low bar and allow shoulders to go forward, keeping arms straight. Extend body completely to reach a horizontal position. Shoulders are slightly forward of low bar toward high bar. Bring body to bar. When hips contact bar, flex hips and continue with back hip circle.

SP In the beginning the spotter can assist at the abdomen and upper thigh area by lifting person to horizontal position. The back hip-circle portion should be spotted like a regular back hip circle. (See Fig. U-27, page 183)

CE 1. Not allowing shoulders to be over hand position.
2. Not hitting horizontal position with body completely tight.
3. Flexing at the hips before contacting bar.

MO Anything that can be done from a front support position.

VA Free back hip-circle mount.

Figure U-10

172

GLIDE KIP MOUNT (Fig. U-11)

SL Low Intermediate

PT Stand under high bar facing low bar or stand in front of low bar facing toward low and high bars. To learn, start with hands in forward grip on bar (eventually stand about three feet behind bar) and jump to bar. The jump into the glide gives the performer more momentum and more time to bring her feet to the bar before the kip.

Arms extended and shoulders relaxed, jump up and forward, lifting the hips backupward. Lift the legs upward so that they will be a few inches above the mat. Keep arms and shoulders extended and allow body to glide under the bar to an extended position. As full body extension is achieved, immediately flex hips, lifting ankles to the bar. As body begins backward swinging motion in pike position, force legs up along the bar by partially extending hips and forcefully pushing downward with extended arms. As hips reach bar level, the legs continue moving outdownward. The hips at this point extend further. The pushing-down action from the extended arms must be followed through until the performer finishes in a front support position with the arms and shoulders fully extended and chin up. Just before completing the skill, rotate grip slightly forward.

SP Two spotters, one on each side of performer in front of bar. Reach under bar and place inside hand on lower back and outside hand on back of upper thighs (help keep hips close to bar). Inside hand helps performer get to front support position after kipping movement of legs and hips is initiated.

CE 1. Failure to thrust hips back and up on jump to bar.
2. Failure to keep arms and shoulders extended on glide.
3. Keeping legs too high on glide.
4. Failure to extend body at end of glide.
5. Failure to forcefully lift legs to bar as soon as glide is completed and to keep hips from dropping backward.
6. Failure to force legs upward until hips reach bar (many beginners have the tendency to kip down and out rather than up and out).
7. Failure to keep arms straight and to push down on the bar to reach the front support position.

MO Same as for front support plus variations on following page.

Figure U-11

VA 1. *Glide kip with legs in straddle position* (Fig. U-12)

Figure U-12

2. *Glide, single-leg shoot through to stride position* (Fig. U-13)

PT Follow same procedures as for kip, but when body has reached extended position in glide, force one leg between hands so that it can continue over the bar. Keep legs free of the bar and finish in a wide stride position.

CE 1. Not forcing leg through arms while hips are forward.
2. Not extending hips as body is ready to pass over bar to final position.

Figure U-13

3. *Glide kip, catch high bar* (Fig. U-14)

SL Intermediate

PT Same procedures as for regular kip. As most of kip is completed (hips to bar), reach for the high bar. Look at the high bar as the initial kipping action is started.

SP Stand between bars. As feet are brought to bar, place outside hand on small of back to

174

prevent a fall and inside hand under the bar on the back of the thighs. Maintain contact and help lift the performer to the high bar, making sure she has a firm grip on it.

CE 1. Failure to complete at least half the kip on the low bar before quickly catching the high bar.
2. Failure to look at high bar when catching it.

Figure U-14

4. *Glide to double-leg shoot through to rear support* (Fig. U-15)

SL Intermediate

PT Same procedures as on a regular glide to extended position. As this position is reached, force both legs between hands. Allow body to ride under the low bar in piked position until the backs of the upper thighs are under the bar. Then forcefully pull with hands, maintain the pike, and pass through an L-support position to rear support on low bar. As the body moves over the top of the low bar, rotate grip forward and lift head and chest.

SP Same as for regular kip but assist at shoulders while inverted in pike position throughout entire skill.

CE 1. Not forcing legs through arms while hips are forward on the glide position.
2. Failure to maintain pike.
3. Failure to rotate grip when coming over top of bar.

Figure U-15

175

5. *Back kip (reverse kip)* (Fig. U-16)

SL Intermediate

PT The back kip is a combination of the glide, double-leg shoot through (third variation of the kip), and a back seat circle.

Figure U-16

Opened pike too soon

SWITCH GLIDE KIP (straddle position) (Fig. U-17)

SL Intermediate

PT From a straddle glide keep hips slightly flexed, rotate hips and shoulders, and turn head to right while releasing right hand. Regrasp bar, trying not to let hips ride forward. Quickly change grip of left hand to a forward grip, and continue into the second glide. Bring ankles to bar and finish kip. (Some girls prefer to finish with a mixed grip rather than make the second change during the kip.)

SP Same as for a regular kip. You may assist at the waist on the turn if necessary.

CE 1. Inadequate first glide.
2. Allowing hips to ride forward toward bar on turn.
3. Poor timing in hand switch and kip.

Hand change

Figure U-17

FRONT HIP CIRCLE (done with reuther board) (Fig. U-18)

SL Advanced Beginner

PT Approaching with a run and hurdle from the board, spring vertically (momentum will carry the body forward) and contact the low bar on upper thighs with body completely stretched, arms overhead, and head up. Maintain this position momentarily, then allow the upper body to initiate the forward movement. Just before the body reaches the inverted position, pike sharply, grasp the bar with a forward grip. As the body continues moving around the bar, extend the arms fully, keep head and chest up, and finish in a front support.

SP Two spotters, one at each side standing in front of the low bar between the reuther board and bar. Allow just enough room for the performer to pass through. As performer leaves the board, each spotter grasps a leg above the knee to make sure that she contacts the bar on upper thighs. After hip circle is started, reach hand under bar and place inside hand on hips and outside hand on the back to keep hips close to the bar.

176

CE 1. Failure to contact body in proper position on thighs, with body completely arched and head up.
2. Failure to pause momentarily, then begin forward movement with upper body.
3. Piking too soon or too late during hip circle.
4. Failure to grasp bar, extend arms, and rotate grip forward to top of bar and to finish in a front support with head and chest up.

MO 1. All those skills listed from the front support mount.
2. Cast back to squat stand, grasp high bar, underswing half turn to hip circle on low bar.
3. Cast back to squat stand, grasp high bar, sole circle half turn to hip circle on low bar.

VA Perform double front hip circle grasping legs below knee while rotating around the bar one and three-quarter times; then grasp bar and finish in front support as for front hip-circle mount.

Hint: When rotating, keep arms slightly bent and forearms close to the bar in order to keep body close to the bar. Then straighten the arms forcefully as hands are placed on the bar to push body to a front support position.

Figure U-18

SQUAT OVER LOW BAR, GRASP HIGH BAR, UNDERSWING HALF TURN (Fig. U-19)

SL Intermediate

PT Using reuther board, jump vertically over the low bar, driving knees to chest, forcefully push with hands on releasing the low bar, and grasp the high bar with a forward grip. As the hips clear the low bar, forcefully extend body (emphasizing hip extension) and, just as hips reach the fully extended position, release right hand, turning hips and shoulders 180°. Regrasp the bar with right hand. At this point of the skill, body should be fully extended behind hands, which are in a mixed grip (left hand undergrip, right hand overgrip). The left hand does not release the high bar.

SP Two spotters, one standing in front of low bar and one standing between bars. The spotter in front of the bar helps performer clear the low bar by lifting her hips. The spotter between the bars places her inside hand on the small of the back and outside hand on the thighs until the performer grasps the high bar and has fully extended. This spotter may also assist with the turn.

CE 1. Insufficient spring from the board.
2. Insufficient push with hands from the low bar.
3. Stopping movement when making contact with the high bar.
4. Not fully extending hips on the underswing.
5. Turning too soon or too late from the extension.

MO 1. Hip circle on low bar.
2. Drop to low bar, then kip.
3. Hip circle on low bar to eagle catch.

177

Figure U-19

STRADDLE OVER, STRADDLE BACK (Fig. U-20)

SL   Advanced Intermediate

PT   From takeoff on reuther board, push forcefully down on the low bar as hips thrust backupward and legs lift in a wide high straddle. Immediately reach for the high bar and go into a forceful long hang, forcing hips forward and heels backward. After momentary hesitation, bend arms slightly and pull on high bar as hips are forced backward. Lift heels up, forcing a wide straddle as body moves backward over low bar. Regrasp low bar, keeping hips back for a nice glide kip.

SP   This skill is difficult to spot since legs are in a straddle position. Stand in front of low bar, ready to step in after performer leaves board. Depending on size of spotter and performer, grasp waist and lift up and forward over low bar, or place hands on back and upper thighs and lift up and over. On return straddle over the bar, grasp waist area again and assist in lifting up and back over low bar.

CE   1. Inadequate punch off board, straddle of legs, or push from low bar with hands.
2. Failure to hit a taut long-hang position.
3. Staying in long-hang position too long (causing loss of momentum).
4. Insufficient pull of arms and leg lift to straddle on return over low bar.
5. Failure to keep hips back so glide kip can be completed.

Figure U-20

178

MO Anything that can be done from a front support position.

VA Straddle or squat over and immediate kip to high bar from long hang.

HALF TURN OVER LOW BAR, KIP TO HIGH (Fig. U-21)

SL Advanced

PT From a punch off the reuther board, jump with stretched body over the low bar, making a half turn and grasping high bar with a forward grip. Forcefully bring ankles to high bar simultaneously with catch and kip to high bar.

SP Stand between the bars (on mats if needed). As body rotates in half turn, put near hand (one closest to high bar) on back, help lift. Far hand goes on back of legs or rear to give support in the kip.

CE 1. Insufficient punch and straight body lift.
2. Catching high bar in mixed grip.
3. Dropping legs rather than lifting to high bar.

MO Cast wrap, sole circle, or any skill done from a front support.

Figure U-21

HANDSTAND MOUNT ON LOW BAR (Fig. U-22)

SL Advanced

PT After takeoff on reuther board, grasp low bar. Keeping head up and back and arms straight, flex hips and stay in piked straddle position until hips are over hands. At this point lift legs together to a completely extended handstand position. (The board has to be punched as if going to vault to get enough lift.)

SP Stand between bars slightly to side of performer. Grasp waist area as piked straddle is achieved. Help lift hips and legs up into handstand position.

CE 1. Insufficient punch off board.
2. Not getting hips over hands before going into handstand and not keeping arms straight.

MO 1. To rear seat support on high bar, then front or back seat circle.
2. Do not allow body to touch high bar—just hit handstand position then drop to hip circle on low bar.
3. Straddle legs down to sole circle on low bar.

Figure U-22

Moves on One Bar

All the following skills should be mastered on the low bar before transferring to the high bar. If there are no uneven parallel bars available, these skills can be learned on a horizontal bar lowered to the height of the uneven low bar, or one bar from a set of even parallel bars can be removed.

SWAN BALANCE (Fig. U-23)

SL Beginner

PT From a front support position, balance body on upper thigh area and lift arms overhead. (Every individual's exact balance point is different, so you must experiment to find yours.)

SP Stand between bars and control the performer's balance by holding ankles, or stand in front of the bar and spot shoulder area to keep upper body from falling forward.

MO 1. Go back to front support position; hands regrasp bar in forward grip; perform any of the skills listed from the front support position.
2. Front hip circle.

Figure U-23

180

SINGLE-LEG FLANK TO A STRIDE LEG SUPPORT (Fig. U-24)

SL Beginner

PT From a front support position with a forward grip, lift left leg upward and sideways over the low bar. Remove left hand, allow leg to pass over, replace hand on the bar, and immediately hold a stride leg support. Weight is on hands, the rest of the body is completely free of the bar. When lifting left hand off the bar, shift weight to right hand. Right arm must remain locked (straight) at all times. The movement, once learned, should be a fast one.

SP 1. Stand in front of performer, grasp upper arm or elbow of right arm, and help keep arm straight until skill is completed.
2. Stand between bars. Hold ankle that will not be flanking and waist of hand that will not be leaving bar.

CE 1. Failure to keep shoulders slightly forward of bar until stride position is attained.
2. Failure to keep right arm straight at all times.
3. Failure to lift left leg high enough to clear bar.
4. Failure to keep legs straight.

MO 1. Single-leg swing down and up.
2. Single-leg flank dismount with quarter turn.
3. Mill circle.
4. Mill circle, catch high bar.

Figure U-24

CAST (push away and return to bar) (Fig. U-25)

SL Beginner

PT From front support position, with hands in a forward grip, flex hips, bring legs under bar (allow arms to slightly flex) and move shoulders forward of the bar. Thrust legs backupward forcing body (except hands) away from the bar, and extend arms. Return to the bar in a fully extended (arched) position.

Hint: Try to swing legs high enough to have calves make contact with the high bar.

SP Stand between bars. Inside hand reaches under the bar and is placed behind elbow (palm against elbow) to force the shoulders forward. Place the outside hand on the upper thigh to help lift body away from the bar.

CE 1. Allowing arms to bend after hips leave the bar.
2. Not keeping head up and shoulders forward of the bar.
3. Insufficient thrust of legs.
4. Allowing legs to bend.
5. Not returning to the bar in an arched position.

MO 1. Back hip circle.

2. This movement is also used for the following skills, but body does not return to the bar in an arched position before continuing with the skills.
   a. Single-leg shoot through to stride support.
   b. Double-leg shoot through to rear support.
   c. Squat stand.
   d. Straddle stand.
   e. Stoop stand.
   f. Squat-over dismount.

Figure U-25

SINGLE-LEG SHOOT THROUGH (Fig. U-26)

SL Beginner

PT From a front support with a forward grip, cast away from the bar, keeping arms straight and shoulders forward of the bar. As the body is suspended away from the bar, forcefully lift hips and bring one knee to chest; then extend if forward over the low bar as body is returning to the bar. Finish in a stride position with entire body weight on hands.

SP Two spotters, one in front of the low bar, one between the bars. The spotter between the bars stands on the nonbending leg side. Grasp leg above knee with inside hand and ankle with outside hand, and help keep body suspended by lifting leg until the other knee is bent and extended over the bar. The spotter in front of the bar supports upper arms to make sure shoulders remain forward of the bar at all times and to prevent performer from collapsing.

CE 1. Insufficient cast.
2. Failure to keep shoulders forward of the bar.
3. Allowing arms to bend.
4. Failure to bend knee to chest and to extend it over the bar in one rapid movement.
5. Allowing knee to be turned out rather than bringing it directly to the chest.

MO 1. Mill circle.
2. Mill circle, catch the high bar.
3. Single-leg flank dismount with quarter turn.

Figure U-26

182

BACK HIP CIRCLE (Fig. U-27)

SL Beginner

PT From a front support position with the hands in a forward grip, cast away from the bar and return in a straight body position, contacting the bar at the lower abdominal area. As soon as the body contacts the bar, flex hips and force legs forward. Bend arms slightly to keep hips close to the bar and rotate around the bar at hip area. As soon as the body has completed three-quarters of the circle, rotate hands (grip) around the bar and extend arms to finish in a front support position.

SP Stand in front of the bar. Reach under the bar and place inside hand on back as body returns to the bar from the cast and outside hand on back of upper thigh to help rotate and keep hips close to the bar. After hips have circled bar, slide outside hand up to arm to help maintain front support position.

CE 1. Poor cast.
2. Failure to pike as hips contact the bar (many beginners pike too soon).
3. Failure to slightly bend arms and continually pull hips to the bar.
4. Failure to keep legs straight at all times.
5. Failure to rotate hands (grip) around the bar, fully extend arms and shoulders, and open body to finish in a front support position.

MO Any skill from the front support position.

Figure U-27

SINGLE-LEG SWING DOWN AND UP (Fig. U-28)

SL Beginner

Note: This particular skill is not one that you will find in a competitive routine. It is merely a lead-up skill for other moves.

Figure U-28

PT From a stride support, right leg in front, hands in a forward grip, shift hips backward, bending right leg so that knee hooks over the bar, and swing back and down under the bar. As momentum under the bar stops, swing left leg down and backupward forcefully; push against the bar with hands and return to the stride position. Just as thigh of right leg moves over the bar, slightly bend elbows, rotate hands to the top of the bar, and extend arms, right leg, and upper body to finish in a stride position.

SP Stand between bars to left of performer. As body swings under bar, place outside hand on back to prevent a fall, and as body starts upward motion, reach under the bar and place inside hand on upper thigh to assist with the pumping action of the left leg.

CE 1. Allowing arms to bend and body to curl forward on the back swing.
2. Not using left (pumping leg) forcefully.
3. Failure to rotate grip as body returns to the stride support position.
4. Failure to extend right leg and upper body as body reaches the stride position.

MILL CIRCLE (Fig. U-29)

SL Beginner

PT From a stride support (right leg forward) *using the reverse grip,* lift body up from the bars and support weight on hands. Keep chest and head up; arch back slightly. Shift weight forward by leading with right foot as if to step forward and extend hips. This movement should force most of the body weight over the bar and allow body to rotate around the bar. For added momentum, lift back leg so that legs are in a wide split position. Keep legs apart and body straight throughout skill. As upper body is coming to the original position, rotate hands forward around the bar, forcing wrists forward, lifting upper body (slightly arching the back to stop momentum), and finish in a stride support.

Note: To learn, it sometimes helps to bring legs together while in the inverted position; however, you must keep weight on hands, and legs *off* bars.

SP Stand between bars, reach under the bar with inside hand, and grasp elbow or wrist with palm to help keep performer's arms straight and to force body around the bar by pushing forward and then upward as the performer comes to the original position. Outside hand supports the back during the last quarter of the skill. A second spotter can reach under the bar and place inside hand on back of thigh to push leg forward at the start of the skill.

CE 1. Failure to lift body off the bar and support weight with hands before starting forward motion.
2. Failure to step out to allow hips to pass forward of the bar and to develop momentum.
3. Not keeping head and chest up throughout skill (chin should drop a bit just before finishing the skill).
4. Allowing upper body to curl when rotating.
5. Bending arms and legs during skill.

Figure U-29

6. Not moving hands around bar with body and not forcing them forward during the last quarter of the skill.

MO 1. Single-leg flank to rear support position; then grasp high bar and move to high bar by performing a stem rise, pullover, or kip.
2. Single-leg flank dismount with quarter turn.
3. Single-leg flank with half turn to front support facing high bar.

VA *Mill circle, catch high bar* (Fig. U-30)

SL Advanced Beginner

PT Same procedures as for the beginning of the mill circle. When body is inverted under the bar, begin looking for high bar and, when body has almost reached the original position, reach for the high bar, keeping the body straight (*hips forward*).

SP Stand between bars. As soon as the performer has passed the inverted position, place inside hand on lower back and outside hand on upper back, and help performer to the high bar. Maintain contact until grasp has been made on high bar.

Figure U-30

CE 1. Poor mill circle.
2. Failure to keep eyes open and look for the high bar.
3. Reaching for the bar too soon, or with one hand at a time.
4. Failure to keep hips moving forward throughout entire skill.

MO 1. Single- or double-leg stem rise.
2. Pullover from low to high.
3. Kip from low to high bar.

FRONT HIP CIRCLE (Fig. U-31)

SL Beginner

PT Assume front support position with the hands in a forward grip and body resting high on upper thighs; keep head up and lean forward, leading with chest and keeping entire body extended. Just before body reaches the inverted position, flex (pike) upper body, bend elbows slightly, and continue rotating around the bar. Push down forcefully on the bar with hands, and just before body returns to the original position, forcefully rotate hands forward, extend arms and shoulders, and finish in a front support.

SP Two spotters between bars. Reach under the bar with inside hand and spot lower back and hip area. As body passes the inverted position, place outside hand on back. (Transfer inside hand to legs to control forward movement, if necessary.)

CE 1. Not starting with thighs high enough on the bar (insufficient extension of shoulders and arms).
2. Failure to keep head and chest up, to extend shoulders, and to arch back.

3. Piking too soon or too late.
4. Failure to keep hips in contact with the bar throughout skill.
5. Failure to extend arms and shoulders up on returning to original position.

MO Any skill from the front support position.

Figure U-31

VA 1. *Free front hip circle (starting with hands over head)* (Fig. U-32)

    SL Beginner

    PT Front support, body high on bar, arms overhead. Forcefully swing arms down, backward, and upward as body follows in a fully arched position. Just before reaching the inverted position, pike upper body and grasp the bar in a forward grip; continue movement to front support as for hip circle.

Figure U-32

2. *Front hip circle, catch high bar* (Fig. U-33)

Figure U-33

186

SQUAT STAND (Fig. U-34)

SL Beginner

PT From a front support with hands in a forward grip, push away (cast) from the bar forcefully. While body is extended and suspended, lift hips and bring knees to chest; then place toes on bar between hands. Lift head and chest, grip the bar tightly, and keep hips low to maintain balance.

Figure U-34

SP One spotter between bars, other spotter in front of bar. The spotter standing between the bars reaches over the bar with inside hand to support upper arm and keep shoulders forward of the bar. Place outside hand on back of thigh (palm up) to help lift as performer squats to bar. Spotter in front of bar supports upper arm to keep shoulders forward of bar.

CE 1. Poor cast.
2. Insufficient height on cast to allow knees to be brought to the chest.
3. Slow leg action in cast, to squat, or body.
4. Not keeping shoulders forward of the bar.
5. Failure to lower hips and to keep head and chest up as feet contact bar.

MO 1. Stand, half turn (180°), front support on high bar, back hip circle.
2. Stand, reach back and grasp high bar, dislocate.
3. Stand, reach back and grasp high bar, back straddle catch.
4. Stand, grasp high bar, 180° turn, sole circle, underswing with half turn.
5. Stand, reach back and grasp high bar, jump to L support, drop back, flank-cut catch or drop back, flank dismount (or straddle cut catch or dismount).
6. Stand, reach back and grasp high bar, jump to L support, front or back seat circle.

DOUBLE-LEG SHOOT THROUGH (Fig. U-35)

SL Beginner

PT From a front support with a forward grip, cast forcefully, bend both legs, drawing knees to chest, and immediately extend legs forward over low bar. Keep arms straight throughout skill and squeeze bar with hands. Finish in an L support or rear support with weight supported on hands.

Figure U-35

SP Two spotters. One in front of the low bar holding upper arm to keep shoulders forward of the bar. The other spotter between the bars with inside hand over or under bar (depending on height of spotter) grasping elbow to help keep shoulders forward and outside hand under back of upper thigh to help performer squat over bar to support position.

CE 1. Poor cast.
2. Slow leg action on drawing knees to chest and extending them forward over the bar.
3. Not keeping shoulders forward of the bar.
4. Allowing toes to contact the bar when shooting through.
5. Failure to hold the L support.

187

MO 1. When performed on low bar:
    a. Drop back and up to L support.
    b. Drop back and up and catch the high bar.
    c. Back seat circle.
    d. Change hands to reverse grip and perform forward seat circle.
    e. Dislocate to glide kip catch.
   2. When performed on the high bar:
    a. Back seat circle.
    b. Change hands to reverse grip and perform front seat circle or dislocate.
    c. Drop back, flank-cut catch or flank-cut dismount.
    d. Drop back, straddle-cut catch or straddle-cut dismount.
    e. Drop back (perform three-quarters of back seat circle, then drop to glide kip on low bar).

CAST-FREE STRADDLE SUPPORT (Fig. U-36)

SL Intermediate

PT Same procedures as for double-leg shoot through except that the legs are forcefully raised to the side and then forward over the bar to the outside of the hands and remain completely free of the bar. Support on hands only. Hips must be raised forcefully, then lowered as the straddle position is achieved.

Figure U-36

SP One spotter stands in front of the bars to support upper arms and to keep shoulders forward of the bar. A second spotter can stand between bars behind performer and, as she straddles, places hands on back of upper thighs and assists her in clearing the bar.

MO 1. On low bar: underswing, half turn to glide kip to front support, or double-leg shoot through.
   2. On high bar: underswing, half turn and hip circle on low bar.

DROP DOWN AND UP (Fig. U-37)

SL Beginner

PT This very basic skill should always be taught, as it teaches timing and control in the piked position; it is also the beginning, middle, or end of several skills. Start in a rear seat support with hands in a forward grip. Lift body off bar while lifting ankles to face. With arms completely straight, drop back and under the bar, keeping hips fairly close to the bar. As soon as the momentum stops, forward motion will begin. At this point push down on the bar forcefully, remain in the tight pike, and move grip slightly forward as body moves back to starting position. Hips will extend at this point to finish in a rear sitting position.

SP Stand to the side of the performer between bars. Place inside hand on buttocks and outside hand on back. Go with the movement, and assist by pushing on back during latter part of return movement.

CE 1. Bending arms at any time during skill.
   2. Allowing upper body to go forward in the beginning rather than lifting legs to upper body.
   3. Trying to return to rear sitting position too soon rather than taking full advantage of the swinging action.

VA Drop down and, on return, catch high bar.

Figure U-37

FRONT SEAT CIRCLE (Fig. U-38)

SL   Beginner

PT   From L support with reverse grip, lift hips back and up so the body is in a tight pike and the lower part of the leg is close to (but not touching) the bar. Lean forward, keeping arms straight and body in tight pike, and rotate around the bar allowing the hands to rotate also. The body rotates without legs or thighs touching the bar. Look at knees during skill. As the body passes the inverted position under the bar and is approaching the original position, rotate the hands forward (thumbs leading), slightly raise the shoulders, and forcefully extend the arms to finish in the original position. Tilt head up; eyes spot stationary object at eye level.

SP   Two spotters stand between bars. Reach under bar and grasp elbow or wrist with inside hand. Force body forward. As body comes under bar, place far hand on back to assist in lifting to original position.

CE   1. Failure to keep body free of bar throughout skill.
2. Failure to lift hips as high as possible before beginning forward movement.
3. Failure to remain in a piked position throughout skill, opening up only slightly upon returning to original position.
4. Failure to keep arms perfectly straight, especially at the beginning of the skill.
5. Failure to rotate hands around bar and then rotate thumb and wrist forward during the last quarter of the skill.

MO   1. On low bar:
a. Change hands to reverse grip, back seat circle.
b. Sit, grasp high bar, kip to high bar.
c. Sit, grasp high bar, kip to double-leg shoot through, drop back, drop kip on low bar.
2. On high bar:
a. Dislocate, hip circle on low bar.
b. Change the hands to a forward grip, back seat circle.
c. Change the hands to a forward grip, drop back, flank-cut catch or dismount.
d. Change the hands to a forward grip, drop back, straddle-cut catch or dismount.

189

Figure U-38

VA *Front seat circle, catch high bar* (Fig. U-39)

    SL Beginner

    PT As soon as the body passes the inverted position, open the tight pike position, extend hips, and reach for the high bar.

    SP Same as for mill-circle catch.

Figure U-39

BACK SEAT CIRCLE (Fig. U-40)

SL Beginner

PT From an L position with the hands in a forward grip, force knees to head so that body forms a tight pike-with hips over bar. Shift weight backward and continue rotating around the bar in a tight pike. Move hands around the bar with rest of body; just as body is three-quarters way around, rotate hands forcefully forward, lift head and spot object at eye level (over the bar), and finish in the original position.

SP Stand in front of the low bar. Reach under the bar with inside hand and

Figure U-40

190

grasp performer's upper arm. As the performer rotates, place outside hand on upper leg to help keep hips away from bar and body in tight pike.

CE 1. Failure to keep body (except hands) free of bar throughout skill.
2. Failure to go into deep pike and remain in this position throughout the skill.
3. Failure to keep arms perfectly straight, especially on the drop backward.
4. Opening pike before returning to L position.
5. Failure to rotate hands around the bar.

MO Same as for front seat circle.

SOLE CIRCLE BACKWARD (Fig. U-41)

SL Advanced Intermediate

PT From stoop position (could be done in straddle) with hips directly above bar, compress as tightly as possible. Pushing against bar with feet and pulling with hands, continue rotation until original position is attained.

Overcoming inertia is critical here. Many gymnasts will be successful if they squat into the bar the last quarter of the rotation. This pulls the weight closer to the base. Start with the balls of the feet on the bar, so as rotation occurs, the feet can stay longer on the bar.

SP Inside hand: back of thigh to help prevent fall on downward portion. Outside hand: on shoulder to assist with lift upward.

CE 1. Not pushing against bar during entire skill.
2. Not rotating hands continually.
3. Not staying compressed.

MO 1. Back sommie dismount.
2. Forward sole circle to kip.

Figure U-41

FREE BACK HIP CIRCLE (Fig. U-42)

SL Advanced

Lead-up: Do pullover mount without allowing hips to touch. *Work on rotating around hands, not hips.*

PT From a front support position on either bar in either direction, cast away from the bar. As the

191

body returns toward the bar drop the shoulders, slightly pike, rotate the hands quickly, keeping hips clear of bar. As the hips pass under the bar and begin to ride upward, forcefully extend the hips upward (as if kipping) and push with the arms to send hips over the bar.

SP 1. Stand on opposite side of bar facing gymnast. As body comes under bar, push shoulders upward.
2. Stand to side of performer. Grasp hip and upper leg to assist in keeping body free from bar.

CE 1. Keeping shoulders forward after cast.
2. Failure to rotate hands.
3. Not extending hips upward after coming under bar.

MO On high bar:
   1. Cast to any number of skills.
   2. Over lower bar:
      a. Bar beat full turn.
      b. Bar beat squat on handstand on high.
On low bar:
   1. To sole circle.
   2. To handstand.

Figure U-42

Figure U-43

VA *Free hip to handstand*(Fig. U-43)

    SL Advanced

    PT As the body comes under the bar, shoot the hips upward forcefully. This will lift the weight upward and allow the hands to rotate quickly. Pull the body in a straight line (beginning with the head and shoulders) to a handstand.

    SP 1. Stand on mats between the bars, and lift in the hip area.
        2. Stand on low bar with one leg over high bar. Grasp ankles and lift up to handstand.

    MO On high bar:
        1. Pirouette.
        2. Cast.

3. Sole circle.
4. Stalder.
   On low bar:
   1. Pirouette.
   2. Sole.
   3. Lower to front support on high bar and "pop off" to another skill.
   4. Stalder.

FRONT HIP CIRCLE TO HANDSTAND (performed from long hang kip) (Fig. U-44)

SL Advanced

PT As the body completes the front hip circle, the shoulders should continue moving forward past the bar. Thrust the hips and legs forcefully upward. Just before vertical position is attained by the legs, pull the shoulders back over the bar. This action should bring body to a total vertical position.

SP Stand in front of bar (on stack of mats). With inside hand, support shoulders. With outside hand, lift abdominal area.

CE 1. Not allowing shoulders to go forward before swinging to handstand.
2. Arching body.

VA 1. Straddle to handstand position.

MO 1. Sole circle.
2. On high bar, pirouette to hip circle.
3. Quarter turn, squat or straddle dismount.

Figure U-44

STALDER (Fig. U-45—not available at this printing)

SL Advanced

Lead-ups:
1. Straddle seat circle forward or backward.
2. Cast to handstand.

PT It can be performed forward or backward.

Forward: From a handstand position allow the shoulders to move forward of the bars as the legs begin to straddle. The head and feet should drop below the bar at the same level and same time. The body must tightly compress in the straddle position to keep mo-

193

mentum at its greatest. As the hands and body continue to rotate, the shoulders will slightly pass the bar, and at this point the body presses to a handstand position.

SP Out of the handstand into the straddle position, support the back and hips. Out of the straddle to the handstand, lift at the waist.

CE 1. Not allowing grip to rotate smoothly.
2. Not compressing under the bar.
3. Opening from straddle to handstand before shoulders pass the bar.

MO 1. Sole circles.
2. Pirouettes.
3. Do not return to handstand; do back sommie to low bar.

Moves From One Bar to the Other

PULLOVER FROM LOW BAR TO HIGH BAR (Fig. U-46)

SL Beginner

PT Grasp high bar with forward grip. Place right foot on low bar with right knee forward of right foot. Extend left leg over the low bar. Lower left leg, then forcefully swing leg up over the high bar while simultaneously bending arms (pulling) to help get hips to the high bar. Immediately push with right foot; bring legs together as body rotates. Lift head and chest; rotate grip and extend arms to finish in a front support on the high bar.

SP Stand between bars and assist by pushing hips to the high bar. As the performer reaches the support position, grasp ankles to assist with balance.

CE 1. Failure to swing straight leg forcefully up and back over bar.
2. Failure to pull with arms and push with foot against low bar.
3. Failure to rotate grip and extend arms, then lift head to finish in a front support.

MO 1. Any skill listed from a front support position.
2. Cast to a long hang and any move from that position.

Figure U-46

DOUBLE-LEG STEM RISE (Fig. U-47)

SL Beginner

PT 1. Grasp high bar with forward grip; place both feet (toes) on low bar. Extend legs, forcing hips to high bar by forcefully pushing downward on the high bar. Allow elbows to bend

194

slightly to let shoulders pass over bar. Feet remain on the low bar until the body is almost to a front support position. Rotate grip, extend arms and shoulders, and finish in a front support.

Note: The timing or coordination of the leg extension and arm pull is very important on both the single and double stem rise. The hips must move backward, then upward as if moving around a large semicircle.

2. Start in L position (toes on low bar). Keep legs straight at all times. Pull up slightly with arms while pushing against low bar. Lower body to original L; then forcefully pull with hands and push against bar with feet until in a front support position.

SP Stand under high bar. Place outside hand on hip, inside hand on back of upper thigh. Assist in backward, then upward movement.

CE 1. Failure to extend legs backward as body is being pulled to the bar by the arms.
2. Not allowing shoulders to pass over bar.
3. Allowing feet to leave low bar before body is ready to extend to front support position.
4. Failure to rotate grip, extend arms, and lift head and chest to end in a front support.

MO 1. Any skill from a front support position on the low bar.
2. Underswing to stride support.
3. Cast to long hang.
4. Underswing dismount over low bar.
5. Handstand, quarter-turn dismount.
6. Handstand, squat, straddle or stoop dismount.
7. Double-leg shoot through to stand on low bar.
8. Cast to straddle stand or free straddle support.

Notice good grip movement forward at this point

Figure U-47

SINGLE-LEG STEM RISE (Fig. U-48)

SL Beginner

PT Grasp high bar with a forward grip. Place right foot on the low bar and extend left leg upward so that ankle contacts high bar. Keeping arms straight, extend right leg (forcing hips backward); then forcefully push down on the high bar while moving right leg vertically to bring hips to bar. Right foot remains on low bar until body is almost to the front support position. Rotate grip, fully extend arms and shoulders, lift head and chest, and finish in a front support position.

Figure U-48

SP Stand under high bar on performer's left side. Place inside hand on hips and outside hand on right leg to assist in backward and upward movement.

CE 1. Failure to extend right leg (causing backward movement of the hips) as body is being pulled to the high bar by arms.
2. Not allowing arms to bend very slightly to get shoulders over bar before getting into the front support position.
3. Allowing right foot to stop pushing on or to leave the low bar before the body is ready to go into the front support position.
4. Failure to rotate grip, to extend arms and shoulders fully, and to end in a front support position.

MO Same as for double-leg stem rise.

KIP FROM LOW TO HIGH BAR (Fig. U-49)

SL Advanced Beginner

PT From rear support on low bar, grasp high bar with a forward grip. Keep eyes focused on high bar or on object in back of high bar until kipping action is almost completed; then look over high bar. Bring ankles to high bar; then forcefully move legs upward and simultaneously push down on the high bar with hands to bring hips to the high bar. As legs are moving up the bar, then outward, hips are extending. Rotate grip forward, extend arms and shoulders, and end in front support.

SP Place inside hand on back of upper thigh, outside hand on shoulder or upper back, and assist in entire movement to the front support.

CE 1. Allowing head to be forward.
2. Sluggish movement throughout the skill.
3. Kipping downward rather than upward, then outward (failure to force legs up the bar)..
4. Allowing arms to bend (except during rotation of hands to move to front support position).
5. Failure to rotate grip, extend arms and shoulders, and end in a front support.

MO Same as from stem rise.

Figure U-49

UNDERSWING TO STRIDE SUPPORT (Fig. U-50)

SL Beginner

PT From front support on high bar with hands in a forward grip, allow the upper body to drop backward (arms remaining straight), keeping thighs as close to the bar as possible. As the body moves under the bar, slightly bend the arms, lift left leg and lower right leg so that it is extend-

196

ed behind the low bar and left leg is extended in front of the low bar. Extend hips forward, bend arms, and lower body to stride position on low bar with control.

SP Stand under high bar and support hips with outside hand and back of upper thigh of left leg with inside hand.

CE 1. Failure to keep arms straight as body drops behind the high bar.
2. Failure to keep thighs close to the bar on the underswing.
3. Failure to bend arms and control underswing as body passes under the high bar.
4. Failure to extend hips as forward leg passes over the low bar.
5. Failure to lower body to stride support with control.

MO 1. Maintain grip on high bar:
    a. Pullover low to high.
    b. Single- or double-leg stem rise after bringing back leg to the bar.
    c. Bring back leg over bar to rear sitting (hanging) support and kip to high bar.
2. Change hands to low bar:
    a. Mill circle.
    b. Mill circle catch.
    c. Single-leg flank dismount with quarter turn.

Figure U-50

FORWARD ROLL TO REAR SEAT SUPPORT ON LOW BAR (Fig. U-51)

SL Beginner

PT From front support on the high bar with hands in a forward grip, lower body forward (pike), rotate grip forward, and slowly lower body to rest on back of upper thighs on the low bar. Hands remain in a forward grip throughout the entire skill.

SP Stand between bars. Put outside hand on back as pike is achieved and inside hand on back of upper thigh to help lower to low bar.

CE 1. Bending legs.
2. Failure to rotate grip.
3. Failure to maintain a forward grip throughout entire skill.
4. Failure to control movement to rear sitting support on low bar.

MO 1. Maintain grip on high bar:
    a. Pullover low to high bar.

197

b. Single- or double-leg stem rise.
c. Dislocate into glide kip, catch high bar.

Figure U-51

DOUBLE-LEG SHOOT THROUGH TO STAND ON LOW BAR (Fig. U-52)

SL Intermediate

PT From a front support on the high bar with hands in a forward grip, cast away from the bar, keeping head up and shoulders forward of the bar. Immediately tuck knees to chest and extend legs over the high bar; extend hips and place toes on low bar; then extend upper body.

   Hint: Place mat over the low bar to prevent bruises on legs if feet should miss the low bar. Also, student should be able to control the squat stand and double-leg shoot through to L support on low bar before attempting this skill on the high bar.

SP 1. Stand on low bar and hook one leg over the top bar. Support arm with inside hand and assist in cast and shoot through with outside hand.
   2. Stand on object at side of bar and spot as above.

CE 1. Poor cast.
   2. Slow leg action on the cast and over the bar.
   3. Failure to extend hips, raise upper body, and place toes on the low bar.
   4. Panic.

MO 1. Dislocate.
   2. Back straddle catch.

Figure U-52

3. Release grip on high bar and place hands on low bar in reverse grip; sole circle (stoop position) on low bar; change hands to forward grip and go into a glide kip.

4. Jump back to L position on the high bar and perform any skill or dismount listed from the seat circles or drop backs.

SQUAT STAND ON LOW BAR (one hand on each bar—front support on low bar facing high bar) (Fig. U-53)

SL Beginner

PT Start in a front support position on low bar, with one hand on high bar in forward grip and other hand on low bar in forward grip. Lower legs down and forward; then forcefully cast away from bar (pushing with hand on low bar); flex hips, bend knees, and place toes on low bar. Lower hips and keep head up, looking at high bar. Hand on high bar assists in pulling, and hand on low bar helps support some body weight.

SP Start to either side of the low bar. Place hands in the hip area as cast is made. Help by lifting hips up so performer can place toes on bar.

CE 1. Insufficient cast and lift of hips (will hit shins on bar if cast too low).
2. Not using arms in push-and-pull action.

MO 1. Jump into straddle sole circle, underswing half turn.
2. Stoop hop, half turn to high bar.
3. Half turn, back straddle catch.

Figure U-53

Releases

CAST FROM HIGH BAR TO HIP CIRCLE ON LOW BAR (cast wrap) (Fig. U-54)

Lead-up: First learn hip circle from the long hang, then the cast to the long hang to the hip circle on the low bar.

Figure U-54

1. *Hip circle from long hang* (Fig. U-55)

SL Advanced Beginner

PT Hang on high bar. Spotter between bars will initiate swing. As the performer contacts the low bar in a long-hang position, she will forcefully pike (bringing knees toward head). When, and only when, this tight pike position is attained should the performer release the high bar to regrasp the low bar and continue with the hip circle. It might be advisable to have a certain number of swings and pikes before releasing the high bar, such as release on third contact with low bar. As movement continues around the low bar, there is a slight bend of the arms to allow the performer to constantly pull hips to the low bar (as in the hip circle from the cast). As the movement is almost completed, rotate the grip, extend arms and shoulders, head up, and finish in a front support.

SP One spotter between bars initiates swing by pushing hips toward the low bar. As the piked position is achieved, the other spotter in front of low bar places hands on backs of upper thighs to force body around the bar. As performer is reaching the front support position, the inside spotter can grasp legs and upper arm to help her maintain front support position.

CE 1. Allowing the hips to pike (flex) before contacting the bar.
2. Not forcing legs toward head after contactiing the low bar.
3. Releasing the high bar too soon or too late.
4. Failure to maintain contact of hips on the low bar during the hip circle.
5. Failure to rotate grip rearward, extend upper body, and finish in a front support position.

Figure U-55

2. *Cast to long hang* (Fig. U-56)

SL Advanced Beginner

PT From a front support position on the high bar with the hands in a forward grip, bring legs forward under the bar; force legs back-upward and extend arms to push body away from the bar with control. Keep body in a fully extended position and swing under the high bar toward the low bar.

Figure U-56

200

Note: Leg action does not have to be very forceful if arms are extended properly. The important thing to remember is to extend arms so the entire body weight will not have to be supported by hands and shoulders in a jarring or jerky movement to the long-hang position.

SP   Stand behind the high bar and grasp legs and lower body throughout the swing. A second spotter can stand under the high bar to assist the performer if she loses her grip and to stop momentum of the swing by placing her hands on performer's abdomen.

CE   1. Jerky cast allows arms to bend, knees to bend, or legs to separate.
      2. Failure to keep body tight throughout long hang.

At this point, if student feels confident that she can perform each part of the skill by herself, the two may be combined. One spotter should spot the cast to the long hang, and the other one should spot the hip circle.

CE   Of combined skills:
      1. Jerky or insufficient cast.
      2. Failure to keep body tight until hips have contacted the low bar.
      3. Failure to flex hips when they contact the low bar.
      4. Releasing the high bar too soon or too late.
      5. Failure to rotate grip, extend arms, raise upper body, and end in a front support.

MO   1. Skills listed from front support position.
      2. Eagle catch.
      3. Pop glide kip.
      4. Hecht dismount.

BACK STRADDLE CATCH (Fig. U-57)

SL   Intermediate

Lead-up:

Remove one bar from a set of even parallel bars and lower the remaining bar. Stand on a stack of mats or some other stable object that will make the distance from the mat to the bar equal to that of the low to the high bar and touch bar with one hand palm down for balance. Bend knees and spring vertically and backward, moving legs to a wide straddle position. Immediately grasp the bar between legs with body hands in a forward grip. The first few times the spotter should stop the performer in a straddle position on the bar. This will assure both spotter and performer that the jump, straddle, and grasp of the bar are being executed correctly. It also gives the performer confidence. When performer feels confident enough, spotter can assist her to clear bar and come to a stand on the mats behind bar with hands still in contact with bar.

SP   Reach over bar and grasp waist of performer. When she is ready to clear the bar, assist her by lifting and pulling hips back.

PT   The performer should now transfer this skill to a regulation set of unevens. Jump vertically, lifting hips up and back. Lift legs to a wide straddle position. Immediately grasp the high bar after the jump and straddle. Force heels out and back as legs come together to enable body to reach a fully extended position before going into the long-hang position.

SP   Stand in back of high bar and as performer straddles and grasps the bar, reach for or make contact with back of upper thighs to prevent a fall or to slow the long-hang swing action until the student is able to perform the skill without contact spotting.

CE   1. Jumping back rather than vertical then back (letting hips drift back toward the bar before jumping), failure to keep upper body over feet.
      2. Not grasping the bar with both hands simultaneously and immediately after jumping and straddling.

3. Insufficient straddle and failure to lift feet high enough to insure clearing the bar.
4. Failure to force heels back after clearing the bar to come into the long hang with a fully extended body.

MO 1. Hip circle on the low bar and then any skill from that position, such as an eagle.
2. Drop kip.
3. Hecht.

Figure U-57

VA *Half turn, back straddle to kip on same bar* (Fig. U-58)

Figure U-58

UNDERSWING WITH HALF (180°) TURN TO A HIP CIRCLE ON LOW BAR

Lead-up: 1. Underswing on low bar with half turn to stand with hands still in contact with bar.

PT Assume a front support with hands in a forward grip; keep arms straight and thighs close to the bar, and drop back from the bar into a pike position after hips pass under the bar; extend body fully by forcefully extending hips upward and point toes in the direction of the turn. Twist hips toward the side of the turn, and as body is extending, release one hand, turn shoulders, and immediately grasp in a forward grip. (Hands now in a mixed grip.) Allow feet to contact mat but keep hands on low bar.

202

Lead-up: 2. *Sit on low bar facing high bar, hands on the high bar in a forward grip or mixed grip.* (Fig. U-59)

PT Lift ankles toward the high bar and immediately extend hips (entire body) and slightly bend arms to assist in upward and then outward extension of the body. Just as body reaches full extension, initiate the turn with hips and shoulders, leading the turn with toes. Release one hand (if turning toward left side, release right hand) and regrasp high bar in a forward grip. (Hands are now in a mixed grip.) Continue into long hang toward the low bar. May also start with mixed grip as shown in Fig. U-59.

SP (Performer turning left) Stand between bars to right side of performer. Assist the half turn by placing hands on hips and turning hips to the left. Performer will release right hand. As the turn is completed, a second spotter can step in and assist performer through the long hang by placing hand on abdomen and upper thigh.

Figure U-59

UNDERSWING WITH HALF TURN FROM FRONT SUPPORT ON HIGH BAR (back facing low bar) (Fig. U-60)

SL Low Intermediate

PT Drop back from bar, keeping thighs close to bar and arms straight. Pike, then extend body fully and make half (180°) turn and go into long hang.

CE 1. Failure to keep thighs close to bar as underswing is initiated.
2. Failure to maintain straight arms throughout skill.
3. Failure to fully extend hips to force body upward and outward before the turn.
4. Turning too soon or too late.
5. Failure to maintain full body extension with feet well behind body when coming into the long hang toward the low bar.

MO 1. Hip circle on the low bar. (Fig. U-60)
2. Any other skill listed from the long-hang position.

Figure U-60

VA 1. *Sole circle* (Fig. U-61)

SL Intermediate

PT From a stand on low bar facing high bar with hands in a forward grip, jump into a straddle stand position on high bar (insteps on bar); pause momentarily, then underswing, half turn into long hang, then hip circle on low bar.

Hint: It is very important in this skill to keep shoulders and arms fully extended and pull against the bar with arms on the underswing to keep feet on bar; also feet (ankles) must extend and push against bar. Keep feet on bar until last possible moment, then extend legs with a foreupward thrust of hips to fully extend body before the turn.

Figure U-61

2. *Underswing with half turn from free straddle support* (Fig. U-62)

SL Intermediate

PT Stand on the low bar facing the high bar, hands in a forward grip; jump into a free straddle-support position (legs over the bar), underswing, half turn into long hang.

204

Figure U-62

Figure U-63

UNDERSWING HALF TURN TO HIP CIRCLE ON LOW BAR FACING IN (Fig. U-63)

SL Intermediate

PT Same principles as all other underswings; only difference is direction.

CE 1. Not riding hips up high enough over low bar.
   2. Piking before hitting the low bar. (Should keep hips forward until contact; then pike into hip circle.)

SP Stand between bars to assist in slowing movement before hips hit bars by placing hands on abdomen and upper thigh.

EAGLE CATCH (Fig. U-64)

SL Intermediate

Lead-up:

From a relaxed hang at hips over the low bar, spotter rocks performer forward and backward. On a prearranged signal, e.g., three swings, the performer forcefully lifts the upper body and swings arms vigorously forward, sideways, and backward to grasp the high bar in an eagle grip. As the upper body lifts, feet are forced backward so that the performer can pop off the low bar in an arched position. *Performer must not look for the high bar* but should tilt head upward on the pop and look directly forward.

SP Stand between bars and grasp performer around upper thighs and help lift to high bar.

PT From a very tight wrap in a hip circle on the low bar, as the body completes approximately three quarters of the hip circle, forcefully lift upper body, force heels backward, tighten hips and reach up, out and back to grasp the high bar in an eagle grip. As body reaches 45° angle from bar, pop begins.

SP As performer is coming off the low bar, place inside hand on front of upper thigh and outside hand on hips or lower back.

CE 1. Popping too soon or too late.
   2. Insufficient pop—not forceful enough.
   3. Turning head to look at high bar.
   4. Failure to keep reaching back until hands contact bar.

Pop at 45° angle above bar

Figure U-64

EAGLE CATCH, DROP KIP (Fig. U-65)

SL Intermediate

SP Stand between bars. As catch is made, place inside hand on upper thigh and outside hand on back and assist by slightly supporting body weight until hands catch low bar.

206

CE 1. Not forcing heels back and keeping body tight in general on eagle.
2. Holding onto high bar too long.
3. Failure to push hips backward when dropping for kip.

Figure U-65

DROP BACK, FLANK-CUT CATCH ON HIGH BAR (Fig. U-66)

SL Intermediate

Lead-up:

Flank-cut dismount described under dismounts.

PT From L-support position on the high bar with the hands in a forward grip, lift knees toward head (without bending legs) so that body is in a tight pike. Drop back under the bar in this position, maintaining straight arms. As body swings under the bar, maintain a tight pike position, pump hips back and, as the body begins upward movement (toward original position), push on the bar forcefully to raise body almost to the original position before flanking legs to the left. Keeping the upper body erect, force both legs to the left side after releasing left hand. Extend hips fully, regrasp the high bar, and continue into the long hang. After legs have flanked to the left, focus eyes over the high bar and keep focused there until hand regrasps bar and long hang is under way.

Figure U-66

SP As the performer goes into an underswing pike position, the spotter may grasp hips or backs of upper thighs and assist the upward pumping movement before flanking. If the flank is to be executed to the left side, then spotter must stand to the right of the performer, and grasp waist.

CE 1. Failure to keep arms straight throughout the skill.
2. Failure to keep body (except hands) free of the bar throughout the skill.
3. Failure to force knees to head and remain in a deep pike until flank is executed.
4. Failure to push against bar with hands to get as high as possible before flanking.
5. Failure to keep upper body erect during flank cut.
6. Failure to extend hips as legs clear the bar so that the body will be in a full extended position before going into long hang.

MO Any skill from a long hang position mentioned previously.

VA *Drop back, straddle-cut catch* (Fig. U-67)

　　SL Advanced Intermediate

　　Lead-up:

　　　Drop back, straddle-cut dismount—described in dismounts.

　　PT Technique is the same as for the flank-cut catch except that the legs straddle, and both hands leave the bar and regrasp; eyes look directly at the bar when straddling.

　　SP Spotter stands directly behind the performer. Places hands on back of upper thighs to assist in straddle.

Figure U-67

STOOP CATCH FORWARD (Fig. U-68)

SL Intermediate

PT Start with soles of feet on bars and hands in reverse grip. Push against bar with feet and pull with hands as body moves forward. Eyes can look at knees until hips pass under bar; then look for high bar. Stay in tight pike position until three-quarters circle completed; then release hands from low bar to catch high bar.

SP Stand in front of low bar and, as performer moves forward, place inside hand on back and out-side hand on upper thigh. As body continues under bar, duck under bar (with hands still in same place) and assist with a lifting action until performer catches high bar.

CE 1. Starting with tips of toes on bar. (When going forward in a sole circle, you should start with the middle of the feet on the bar and, when going backward, start with the toes on the bar.)
2. Failure to extend legs and arms (especially in shoulder area) throughout entire skill.

MO 1. Double stem rise.
2. Drop kip.

VA 1. Straddle, sole-circle catch.
2. Straddle, sole circle, half-turn catch.

Figure U-68

STOOP, HALF-TURN CATCH (stoop, hop, half turn) (Fig. U-69)

SL Intermediate

PT From front support on low bar, cast to stoop position on low bar (on toes). Shift hands (in for-ward grip) slightly forward before backward motion begins. Keeping legs and arms completely straight, drop back in tight pike position. Look at knees at this point. As body passes under the bar, feet leave bar and shoot upward and outward. At this point hips are extended force-fully and eyes look for high bar. Both hands release low bar with right hand swinging across body to back of high bar, catching in forward grip, and left hand catches high bar in reverse grip as body completes half turn. Keep legs together and tight through skill.

SP Stand in front of low bar. As performer drops back in stoop position, place inside hand on upper thigh and outside hand on lower back. As body goes under bar, duck under, keeping hands in contact with performer and assisting with the lift and turn by pushing hip and back area.

CE 1. Bending arms or legs on stoop under bar.
2. Failure to extend hips and shoot legs up and out after passing under bar.
3. Holding onto low bar too long and failing to look for the high bar.

Hint: Learn stoop catch first before adding half turn.

MO 1. Hip circle on low bar.
2. Straddle or stoop legs over low bar; then kip to high bar.
3. Lift toes to low bar, change grip, stem to high bar.
4. Drop kip.

Figure U-69

BACK SOMMIE TO DROP KIP ON LOW BAR (from L support facing low bar) (Fig. U-70)

SL Advanced

PT From an L support on the high bar, hands in a forward grip, drop back and perform a partial seat circle. Look at knees. Before forward movement begins (in the piked position), tilt head

Figure U-70

210

up and back so eyes can spot the low bar. Release the high bar, partially extend hips so that body is at a 90° angle, and drop to the low bar, grasping bar with a forward grip. Go into a glide position and kip to the low bar.

SP Stand between bars. As performer is reaching piked position under bar and is ready to slightly extend and drop to low bar, place inside hand on back and have outside hand ready to place on back of upper thigh. Use two spotters.

CE 1. Tensing up on back seat-circle portion of skill.
2. Failure to look up and back after reaching piked position under bar and looking for low bar.
3. Failure to keep hips flexed at 90° when dropping to catch the low bar.
4. Not completing enough of the back seat circle, or completing too much of the back seat circle (riding it up too far).
5. Failure to release high bar and regrasp low bar in forward grip.

VA From rear support on low bar, hands in forward grip on high bar, kip to high bar with double-leg shoot through, drop back under and drop to kip on low bar.

PARTIAL BACK SEAT CIRCLE, EXTEND OVER LOW BAR TO DROP KIP ON LOW BAR, END FACING HIGH BAR (Fig. U-71)

SL Advanced

Lead-up:

From L support on low bar, drop back and practice extending in 90° angle to stand on mat.

PT From L support on high bar with back to low bar, hands in a forward grip, drop back as if to perform a partial back seat circle, eyes looking at knees. As forward movement begins from the piked position under the bar, partially extend hips so body is at a 90° angle. Pass over the low bar in this position, tilting head to look at the low bar. Release high bar and grasp low bar in a forward grip. Keep arms extended and glide under low bar; then kip to low bar.

High bar

Figure U-71

SP Two spotters, one between bars, one outside low bar. Spotter between the bars should grasp shoulder with inside hand and front of upper thigh with outside hand and help performer over the low bar. Spotter on outside of bar should place outside hand on lower back and inside hand on back of upper thigh and help to glide kip.

CE 1. Failure to begin forward movement from piked position before slightly extending hips and looking for low bar.
2. Extending hips too much on shoot over low bar (opening body too much).
3. Failure to release high bar as body extends (slightly) to pass over low bar.
4. Failure to grasp low bar in a forward grip, maintain open pike, and continue into glide kip.

TWISTING-MOVES PRACTICE (Fig. U-72, U-73, U-74)

Attach a single bar to a 2 X 4 X 4 piece of wood at each end. Students can practice hand change positions the following ways:

1. Kick to handstand—pirouette.
   a. Can start in forward grip—rotate outward (Fig. U-74)
   b. Can start in forward grip—rotate inward (Fig. U-73)
2. On floor face down, rotate (roll) body and hands as if in bar beat full—in the actual move the body will not be rolling to the right or left; however, the exercise gives the gymnast a feel of releasing and regrasping without having to worry about hanging the hips (Fig. U-72).

Figure U-72

→ Figure U-73

→ Figure U-74

HANDSTAND PIROUETTE (handstand half turn) (Fig. U-75)

SL Advanced

PT Can be done with hands in forward grip or mixed grip. Stand on low bar with hands on high

212

bar in forward grip. Press hips into high bar, then away. Bend knees, flex hips, and forcefully push off of low bar with legs and feet. Keeping arms straight, force hips upward with legs in a straddle position. As hips reach overhead position, bring legs together to fully stretched handstand position. As body passes vertical point, start rotation with right shoulder, release the left hand, and regrasp bar; then change right hand to forward grip. *Keep body tight throughout.* (Do not allow body to have large arch in back.) When pressing into handstand keep head up and back. When starting the half turn, look at the bar or hands.

SP 1. Have student practice on single bar and turn onto landing mat, port-a-pit, or pit. If these devices are not available, stand on low bar with one foot, other leg hooked over high bar. Hold upper arm with your inside hand and lift in hip area with outside hand. Have someone on mat to slow down momentum or swing into the low bar.
     2. After confidence is built up: stand to back of high bar to assist in control of swing coming into low bar.

Hint: To learn handstand, pile mats in front of low bar to simulate distance and height to high bar. Jump from mats into handstand on low bar. Could also use parallel bars. Take off one bar, lower other and use mats stacked up. Also, it is to performer's advantage to learn the handstand quarter turn dismount off high bar before adding half turn.

CE 1. Insufficient push with legs to get to handstand position.
     2. Failure to keep arms straight.
     3. Trying to bring legs together from straddle position before hips are over hands.
     4. Not keeping body tight after handstand position is reached.

MO 1. Hip circle on low bar; then anything from that position.
     2. Hecht dismount.
     3. Hit low bar, back uprise or drop kip.

Figure U-75

BACK UPRISE (Fig. U-76)

SL Advanced

PT From a front support on the high bar cast to low bar; from piked position on low bar forcefully drive the body straight backupward. As the body passes the 45° angle upward from vertical, slightly pike hips and pull with straight arms to front support position.

SP On back swing lift lower legs back, then up.

CE 1. Piking too much, which will cause body weight to drop.

2. Trying to move upward too soon. Body must pass 45° angle position.
3. Bending arms, which does not allow the shoulders to rise above the bars.

Figure U-76

VA *Back uprise from low to high* (Fig. U-77)

  SL Advanced

  PT From high bar cast to low bar. Then from pike on low bar totally straighten body to lift as high as possible in horizontal position. Pull immediately forward with straight arms, allowing shoulders to pass over bar, and bring body to front support. Usually followed by a back hip circle.

Figure U-77

BACK-UPRISE FULL TURN (Fig. U-78)

SL Advanced

PT Perform back uprise as in Fig. U-76. When the head is above high bar on return lift, push forcefully on bar, continue to rise; release arm in direction of turn while giving second push with other arm, then release and forcefully pull across body as body rotates. Head turns over shoulder in the direction of the turn. Both hands catch bar simultaneously with the body in a long hang position.

SP Stand to side of performer (on pile of mats if needed). As gymnast begins turn, place hands on hip and waist area to assist with the turn.

CE 1. Starting the turn before head rises above bar.
2. Not giving extra push with second hand before releasing bar.
3. Not releasing bar with second hand after push.
4. Not keeping body tight.

Figure U-78

CAST-WRAP FULL TURN (Fig. U-79)

SL Advanced

PT As the body completes three quarters of the hip circle, forcefully lift off bar, forcing the far arm to come across the body so that it can catch the high bar simultaneously with the other hand in a mixed grip. The body must stay totally tight during the rotation. (Relaxing will only lower the body weight and center of gravity.)

SP Grasp at waist area and assist in the turn.

CE 1. Throwing the first arm in rotation direction more forcefully than the second arm.
2. Trying to rotate arms in one direction and body in the other.
3. Coming off the bar with body not tight.
4. Releasing only one hand.

Figure U-79

BAR-BEAT FULL TURN (Fig. U-80)

SL Advanced

PT From a front support on the high bar cast to pike position on low bar, hands in forward grip as the body begins the backupward movement in a tightly stretched position; the first hand of the turning side releases and the head looks toward the armpit of the other arm. The second releases as the first hand regrasps (not fully), and the hand positions change once more to complete the full turn. The body should be fully stretched in the horizontal position and at this point ready to perform the next move.

SP Stand on mats between the bars and assist in rotation at the hip area.

  Hint: Place rubber tubing around bars or foam on gymnast's hips to help prevent bruises from initial inadequate turning attempts.

VA 1. Hands could start in mixed grip as cast is performed to assist in faster rotation.
  2. Could be done from a sole-circle underswing half turn to bar-beat full turn.
  3. Bar-beat full turns consecutively.

Figure U-80

FRONT SOMMIE FACING HIGH BAR (Fig. U-81)

SL Advanced

PT From a front support position on the low bar facing the high bar, cast the hips upward with legs straddled. As hips pass over bar push against and release low bar; look between legs to grasp high bar. Catch in straddle, then end in long hang.

SP Stand on mats between bars:
  1. With inside near hand on upper back, assist rotation.
    With far outside hand on back of upper thigh, assist with lift.

216

2. With inside hand on wrist, help carry to high bar.
   With outside hand on rear, help lift total weight.

CE 1. Insufficient cast of hips.
    2. Insufficient push from low bar before reaching for high.
    3. Releasing low bar too late.

VA Do from bar beat.

MO 1. Move legs from straddle to kip to high bar.
    2. Half-turn drop kip on low bar.
    3. Underswing half turn, wrap, eagle, etc.

Figure U-81

FRONT SOMMIE FACING AWAY FROM HIGH BAR (Fig. U-82)

SL Advanced

PT From front support cast hips toward high bar to a between bar position. Straddle legs. Release low bar, look between legs to high bar. Reach forcefully for high bar and catch in straddled position.

SP Stand between bars:
    1. With hand on back, help rotate.
    2. With near hand on wrist, guide to bar.

CE 1. Cast of hips too far over low bar.
    2. Release bar too late.

MO Drop kip.

Figure U-82

217

Dismounts

SINGLE-LEG FLANK WITH QUARTER (90°) TURN (Fig. U-83)

SL Beginner

PT Assume a stride position on low bar, right leg in front, right hand in a reversed grip, left hand in either a forward or reversed grip. Lift (flank) left leg sideways, upward, and over the bar. As leg is being lifted, support weight with right hand, and take left hand off the bar and lift it sideways. As left leg passes over the bar, extend hips, execute quarter turn and land on mat with right hand still contacting bar. Turn head to right and land with knees slightly bent to absorb shock and for balance.

SP Stand behind performer on supporting-arm side. Place outside hand on elbow of left arm and have inside hand ready to help lift right leg and clear bar.

CE 1. Failure to lift leg high enough to clear bar and to keep legs straight at all times.
2. Failure to keep supporting arm (right in this case) straight at all times.
3. Failure to lift arm as leg passes over bar.
4. Failure to extend hips as leg passes over bar.
5. Failure to keep upper body erect at all times.
6. Failure to maintain contact with the bar with supporting hand until feet have reached the mat and balance is attained.

VA Single-leg flank dismount with three-quarter turn.

Figure U-83

UNDERSWING ON LOW BAR (Fig. U-84)

SL Beginner

PT From a front support position on the low bar with a forward grip, keep arms straight, thighs close to the bar, and drop back behind the bar, lifting legs upward. After hips pass under the bar, fully extend body by thrusting hips and legs foreupward, then outward as hands release the bar. Land with knees slightly bent, arms over head, and head between arms.

SP Stand in front of low bar beside performer. Reach under bar with inside hand and grasp performer's back. As the underswing begins, place outside hand on back of the upper thighs to help lift legs upward. Maintain contact until the performer has landed.

CE 1. Failure to keep arms straight as body drops back, then to bend arms slightly as body is extending to push body away from bar.
2. Failure to lift legs upward to keep thighs close to the bar until hips pass under the bar.

218

3. Failure to push away from the bar (release the hands) as body extends upward and outward.

4. Allowing upper body to fall forward upon landing (mainly due to allowing hips to flex).

Figure U-84

VA 1. *Underswing from high bar over low bar* (Fig. U-85)

SL Beginner

PT Same principles of movement as for underswing from low bar.

SP One spotter between bars to help clear low bar; place inside hand on hip, outside hand on upper back. Second spotter, in front of bar, places inside hand on hip as performer is clearing the bar and outside hand on back of upper thigh. Maintain contact until landing position is achieved.

Figure U-85

2. *Underswing from high bar over low bar with half (180°) turn* (Fig. U-86)

SL Beginner

Figure U-86

PT Underswing from front support on high bar; as body reaches fully extended position, make half turn leading with toes and turning hips in the direction of the turn. If the turn is being made to the left, head should turn to the left as the turn is initiated. Performer should land facing low bar.

SP Same as for preceding underswing variation. Spotter in front of bar stands at nonturning side of performer.

3. *Underswing may also be performed with quarter or three-quarter turn.*

HANDSTAND QUARTER (90°) TURN FROM FRONT SUPPORT ON HIGH BAR (Fig. U-87)

SL Beginner

PT From a front support position on the high bar, flex upper body and grasp the low bar with left hand in a forward grip and right hand in a reverse grip (hands shoulder width apart). Lower legs and immediately swing them upward to move body into a handstand position on the low bar. As body slightly overbalances, initiate quarter (90°) turn by shifting weight to right straight arm and rolling hips to the right. Keep head up and back and, as turn is initiated, look to the right, still keeping head up and back. Release left hand, lift upper body, and allow feet to land on mat. (There will be a slight hip flexion on descent.) Upon landing, right side of body will be facing the low bar, and right hand will remain on the low bar until balance is achieved.

SP One spotter stands between bars and helps the performer pass through a handstand position by pushing on abdomen. A second spotter stands between the bars to the right of the performer with both hands ready to make sure legs clear bar. A third spotter in front of low bar grasps performer's left arm to make sure hand does not leave the bar until she has landed properly.

CE 1. Failure to drop legs and forcefully swing them upward to allow body to reach handstand position before making the turn.
2. Failure to keep arms straight at all times.
3. Not releasing the left arm at all or too late.
4. Failure to lift upper body and keep body fairly extended after the turn until landing.
5. Failure to maintain contact with low bar until landing.

Figure U-87

220

HANDSTAND SQUAT, STOOP, OR STRADDLE (Fig. U-88)

SL Intermediate

PT Squat. From front support on high bar, flex upper body and grasp low bar with hands in a forward grip, shoulder width apart. Lower legs and forcefully swing them upward so that the body leaves the high bar and moves into a handstand support position on the low bar. Overbalance slightly (heels past hands), keeping shoulders over hands, then squat, straddle, or stoop, lifting the head and chest while forcefully pushing away from the low bar. Land in front of the low bar. Extend body fully before landing.

SP Stand in front of low bar (on mats if necessary). Grasp hip and abdominal area with far hand to help move hips over hands. With near hand on upper arm, help to lift arm and chest up as performer's shoulder passes hands. Far hand can now move to the rear to make sure hips and feet clear bar.

CE 1. Failure to maintain straight arms throughout skill.
      2. Failure to keep head up when in handstand position.
      3. Failure to forcefully thrust legs upward and over high bar to allow body to go through handstand position.
      4. Failure to slightly overbalance before continuing with squat, straddle, or stoop.
      5. Failure to lift head and chest and push body away from the bar as the squat, straddle, or stoop is executed over the low bar.
      6. Failure to extend body before landing.
      7. Failure to keep head up at all times.

Figure U-88

221

DROP BACK, FLANK-CUT DISMOUNT
(Fig. U-89)

SL Beginner

PT From L position on the high bar with the hands in a forward grip, lift knees toward head (as if to start a back seat circle) and, keeping arms straight, drop back and swing under the high bar in a pike position. As movement upward begins, push downward on the high bar to force body as far foreupward as possible. Keeping upper body erect, release left hand and allow legs to flank to the left side of the body. When body is fully extended with feet under it, release right hand and land with knees slightly bent and slight hip flexion.

SP Same as for flank-cut catch. Maintain contact until balance is achieved upon landing.

CE 1. Failure to keep arms straight throughout skill.
2. Failure to keep body (except hands) free of the bar throughout the skill.
3. Failure to stay in a pike position. until the flank is executed.
4. Failure to push against the bar with hands to get as high as possible before flanking.
5. Failure to extend hips as body flanks and to push down on bar with right hand before releasing it to dismount.

   Hint: Learn on low bar first.

Figure U-89

VA *Drop back, straddle-cut dismount* (Fig. U-90)

   SL Low Intermediate

   PT From L support on high bar with hands in a forward grip, drop back and swing under high bar (same as in flank-cut dismount). As backupward movement begins, forcefully push on high bar with hands to raise body as far as possible before legs straddle. It is very important to keep upper body erect when legs straddle and hands release bar.

   SP Same as for straddle-cut catch. Maintain contact until balance is achieved upon landing. Grasp waist area upon landing.

Figure U-90

HANDSTAND QUARTER-TURN DISMOUNT OFF HIGH BAR (Fig. U-91)

SL Beginner

PT Stand on low bar, with hands in forward grip on high bar. Bend knees, flex hips, and force-fully push off low bar with legs and feet. Keeping arms straight, force hips upward with legs in a straddle position. As hips reach overhead position, bring legs together to fully stretched handstand position. As body passes vertical position, remove left hand and make quarter turn. As feet lower past high bar, keep eyes focused forward and release right hand. Land with hips and knees slightly flexed to absorb the shock.

Figure U-91

SP Same as for pirouette (Fig. U-75, page 212-213). After skill is learned, stand behind bar and assist at waist area during landing.

CE 1. Insufficient push with legs to get to handstand position.
2. Failure to keep arms straight and allowing back to arch.
3. Not keeping entire body tight after hitting handstand position.

HECHT (Fig. U-92)

Lead-up:

From a front support position on the low bar, relax in a piked hanging position. On a previously arranged signal between the performer and spotter, lift the upper and lower body *forcefully* and *simultaneously* while reaching foreupward with the arms. (This movement will be referred to as the pop.)

SL Intermediate

SP One spotter on each side of the performer in front of the bar. Grasp the upper arm with outside hand before movement begins. As the popping action is made, pull the performer off the bar, placing inside hands on the performer's abdomen to help lift the entire body over the bar. Contact must be maintained until performer has landed properly.

Dismount:

PT The hecht is usually prefaced with a cast (from a front support on the high bar) through the long hang position to a hip circle on the low bar, then off. After the skill has been mastered from the cast, then it may be performed from other skills, such as the back straddle catch-hecht dismount. It is essential to have a tight hip circle (so that the momentum developed in the cast to the long hang will not be lost) to allow the pop to be forceful enough to lift the body forward and up. As the body passes over the low bar, keep legs straight and hips tight. Keep lifting arms, head, and upper body so that legs and feet may be pulled under body to ensure proper landing. Popping action starts when upper body is at 45° angle to the floor.

SP After the hip circle is almost completed and the pop is about to occur, place inside hand on lower back and outside hand on abdomen and help lift and pull over the bar. Since this is a very fast move, the spotters must be very alert and ready to spot the performer if she should come off of the bar too soon or too late.

45°
Angle

Figure U-92

CE 1. Insufficient cast and poor hip circle.
2. Popping too soon or too late.
3. Failure to reach foreupward and to the side with arms and to continue reaching until feet are on mat.
4. Failure to keep body (especially hips) tight when popping.
5. Lifting hips and allowing knees to bend when passing over the bar.
6. Failure to keep head and upper body moving upward until feet have contacted mat.

VA *Straddle hecht*

> **PT** Same technique as above; as popping action starts, straddle legs instead of keeping them together.
>
> **SP** Use same spotting technique.

HECHT WITH FULL TWIST (Fig. U-93)

SL Advanced

PT When the upper body reaches a 45° angle between the floor and low bar from the cast wrap, the popping action begins as if doing a regular hecht. At this point look to the left and force right arm across the face. Keep the entire body taut with left arm close to chest, body will pass over bar. Notice that half of the turn is made as the body is popping upward and the remainder of the turn is made after clearing the bar. Just before landing, try to look at an object at eye level. Flex hips and knees slightly before landing.

SP As popping action is about to occur, place inside hand on left waist and outside hand on right waist. Pull body with inside hand toward you and push with outside hand. As performer rotates, hands will slide around waist area, regrasping opposite sides, then finishing with outside hand on abdomen and inside hand on lower back. The spotter must lift and quickly rotate the move forward so she does not stop the momentum of the performer.

CE 1. Turning too late or too soon.
2. Not keeping body tight after pop.
3. Not using arms to assist in turn.

Figure U-93

BACK SOMMIE FLY-AWAY (Fig. U-94)

Note: This skill is usually done from a bar-beat straddle over low to a long hang to a sommie.

SL Advanced

PT From a long-hang position thrust the entire body forward to slightly above horizontal position. This allows the center of gravity to be high enough for rotation to begin when the knees are brought to the chest. At this point quickly bring knees to chest to develop momentum and simultaneously release bar. After the body has rotated and the back is horizontal, lift the chest and extend legs before landing.

SP Stand to side of performer. Place inside hand on lower back, outside hand on back of upper thighs. Inside hand supports, outside hand rotates.

CE 1. Attempting tuck too soon. Hips must be at least horizontal to rotate properly.
2. Not extending chest and legs simultaneously for solid landing.

VA 1. Bar-beat straddle over back sommie.
2. From a squat on low bar jump to hang and dismount.

Figure U-94

FRONT SOMMIE DISMOUNT (Fig. U-95)

SL Advanced

PT Cast from high bar to low doing only a bar beat, then forcefully lift total body backupward toward high bar. As feet hit above low-bar position, release hands, forcefully pull body to tuck position, rotate three-quarter circle forward, then open to stand.

SP With outside hand, grasp abdominal area and lift. Place inside hand on upper back to assist in rotating; both hands move to waist area for support in landing.

CE 1. Not lifting body high enough before rotating.
2. Underspinning, generally causing a fall backward.
3. Overspinning, generally causing a fall forward.

VA Perform from high bar from cast.

226

Figure U-95

TOE ON FRONT OR FRONT SOMMIE DISMOUNT FROM SOLE CIRCLE BACKWARD (Fig. U-96)

SL Advanced

PT Jump to a short straddle or stoop sole circle and rise in that position until the hips have traveled above the bar on the other side. The feet should shoot upward and hips work as if kipping to extend body. Bend knees, release high bar, and force body into tight tuck with arms rapidly moving forward to grasp or be near lower legs. As the hips pass the horizontal plane, extend body for landing.

Figure U-96

227

SP Use inside hand to catch back; place outside hand on abdomen. When learning from low bar, use outside hand to catch across abdominal area; lift inside hand on back to help rotate.

CE 1. Releasing bar and tucking before hips above horizontal.
2. Opening too late, causing body to fall forward.
3. Opening too soon, causing body to fall backward.

ROUTINE COMPOSITION FOR CLASS

Since the majority of our girls are weak in the upper arm and shoulder area, routines for class should be composed of just a few skills at first. As strength and endurance are developed and skill ability is increased, the routines can be lengthened.

The routine should be composed of a mount, skills on one bar, skills going from one bar to the other (also facing each direction), and a dismount.

Some of the routines are partial routines and can be performed on one bar. This will give those students who do not have unevens a chance to perform a partial routine even though it involves skills on only one bar.

Beginning Routines

1. Jump to front support, back hip circle, single-leg flank to stride support, single-leg flank dismount with quarter turn.
2. Pullover on low bar, back hip circle, single-leg flank to a stride support, mill circle, single-leg flank dismount with quarter turn.
3. Stand facing low bar. Jump to front support, single-leg flank to stride support, single-leg swing down and up, grasp high bar, pullover on high bar, underswing to stride support on low, single-leg flank dismount with quarter turn.
4. Stand facing low bar. Back pullover on low bar, back hip circle, single-leg flank to stride support, single stem to high bar, underswing to stride support on low bar, mill circle, single-leg flank back to front support on low, underswing dismount.
5. Beat swing squat mount (to toes on bar), double-leg stem rise to high bar, underswing to stride position on the low bar, mill circle, reach back, grasp high bar, pull over to high bar. Forward roll to stride position on low bar, single stem rise to high bar, underswing dismount over low bar.

Advanced Beginning Routines

1. Beat-swing straddle mount, single stem to front support on high bar, cast to hip circle on low bar, single-leg shoot through to stride position on low bar, mill circle, catch high bar, back hip pullover to front support on high bar, back hip circle on high bar, handstand quarter-turn dismount.
2. Stand outside bars facing high bar. Glide kip on low bar. Back hip circle, squat stand, stand and jump to front support on high bar, underswing on high with half turn to hip circle on low bar. Single-leg shoot through to stride position, mill circle, catch high bar. Single stem to high bar, handstand quarter-turn dismount.
3. Stand outside bars. Glide kip to front support, squat stand, jump to free straddle support on high bar, underswing half turn to hip circle on low bar, single-leg shoot through, mill circle, catch, single stem to high bar, cast to hip circle on low bar, double-leg shoot through, back seat circle, drop back and up to catch high bar, kip from low to high, double-leg shoot through and flank dismount.

ROUTINE COMPOSITION FOR COMPETITION

Routines on the uneven parallel bars should consist of swinging movements from one bar to the other. Approximately ten to sixteen skills, including the mount and dismount, should be used in a sequence that will take the performer under and over both bars and in both directions. Skills that

228

require the performer to release the bar and regrasp the same bar or the other bar are more desirable.

The performer should include six elements of difficulty, three of which must be of superior difficulty (refer to FIG Code of Points). All skills should flow from one to the other, with planned hesitations *only* before extremely difficult movements.

Performers should try to be creative when developing their routines since credit is given for originality.

Intermediate Routines

1. Stand between bars facing low bars. Glide kip, catch high bar, drop kip with double-leg shoot through to rear support. Forward seat circle, catch the high bar, kip from low to high, free back hip circle to long hang into hip circle on low bar, eagle catch. Squat onto low bar, back straddle catch, hecht dismount.

2. Approach from behind bar. Run and dive into front hip circle, cast to stoop position, sole circle forward, catch high bar, drop kip to low, catch high bar. Beat-swing stoop over low bar to rear support, kip to high bar. Double-leg shoot through, dislocate, hip circle on low to eagle, drop kip and catch the high bar, stoop legs over the low bar to rear seat support, kip with double-leg shoot through and immediately straddle-cut dismount.

3. The routine done in Figure U-97 is as follows:

   1-4   Kip, double-leg shoot through catch high bar.
   5-13   Kip, double-leg shoot through to high bar with partial back seat circle drop to low bar kip, catch high bar.
   14-18 Double stem to high bar immediate stoop through.
   19-25 Drop back straddle cut catch to hip circle on low bar stopping momentarily in front support.
   26-37 Front hip circle, immediately stoop on low bar, change grip, stoop sole-circle forward, change grip, kip with double-leg shoot through over low bar, catching high bar with right hand and low bar with left hand.
   38-40 Press to squat position and turn 180° to face high bar.
   41-45 Immediately jump to free aerial straddle and underswing with half turn to hip circle on low bar followed by eagle.
   46-51 Bring feet to low bar, push through to stand on low bar, then jump to underswing and straddle-cut dismount.

Figure U-97

chapter eight

SIDE HORSE VAULTING

Vaulting for girls can be a very exciting event because it involves the body floating momentarily through space before and after contacting the horse. Too often we find girls petrified of the horse; they frequently sound like broken records with, "It's too high," or "The board is too far back." These remarks are usually accompanied by jammed fingers, sore wrists, or ugly bruises on the shins. Incidents of this nature should not happen frequently if proper vaulting techniques and safety precautions are stressed from the beginning. There are, invariably, those girls who will not get over the horse before attempting the vaults fifty times; however, it should be remembered that all girls are not designed to be champion vaulters.

SPECIAL CONDITIONING EXERCISES

1. Consecutive vertical jumps from the balls of the feet.
2. Sprints
3. Handstand snap downs (mule kicks) to a squat, stoop, and straddle stand.
4. Run and punch off board into layout dive roll onto a landing mat.

SAFETY HINTS

1. Runway should be free of obstructions.
2. Frequently remove dust of any type or other slippery substances from the runway.
3. If necessary, rope off runway so that other people in the area will not interfere with the vaulter's run.
4. Proper shoes (gymnastic slippers with rubber soles) should be worn. Pads can be inserted in the shoes to minimize sore feet and shin splints.
5. Use damp towel or resin to step on before running to prevent slipping.
6. Reuther board should have rubber grips on the bottom to prevent it from sliding, or use a board spacer.
7. Use mats (double thickness when possible) or landing mat on far side of horse where vaulters normally land.
8. Two or more spotters should be used, especially for beginners.
9. Performers should inform spotters beforehand of the vault they intend to perform so that spotters may be in the correct position.
10. Use mats when possible on runway to help prevent shin splints.
11. Use trampoline to save wear and tear on legs when doing a lot of handspring vaults at one time.
12. Have a definite skill program.

VAULTING TECHNIQUE

Vaulting can be divided into four major categories:

1. Approach (run).
2. Takeoff (hurdle and contact with the reuther board).
3. On horse contact.
4. After flight and landing.

At the beginning level, our major concern should be with the run and takeoff. The run can determine the performance of the rest of the vault, so we must master this motor skill and be concerned with the following techniques for a good run.

RUN (Fig. V-1)

PT 1. Slight forward lean with the head held in a natural position.
2. Eyes focused on the reuther board (place of foot contact).
3. Proper use of arms—foreupward and backupward in opposition to the legs.
4. Strong push downward and backward with balls of feet, never allowing heels to come in complete contact with the floor.
5. Adequate knee lift so that when feet contact the floor the push will be forceful enough to develop forward velocity.
6. Steady stride with increasing velocity, reaching maximum speed a few steps before the hurdle is taken.

CE 1. Body leans too far forward or backward.
2. Run is flat footed.
3. Arms not used properly.
4. Knees turned in; heels out.
5. Knees turned out.
6. Run not forceful.
7. Speed not increased gradually.

The distance or number of paces that each vaulter uses varies among individuals. To ensure a reasonable consistency in contacting the board, the distance should be carefully measured. This can be done by stepping off the number of feet or by using a tape measure. The distance should be long enough to allow the performer to reach maximum speed about fifteen feet (three to four steps) before the hurdle for beginning vaults and thirty feet for more difficult vaults.

The speed of the run will vary with each performer, and to some degree it will depend on the vault to be executed.

After learning to run properly, add the hurdle and contact with the reuther board. It is advisable to learn the hurdle first from a step, then gradually add steps, from a slow run and finally from a vaulting run.

Figure V-1

COMPONENTS OF A GOOD HURDLE AND TAKEOFF (Fig. V-2 and V-3)

PT 1. The hurdle should be long and not too high so as not to lose forward velocity and to maintain balance. As the hurdle step is taken, arms go down to sides of body.
2. The knee lift is only slight to allow both legs to come together quickly.
3. The balls of both feet must contact the board parallel and simultaneously with a very slight knee bend (heels never touch). Since the action of the reuther board is very fast, a great knee bend upon contact would cause a very long (and sluggish) takeoff.
4. Shoulders should be slightly behind the toes when contact is made on the board.
5. As feet contact the board, the arms reach forward and upward to assist on the vertical lift.
6. Immediately extend knees explosively to ensure a high vertical lift.
7. Ankle extension is also very important; extend ankles fully in order to allow the tips of the toes to leave the board last.
8. As the hurdle step is taken, transfer eyes from the board to the horse or beyond the horse, depending upon the type of vault being executed.

CE 1. Hurdle too high, too low, too short, or a combination of any of these.
2. Slowing the run before the hurdle.
3. Bending the knees too much upon contacting the board.
4. Landing flat footed on the board.
5. Allowing the body to lean forward (mainly upper body) when feet contact the board.
6. Little or no ankle or hip extension.
7. Poor arm direction or uncoordinated arm and leg action.

Hint: Practice run and hurdle to a jump onto a stack of mats or the trampoline before using the horse.

Figure V-2   Figure V-3

The position of the body in preflight will be discussed under the individual vaults. It is essential that there be a visible distinction (time lapse) from reuther board contact to horse contact.

Usually *on-horse contact* and *afterflight* are not mastered until the intermediate to advanced stage of vaulting; since all vaults involve these parts, however, it is essential to stress some of the basic components of the last half of the vault.

ON-HORSE CONTACT

PT 1. On most vaults, the hands contact the horse shoulder-distance apart and in the middle of the top of the horse.
2. When the hands contact the horse, the shoulders should be almost directly over the hands, sometimes behind, but *never forward of the hands.*
3. The touch on the horse should be of a very short duration.
4. The shoulders should never be allowed to sag as hands contact the horse.

CE 1. Hands on horse too long, usually resulting in downward slant after flight.
2. Insufficient push off the horse, or push poorly directed.
3. Other faults due to poor takeoff, such as contacting the horse on the near side (caused by a forward lean).

AFTERFLIGHT

In general, the greater the preflight and push, the greater the afterflight. The body should be extended in the air before landing; this mainly refers to squat, stoop, and straddle vaults. The afterflight should be upward as well as outward; a higher afterflight allows more time to position the body for a good landing.

LANDING

1. Landing should be solid but light.
2. Bend knees slightly to absorb shock and to help maintain balance.
3. Arms are slightly forward or sideward (obliquely) for balance, then to side when standing.
4. Slight forward bend of the body at hips.
5. If students can be taught to "stick" (stop upon making contact with mat) vaults, there will be fewer accidents.

LEAD-UP SKILLS

If a side horse is not available, other pieces of equipment can be used for teaching vaulting techniques.

1. Use a pile of mats (about two feet high) and have students take an abbreviated run and hurdle, landing on the mats.
2. Use mats as above and have students run, hurdle, and jump over the pile of mats.
3. Use lowered Swedish box (two to two and one-half feet).
   a. Jump up to stand and off.
   b. Jump to squat stand and off.
   c. Squat vault.
   d. Jump to straddle stand, then off.
   e. Straddle vault.
4. Lower a balance beam and cover it with mats.
   a. Use same procedures as for Swedish box.
   b. Use reuther board and raise beam slightly.

If a horse and reuther board are available from the beginning, be concerned with two things: how high should the horse be, and how far away from the horse should the board be (assuming that the girls have had ample practice on the run, hurdle, and takeoff on the board to a mat). Since quick success is a strong motivational factor in learning, lower the horse below standard height and place the board approximately two feet from the base of the horse.

234

PROGRESSION

JUMP TO SQUAT STAND ON HORSE
(Fig. V-4)

SL Beginner

PT Take an abbreviated run and hurdle. After the vertical lift from the board, raise hips upward so that back is parallel to the floor and tuck knees to chest. Place the hands in the center (middle of top) of the horse with the hands shoulder width apart, arms straight, and fingers spread slightly. Lower hips and allow feet to come to rest on the horse between the hands. Lift chest as feet contact the horse, and focus eyes on object at eye level in front of the horse. Stand and jump off, bending knees when landing. Arms foreupward, then down.

Figure V-4

SP Stand on far side of horse beside performer. Reach across the horse and grasp upper arm and wrist of the performer as she places hands on the horse. Be careful not to hinder her movement.

CE 1. Poor run and hurdle.
2. Landing on the board flat footed.
3. Leaning forward on the board.
4. Knees bending too much on the board, causing the forward momentum to be slowed down.
5. Insufficient vertical lift.
6. Poorly coordinated arms.
7. Placement of the hands on the near side of the horse rather than on the top.
8. Failure to lift hips and bring knees to chest. (Many beginners tend to bring the hips under the body rather than lifting them backupward.)
9. Failure to maintain straight arms and erect shoulders.

SQUAT VAULT FROM AN ABBREVIATED RUN (Fig. V-5)

SL Beginner

PT After the vertical lift, raise hips backupward and tuck knees to chest. After reaching foreupward, place hands on top of the horse. Immediately push downupward on the horse, lifting chest; then lift arms foreupward. Eyes look at the board when running, horse when hurdling, and object at eye level in front of the horse when passing over the horse. As feet pass over the horse, extend legs and hips so that body is straight before landing. Land with hips and knees slightly flexed.

SP Same as for squat stand. Maintain contact until the performer has gained balance upon landing.

CE 1. Same as 1-9 for squat stand.
2. Allowing hands to remain on the horse as feet pass over the horse.
3. Failure to completely extend body before landing.
4. Failure to lift head and chest after pushing off the horse with hands.
5. Allowing arms to go over head and back upon landing (this causes many beginners to fall back toward the horse).

235

Figure V-5

JUMP TO STRADDLE STAND (Fig. V-6)

SL Beginner

PT From an abbreviated run, hurdle. On the vertical lift from the board, lift hips up and back; then force legs to a wide straddle position. As hands contact the horse, lift head and chest and allow feet to contact the horse in a wide straddle position. The shoulders will be slightly forward of the hands due to the stop on the horse in the straddle position.

Figure V-6

SP Stand on the far side of the horse in front of the performer. Reach across the horse and grasp upper arms as performer puts them on the horse. Assist by lifting and pulling to the horse, if necessary, and help control the straddle-stand position.

CE 1. Same as 1-7 of the squat stand.
2. Failure to lift hips high enough to allow feet to straddle onto the horse.
3. Failure to straddle both legs.
4. Failure to lift head and chest when feet come to rest on the horse.
5. Failure to maintain straight arms throughout the skill.

STRADDLE VAULT (Fig. V-7)

SL Beginner

PT From an abbreviated run, hurdle to the board and immediately spring vertically, lifting hips backupward. Reach foreupward with arms to place hands on the top of the horse (eyes look up at this point) while simultaneously straddling legs. Immediately push off the horse with hands and lift upper body. As legs pass over the horse, extend hips forward and bring legs together before landing. Land with knees and hips slightly flexed.

SP Stand in front of horse and performer (one foot slightly in front of the other). As the performer places hands on the horse, grasp her upper arms. As she is moving over the horse, step back and help lift and pull her to make sure she clears the horse. Maintain contact until proper landing.

CE 1. Same as 1-7 of jump to squat stand.
2. Failure to maintain straight arms throughout skill.
3. Failure to push off of the horse and keep shoulders erect almost immediately after contact.
4. Failure to lift head and chest, extend hips, and bring legs together before landing.

236

Figure V-7

BENT-HIP ASCENT STOOP (Fig. V-8)

SL Beginner

PT After vertical lift from the board, raise hips as high as possible and focus eyes beyond the horse. Hands reach foreupward and then are placed on the top of the horse (wide enough apart to allow hips to pass through). Force straight legs through arms with an immediate push from the horse and forcefully lift head and chest. Extend hips forward to allow body to extend completely before landing.

SP Same as for squat vault.

CE 1. Poor run and hurdle.
2. Insufficient lift from board.
3. Failure to lift hips high on vertical lift from board.
4. Failure to maintain straight arms and legs throughout skill.
5. Failure to focus eyes beyond the horse upon hand contact on horse.
6. Failure to forcefully drive legs through arms, to push off the horse with hands, and to lift. head and chest.
7. Failure to force hips forward to allow body to extend before landing.

Figure V-8

237

LAYOUT VAULTING

Once girls have mastered the layout position in vaulting, they have moved into the intermediate vaulting category. The following techniques are suggested as aids for developing a good layout position between the reuther board and the horse.

General Techniques

1. Develop a consistent run and takeoff spot on the board.
2. Increase the speed of the run so that maximum speed will be reached just before th hurdle.
3. Move the board back from the horse so that the takeoff and hand contact on the horse cannot occur simultaneously..
4. At takeoff from the board, shift eye focus to the horse.
5. Just after takeoff from the board (on vertical lift), tighten the entire body, especially hips and legs, and lift heels overhead.

Teaching Aids

1. Practice handstand snapdowns to squat, straddle, and stoop stand to assist in learning the action of legs and hips in the layout vaults.
2. Practice swan jump from board; spotter stands in front of the board to catch the performer at waist areas. This will help develop vertical lift and also help get the feeling of flying.
3. Practice hitting layout position and landing on stack of mats in a squat position.
4. Practice hitting layout and landing in squat on trampoline.
5. Practice layout dive rolls landing on crash pad.
6. Using reuther board and side horse at regulation height, use spotters on near side of horse to help lift performer to proper position.

LAYOUT VAULTS (Fig. V-9)

Since the layout vaults have many common errors that are the same, the following list will be referred to for all vaults; errors peculiar to each vault will be listed under the performance technique of that vault.

Figure V-9

General Common Errors

1. Insufficient run, hurdle, and takeoff from the board.
2. Leaning forward on take-off from the board.
3. Piking on preflight (failure to tighten gluteal, thigh, and back muscles after takeoff from the board).
4. Failure to attain layout position before executing the desired vault.
   a. Below horizontal.
   b. Barely horizontal.
   c. Slightly above horizontal.
   Layout position should be at least at a 45° angle.
5. Failure to place hands on *top* of horse.
6. Allowing arms to bend.
7. Allowing legs to bend (except in squat vault).
8. Landing heavily on the horse with hands.
9. Failure to push off the horse with the hands immediately after contact. If hands remain on horse too long, usually the afterflight will be slow and low.

10. Allowing shoulders to be forward of hand position.
11. Allowing shoulders to shrug as hands contact horse.
12. Allowing feet to touch the horse during any part of the vault.
13. Insufficient afterflight (must be upward as well as outward).
14. Failure to keep head up and back and to lift upper body for proper direction on the afterflight.
15. Failure to extend body fully before landing.
16. Failure to land lightly and with control.

LAYOUT SQUAT (Fig. V-10)

SL Intermediate

PT After attaining a layout position from the vertical lift, tuck knees to chest. Push off the horse with hands while simultaneously lifting head and chest. As body passes over the horse, force hips forward to extend body before landing. Focus eyes on the board before running, upward before takeoff on board, on the horse on preflight, and foreupward on the afterflight. Slightly flex knees and hips upon landing. After push-off from the horse arms go foreupward, then obliquely forward upon landing.

SP Use as many as four spotters, two on near side of horse and two on far side. Spotters on near side help performer attain layout position by placing one hand on her thigh and other on her abdomen. Spotters on far side of horse beside performer help lift and pull performer over the horse by grasping her upper arms. Maintain contact until balanced landing is achieved.

Figure V-10

LAYOUT STOOP (Fig. V-11)

SL Intermediate

PT After attaining a layout position from the vertical lift and contacting the horse with hands, forcefully flex hips and drive legs through arms without bending knees. Push off the horse with hands while simultaneously lifting head and upper body. Force hips forward to completely extend body before landing. Eye focus and arm action is the same as for the layout squat.

SP Same as for the layout squat vault.

239

Figure V-11

LAYOUT STRADDLE (Fig. V-12)

SL Intermediate

PT After attaining a layout position from the vertical lift and contacting the horse with hands, move legs to a wide straddle position. Push off the horse with hands while simultaneously lifting head and upper body. As body passes over the horse, keep hips forward and bring leg together before landing. (Many beginners tend to flex hips after straddle position is attained and then force legs forward. This will decrease their afterflight and means that they must make an extra hip movement, since the body must be fully extended before landing.)

SP Stand on far side of horse in front of performer. As performer places hands on horse, grasp upper arms and help pull and lift (if necessary) her over the horse. Maintain contact until balance is achieved. Have one foot in front of the other so that you can step back as the performer clears the horse so that she can have some afterflight.

CE Allowing legs to straddle before layout position is achieved.

Figure V-12

HANDSPRING VAULT (Fig. V-13)

SL Intermediate

PT During vertical lift reach more upward with arms than for a layout vault so that the flight of the body can be more up then onto the horse for continual motion over the horse. The body should be in an inverted position when hands make contact with the horse. Head must be between arms. As hands contact the horse, shoulders give very slightly so that hands and

240

shoulders can extend forcefully to push body upward, then outward. The body must remain in a layout position until landing. Arms must remain overhead during the afterflight, and head should remain up. Toes should reach out toward the mat and, as they contact the mat, knees and hips flex slightly and arms move to a back oblique position.

SP 1. Two spotters on near side of horse spot same as for layout vault. Two spotters on far side of horse grasp upper arms with inside hands and hips with outside hands.

2. Spotter on near side of horse in front of performer between the reuther board and the horse. As the performer takes off from the board, place hands on waist and hip area and assist her to handstand position. As contact is made with the performer, the spotter should bend knees and lift with legs rather than straining the arms and back. Spotter on the far side of the horse grasps upper arm and hips as for technique above.

CE 1. 1-3 and 5-16 of the general common errors for layout vaulting.
2. Failure to make arms lift high and then onto horse.
3. Failure to reach inverted position as hands contact horse.
4. Allowing the shoulders to sag when hands contact horse.
5. Failure to keep arms overhead, head up and back, and body arched on the afterflight.

Figure V-13

HECHT (Fig. V-14)

SL Intermediate

PT Take a fast run and hurdle. Upon contacting the board, keep eyes focused on the middle of the horse. Keep head close to arms as they reach for the horse. As hands contact the horse, arms should be almost in line with upper body. The entire body should be horizontal. The head and shoulders should follow through with the downward thrust created with the hand push-off from the horse. (This action usually raises the hips and will in turn elevate the entire body.) As body is almost over the horse, raise arms slightly, and arch back slightly; keep the eyes focused on the landing area. Flex hips and allow legs to be brought under body; try to delay knee bend until feet contact the mat.

SP Stand on far side of horse. As performer passes over horse, place inside hand on lower back and outside hand on abdomen to help lift her forward, then upward. Two spotters should be used. Maintain contact until landing.

CE 1. Insufficient run.
2. Insufficient forward lean on takeoff from the board.
3. Failure to keep head between arms as hands contact horse.

241

4. Failure to allow body to follow the downward movement from the hand push-off.
5. Failure to have shoulders slightly behind hands on horse contact.
6. Bending knees before feet contact mat.

Figure V-14

VA *Hecht with full twist*

SL Advanced

PT Approach and push off horse as for hecht. To begin the twist, keep the arm up in the direction of the turn. The lift should continue upward during the twisting action.

SP 1. Stand to far side of horse and help rotate at hip area. (Before one attempts the hecht full, both the hecht and a full should be learned independently.)
2. Hold out arm around waist area and gymnast will rotate in front of arm, using it as a guide.

CE 1. Insufficient punch off board.
2. Insufficient push off horse.
3. Relaxation of body during twist.
4. Failure to keep lifting during the twist.

YAMASHITA (Fig. V-15)

SL Advanced Intermediate

PT Begin front-handspring vault. As body reaches the inverted position on the horse and push-off is about to occur, forcefully flex hips and upper body to bring body to a tight piked position. Immediately extend hips, forcing legs upward and outward while entire body is moving upward and outward in an arched position. Continue reaching for the mat with toes and slightly flex hips and knees upon landing. Eyes spot knees when going into piked position, object overhead when returning to arched position, and then object at eye level upon landing.

SP Same as for front handspring. Be careful not to inhibit piking action of performer by spotting too closely.

CE 1. Same as for handspring vault.
2. Insufficient pike.
3. Piking too soon or too late.
4. Failure to extend legs upward as well as outward after piking.
5. Slow action getting into and out of piked position.
6. Failure to return to an arched position before landing.

Figure V-15

YAMASHITA HALF TURN (Fig. V-16)

SL Advanced

PT When the body has pushed off the horse for a Yamashita, and the back is parallel to the floor in a piked position, push the hips upward, rotating hips and shoulders similar to underswing half turn on unevens, to make a half turn. The body should reach an extended position after the turn and remain extended until landing.

SP Near side, lift at hip area.
Far side, assist at hip and waist area upon landing.

CE 1. Insufficient punch from board.
2. Insufficient push-off from horse.
3. Rolling body around rather than extending forcefully from a pike to a layout.
4. Not extending body before landing.

Figure V-16

243

QUARTER ON, QUARTER OFF (cartwheel, quarter-turnout) (Fig. V-17)

SL Advanced

PT As body punches off the board initiate quarter turn in desired direction; however, turn is not completed until total body is in air ready to make contact with horse. As hands contact horse (almost simultaneously) body will be almost vertical. Then immediately push off, and quarter twist should be made by turning shoulder in desired direction. The quarter turn must be finished in air before landing.

SP Front spotter: Stand between board and horse and lift in abdominal area.
Back spotter: Stand to far side of horse and spot as for handspring or just grasp at waist area.

CE 1. Inadequate punch from board.
2. Making turn immediately off board, therefore not preflight.
3. Bending arms on horse.
4. Inadequate push from hands on horse.
5. Not passing through the vertical.
6. Not keeping the body tight throughout.

Figure V-17

QUARTER ON, THREE-QUARTERS OFF (cartwheel, three-quarters-turnout) (Fig. V-18)

SL Advanced

PT The beginning of vault is the same as for the quarter on, quarter off (Fig. V-17). As body pushes off the horse, the turning-side arm is kept vertical, and the other arm pulls across the chest in the direction of the turn. The total body remains extended until landing.

SP Near side: Lift at hip and waist area.
Far side: Control twist with hand at hip and waist area.

CE 1. Insufficient punch off board.
2. Quarter turn late or early.
3. Bending arms on horse.
4. Insufficient push upward off horse.
5. Body not kept tight throughout.

244

Figure V-18

HALF ON, HALF OFF (Fig. V-19)

SL Advanced

PT From a punch off the board, lift vertically making one half turn before hands contact horse. Upon leaving the board make eye contact with the middle of the horse and keep that eye contact until hands hit. It might help to feel as if you are rotating around that contact. As hands hit, push off and as the body rises vertically complete a half turn, landing as for other inverted vaults. End with back to horse.

Note: The second turn must be done in the same direction as the first, continuing a full turn if used as a compulsory vault. As an optional vault the second turn may be done in either direction.

SP Near side: Lift at hip area, assist with turn if necessary.
Far side: Grasp waist area, assist with turn and landing.

CE Basically the same as for quarter on, quarter off.

Figure V-19

245

HANDSPRING, FULL TURN (Fig. V-20)

SL Advanced

PT After punching the board the preflight to the horse should be slightly lower than for a regular handspring. This is to give a great push upward for time in afterflight to complete the full. As the hands push off the horse, the lift is upward. Keep the turning-side arm vertical and pull the other across the chest to finish in a vertical. Keep body straight until landing.

SP Near side: Lift at hip area.
Far side: Guide body through twisting phase at waist area. Just off horse the gymnast is usually too high to be spotted. Generally spotting occurs on the down phase.

CE 1. Insufficient punch off board.
2. Contacting horse too vertical.
3. Bending arms on horse.
4. Not pushing upward off horse.
5. Relaxing during turn.

Figure V-20

TSUKAHARA (Fig. V-21)

SL Advanced

PT The takeoff, preflight, and on-horse phase are the same as for the half on, with the preflight being just slightly lower. As the hips reach the vertical position and push-off occurs, bend the legs forcefully and reach behind the legs with the hands to pull the body in a tight tuck. When

Figure V-21

246

the back is parallel to the mat (when the eyes spot the ceiling) tilt the head backward to look for the landing mat. At the time start to extend for landing. Since so much momentum has been developed, make sure to land with bent knees and hips to absorb shock.

SP Near side: Lift in hip area (Fig. V-22)
Far side: Push backupward, help rotate at hip area, then grab waist in landing.

CE 1. Not pulling body in tight tuck or pike.
2. Waiting too long to start tuck.

VA 1. Pike position.
2. Layout position.
3. With full twist.

  Hints: 1. Learn off trampoline or with overhead spotting belt.
2. Practice handstand to tuck position off horse or trampoline.

Figure V-22

HANDSPRING, FRONT SOMMIE (Fig. V-23)

SL Advanced

PT As with other vaults involving turns in afterflight, the preflight to the horse must be slightly lower than for a regular handspring. Just before the body passes the vertical, slightly pike. After push-off upward, forcefully drive the arms to pull the body into a tight tuck position. Open same as front on floor.

  Hint: To learn, keep the legs slightly apart in the tuck position and look toward the rear end. This way it is also easier to see the landing mat. Learn off trampoline first.

SP Far side: Push hips upward, then put outside hand on back near hand on hip to rotate. Grasp waist area upon landing.

CE 1. Initiating sommie too soon.
2. Opening too soon or too late.

VA Handspring, front sommie in piked position.

247

Figure V-23

Arm Positions for Full Twisting Vaults off Horse

A few different techniques are being advocated for arms during twisting vaults. The following are used and have been proven successful. Others are still being tried. Since each gymnast's spinning capacity is different, she must use the one that best enables her to spin or twist.

1. Arm vertical in direction of turn. Other arm pulls across chest in direction of turn. Eyes look at armpit.
2. Arm in direction of turn drops behind neck. Other arm pulls across chest. Eyes look at armpit.
3. Arm in direction of turn drops behind neck. Other arm pulls across chest in direction of turn. Eyes look at shoulder.

VAULTING FOR COMPETITION

School

Generally, schools with competitive gymnastic teams require their gymnasts to do only optional vaulting. These vaults could range from a squat to a Tsukahara. The gymnast will receive the best score of her two vaults. Since the values for the vaults seem to be constantly changing, it is best to refer to the Code of Points for Women or the Scholastic Rules Guide.

The USGF and some school organizations do not allow more than half of the vaults performed to be the same. For example, if six girls vault, there can be only six of any one vault.

Club Competition

If the meet is both compulsory and optional, the gymnast performs two compulsory vaults and two optional vaults. The gymnast receives the best score for her compulsory vault. The total of the two (best compulsory and best optional) is her vaulting score. A coach may request in advance an average for the first vault so he or she may have the gymnast perform a different vault or not perform a second vault. In elite competition the gymnast must perform two different optional vaults. At all other levels she is allowed to perform the same optional vault twice.

chapter nine

TRAMPOLINE

The trampoline is a versatile piece of equipment and should be used in all gymnastic curricula. Because of its size, it can present problems when trying to arrange all the equipment in a small area. If this is your particular situation, possibly a unit for tumbling, minitramp, and trampoline can be taught for a couple of weeks, then bars, beam, and vaulting.

The skills to be covered are as follows:

Basic bounce	Swivel hips
Killing the bounce (stopping)	Back drop
Tuck jump	Cradle
Straddle jump	Front sommie
Half turn	Back sommie
Seat drop	Baroni
Knee drop	Front sommie with half twist
Roll over (seat drop—full twist—seat drop)	Layout
Full turn	Full twisting layout

Other uses of the trampoline are suggested at the end of the chapter.

SAFETY PRECAUTIONS

1. Never leave the trampoline unsupervised.
2. Teach students how to properly fold and unfold the trampoline.
3. Replace shock cords when damaged.
4. Have mats on dismount end of trampoline.
5. *Never allow students to bounce alone.*
6. Have alert spotters—spotters should know what skills are being performed.
7. Bounce in the middle of the trampoline (unless doing doubles bouncing).

8. When tired, stop bouncing—individuals should bounce for short periods of time.
9. When dizzy, stop bouncing.
10. Perform skills at own level—*do not attempt new skills without proper instruction.*

SPOTTING TECHNIQUES

1. The basic skills can be learned from a low bounce. As the performer gains confidence, she may attempt the skills from a higher bounce.
2. For some of the intermediate and advanced skills, hand spotting may be used. The spotter must bounce *with* the performer. At a designated count, (usually three) the spotter must flex his or her knees, stay on the bed of the trampoline, and manually rotate the performer.
3. When using an overhead spotting belt, first make sure the ropes attached to the belt are even and fairly tight. (Pull down on the ropes to take up the slack as the performer bounces up.) When the performer is ready to do the skill (usually on a designated count), the spotter pulls very hard on the ropes so the student may complete the skill in the air.

Spotting Belts

There are two types of spotting belts. One is usually a plain canvas strap very much like a regular belt. The second type of belt is a twisting belt which has a regular belt attached to an outside metal frame. The latter allows the performer to twist freely in the air without getting caught in the ropes.

MOUNTING THE TRAMPOLINE

1. Jump to a sitting position.
   a. Stand facing the trampoline. Place hands on the frame. Jump up and turn to sit on frame.
   b. Stand with back to frame and jump up to sitting position.
2. For small children, have some type of sturdy steps or lift them onto the trampoline. *Never use folding chairs.*
3. When children reach the intermediate level, they can mount with a forward roll—being careful to keep head from between springs. If students have used the minitramp, they could mount by rebounding off the minitramp into a dive roll onto the trampoline.

DISMOUNTING

Crawl, scoot, or walk slowly to the end of the tramp. Sit down and hop off onto designated mat.

BASIC SKILLS

It is important to understand that all skills are initiated from the bed of the tramp even though the actual movement is completed in the air. To prove this to students have one on the tramp bouncing. As her feet leave the bed immediately give her a command to do a seat drop or half turn or some other skill. Make sure she does not know what skill will be called. She will find herself unable to do this skill unless she takes another bounce. Sometimes advanced performers can defeat this theory with beginning skills because of the great amount of control and height they have developed in their bounce. In order to show various positions of the body in a skill, we have made it look like the skill starts in one place on the tramp and finished in another. Most skills, however, are performed in the same vertical or horizontal plane.

250

BASIC BOUNCE (Fig. TR-1)

PT Legs: Start with feet a shoulder-width apart. Bend knees and jump by extending legs and ankles completely. Toes should be pointing toward the bed while the body is suspended in air. When landing, toes contact the bed first, immediately followed by the feet. Ankles and knees flex slightly to prepare for the next lift upward.

Note: After students feel comfortable bouncing, they should bring the legs together while in the air.

Arms: Two basic arm movements are used.
  1. Circular—arm movement is similar to the arm pattern of the breast stroke. Start with arms sideways but forward, with elbows slightly bent. As knees bend to begin the upward jump, arms go down and together in front of the body. As the body projects upward, the arms go to an overhead position, assisting with the lift.
  2. Up-down oblique—arms move from a downward position to an upward oblique position when the body is in the air. There is no circular motion in this technique.

Eye focus—Depending on the individual, students should:
  1. Focus on subject at eye level;
  2. Focus on frame of tramp;
  3. Use no focus.

CE 1. Bouncing flat footed—not completely extending the ankles.
  2. Bending knees too much when contacting bed.
  3. Allowing arms to move behind body.
  4. Improper coordination of arms and legs.
  5. Letting eyes wander, turning the head, or looking down at bed of tramp.

Figure TR-1

KILLING THE BOUNCE (stopping) (Fig. TR-2)

PT When contacting the bed of the tramp, quickly flex the knees and hips as if to sit and move arms forward in front of the body.

Figure TR-2

Figure TR-3

TUCK JUMP (Fig. TR-3)

SL Beginner

PT As the body approaches the peak of the bounce, lift knees to chest. As body begins downward movement extend the legs before contacting the tramp bed. Arms may touch knees or ankles while in tuck posiiton.

CE 1. Leaning forward while in tuck position.
2. Insufficient tuck.

STRADDLE JUMP (Fig. TR-4)

SL Beginner

PT Just before reaching the peak of the bounce lift the legs high and wide in a straddle position. Keep upper body straight and touch toes with hands.

CE Beginners tend to lower the upper body forward rather than lifting the legs upward.

HALF TURN (should be practiced right and left) (Fig. TR-5)

SL Beginner

PT Initiate turn from bounce upward and continue to turn after feet leave the bed. The turn should be completed at the peak of the bounce. The head should be turned in the direction of the turn. The arms may be at the side of the body, in the air, or one in the air with the other pulling across the body in the direction of the turn.

CE Not turning the head in the direction of the turn.

252

Figure TR-4

Figure TR-5

SEAT DROP (Fig. TR-6)

SL Beginner

PB (Position on Bed) Open pike position. Legs together and straight with toes pointed. Upper body erect and hands placed by the hips on the bed of the tramp, with fingers pointing toward toes.

PT As body is reaching peak of bounce, lift legs so they are parallel to the bed. Allow upper body to tilt back ever so slightly. Remain in this position until contacting tramp. Push with hands on tramp; then lift overhead to assist in bringing body to upright position.

CE 1. Not lifting legs high enough, causing heels to hit tramp before rest of body.
2. Lifting legs too high, causing performer to land on buttocks and back.

Figure TR-6

253

3. Not keeping legs straight upon contact with tramp. When legs are bent it is more difficult to return to a standing position.

VA 1. Seat drop with legs in a straddle position.
2. Half turn into seat drop.
3. Tuck or straddle jump into seat drop.

KNEE DROP (Fig. TR-7)

SL Beginner

PB Body erect from knees up. Legs bent at knees and in contact with tramp from knees to ankles. Toes pointed to prevent injury. Arms slightly forward and at waist level ready to assist in upward movement.

PT As the body is reaching the peak of the bounce, bend legs, keeping upper body erect. After contact is made in this position, use arms to assist in lifting body to standing position.

CE 1. Sitting back on heels on tramp.
2. Lifting heels too high—lower leg should be parallel to bed.

Combination
1. Seat drop, knee drop, seat drop.
2. Half turn, knee drop.

Figure TR-7

ROLL OR SEAT DROP, FULL TWIST, SEAT DROP (Fig. TR-8)

SL Beginner

PT From a seat drop, push forcefully with the hands on the tramp. As the body moves upward, allow the upper body to drop backward so the body is almost horizontal to the tramp (in the air). Pull the left arm forcefully across the chest and face to assist with the full turn. As the turn is completed, drop the hips backward and downward and bring the upper body forward so as not to land in seat-drop position.

Note: During the twisting move, keep hips and legs as tight as possible.

CE 1. Trying to twist out of a poorly executed seat drop.
2. Trying to twist while in the sitting position.
3. Twisting too soon or too late.
4. Not dropping the turning shoulder directly toward tramp bed where seat drop was performed.

254

Figure TR-8

FULL TURN (Fig. TR-9)

SL Beginner

PT As body is reaching the peak of the bounce, force the outside arm across the body toward the direction of the turn. Look in the direction of the turn. Complete the full turn before landing.

Note: Some people can turn easily and, therefore, do not need the force from the opposite arm. Arms can be at sides for these individuals.

CE 1. Turning too soon or too late.
2. Completely relaxing the body during the turn. The body should be completely vertical and as tight as possible.
3. Turning in the wrong direction—if an individual is not successful turning to the right, have her turn to the left and vice versa.
4. Looking in the opposite direction of the turn.

Figure TR-9

SWIVEL HIPS (seat drop, half turn, seat drop) (Fig. TR-10)

Lead-up:

>Seat drop—stand in air and reach for ceiling.
>Seat drop—vertical position, half turn.
>Seat drop—half turn seat drop.

SL Beginner

PT From a seat drop completely extend the body to a vertical position with arms overhead. Make a half turn looking in the direction of the turn; then flex the hips and go into another seat drop.

CE Failure to push with the hands and *to extend the body fully before turning and sitting.*

Figure TR-10

BACK DROP (Fig. TR-11)

SL Beginner

PB Body in piked position, hips raised from bed. Landing is on middle to upper back, chin tucked toward chest with arms by knees.

Figure TR-11

PT To learn a back drop, hold the arms in front of body as if holding a ball. Lift one leg as if to kick ball, followed by other. Land in piked position on back with chin tucked. The legs lift upward and outward at a 45° angle; hips are forced upward and forward and upper body is arched, with head slightly back and arms overhead.

CE 1. Not keeping head tucked when hitting backdrop position.
2. Landing on buttocks or shoulder area rather than back.
3. Not taking advantage of spring from trampoline to push body upward.

CRADLE (back drop, half turn, back drop)

SL Intermediate

Lead-up:

Back drop with half twist to stand (Fig. TR-12)

Note: For those girls who have worked an underswing half turn on unevens, you can compare body actions from back drop to half turn to the compressed position to the extended position. Another hint might be to do a back drop, come forward as if to do a front drop, half turn to back drop.

PT When the body is returning upward from a back drop, the legs and hips are extended. As the body reaches its peak, rotate hips and shoulders 180°, pike body again, and land on back facing opposite direction. Then extend body to standing position.

CE 1. Poor back drop.
2. Extending too soon—wait until body is in air before twisting.
3. Twisting too late—usually results in landing on side.

Figure TR-12

FRONT SOMMIE (Fig. TR-13)

SL Intermediate

Lead up:

1. Knee drop, forward spin to back. *Make sure students go up out of knee drop before spinning. Letting them turn forward from the bed only creates bad habits and poor technique.*
2. Knee drop, forward spin to seat.
3. Knee drop, forward spin to feet.
4. Regular low bounce to back.
5. Regular low bounce to seat.
6. Regular low bounce to feet.

257

PT As the body is reaching the peak of the bounce, with arms overhead raise the hips forcefully backupward; force arms downward, tuck head, bring knees to chest, and rotate 360°. Just before the feet come under the body, extend legs, chest, and head so as to land on feet in standing position.

CE 1. Turning forward from bed rather than waiting until body is in air.
2. Closing eyes.
3. Not tucking tightly enough.
4. Turning head to side while rotating.
5. Using one arm more than the other. (4 and 5 cause spin to be crooked)
6. Not opening soon enough.

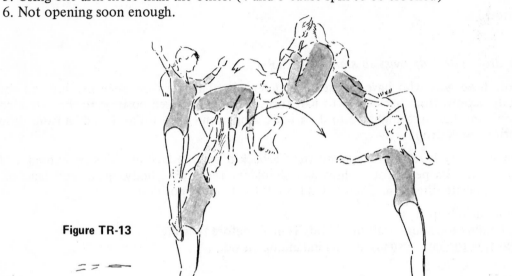

Figure TR-13

VA *Front sommie in piked position* (Fig. TR-14)

Figure TR-14

BACK SOMMIE (Fig. TR-15)

SL Intermediate

PT As the peak of the bounce is reached, with arms overhead forcefully lift knees to chest, keeping head in normal position. Complete spin in air. After the back and head have passed the horizontal position (three-quarters of the skill has been completed and the back is to the ceiling), extend legs and come to standing posiiton.

CE 1. Starting the rotation too soon.
2. Whipping the head back.
3. Turning the head to one side, thus causing an oblique rotation.
4. Not opening the tuck soon enough.

SP 1. Spot with overhead belt.
2. Hand spot—one hand on back of upper leg, other on small of back (Fig. TR-16). On designated count (usually three) stay on bed of trampoline and lift and rotate body with hand on leg, and support, then rotate with hand on back. Grasp waist after rotation.

Figure TR-15

Figure TR-16

259

VA *Back sommie in piked position* (Fig. TR-17)

Figure TR-17

BARANI (Fig. TR-18)

SL Intermediate

PT This move is very similar to a round-off. As the peak of the bounce is reached, the hips thrust backupward and the body moves forward as if to do a front sommie. *The eyes focus on the middle of the trampoline at all times from this point.* The lower body rotates over the head, making a half turn. The hips flex at this point to come to a standing position.

Figure TR-18

SP 1. Use overhead gear with twisting belt.
    2. Spot as for side aerial. One hand on hip, other on shoulder.

CE 1. Not focusing eyes on the bed of tramp throughout skill.
    2. Starting the skill too soon—wait until body is in the air.
    3. Directing hips and legs around rather than directly over head.

FRONT SOMMIE WITH HALF TWIST (Fig. TR-19)

SL Intermediate

PT Start the same as for a front sommie in piked position. Continue until the body has almost an inverted piked position. Eyes focus on knees. At this point extend hips so that legs move through L position. At this point start looking in the direction of the turn. When the body has made the half twist, it will be horizontal to the tramp. Flex the hips and lift the upper body to come to a standing position.

SP 1. Use overhead gear with twisting belt.
    2. Near hand on abdominal area. Lift. Far hand on back to help rotate and control.

CE 1. Not completing three-quarters of the front sommie before beginning the twist.
    2. Not looking in the direction of the turn.
    3. Looking in the direction of the turn to force the arms in another.
    4. Not using arms to start rotary motion.

Figure TR-19

LAYOUT (Fig. TR-20)

SL Intermediate

PT As the body leaves the bed of the tramp completely tighten all muscles, especially the hips. Keep head in normal position and lift forcefully with chest, and body will rotate around head to land on feet.

SP 1. Use overhead spotting gear with regular belt.
    2. Hand spot—on designated count (usually three), stay on bed of tramp, flex knees while placing one hand on hip, one on lower back. Lift and rotate hip area clockwise.

261

CE 1. Whipping head back as body leaves tramp.
2. Not staying taut or tight in hip area throughout move.
3. Not concentrating on a lift with the chest.

Figure TR-20

Figure TR-21

FULL TWISTING LAYOUT (Fig. TR-21)

SL Intermediate

PT Use same takeoff as for layout. Turn the head and shoulder in the direction of the twist and look at the hip area. Pull outside arm across body. Body will continue twisting as it rotates around head. As the body reaches the vertical position, focus eyes on bed of trampoline, and keep them focused there until twist is finished. Flex hips slightly and slightly lift head to come to a standing position.

SP Use overhead gear with a twisting belt.

CE 1. Not keeping body straight and tight throughout entire skill.
2. Twisting too soon (start layout first).
3. Twisting too late.
4. Not using arms for assisting in the turning action of the body.

OTHER USES FOR THE TRAMPOLINE

The trampoline can be used for a number of tasks. One of the main reasons for using the trampoline for learning tumbling and vaulting skills is to save wear and tear on the legs and feet. It also

Figure TR-22

Figure TR-23

helps avoid shin splints and, of course, on some skills eliminates the fear of falling on a hard surface. The following are just a few suggested uses for the trampoline.

Trampoline as an Exercise Barre (Fig. TR-22, TR-23, TR-24)

Depending on the exercises to be done, a large number of girls can work around the trampoline doing leg lifts (Fig. TR-22), stretching exercises (Fig. TR-23), or working on body positions such as the arabesque and grand battement (Fig. TR-24).

Figure TR-24

Trampoline as a Tumbling Aid (Fig. TR-25 and TR-26)

The skills shown below are just some of many that can be learned on the trampoline. Even in beginning tumbling when an individual is having difficulty rolling over on a backward roll, the trampoline can be used to show poor technique. In advanced tumbling it is especially helpful to learn skills such as the front and back sommies, layouts, and twisting moves on the trampoline first. These skills are a bit easier to spot on a trampoline and, of course, landing on the trampoline is much easier on the feet and legs than landing on mats. The back handspring (Fig. TR-25) learned on the trampoline does not offer the performer a true feeling of the skill, so after learning in the middle of the tramp the student can stand on the frame of the tramp (which better assimilates the push action on the floor) and perform the skill onto the bed of the trampoline (Fig. TR-26).

Figure TR-25

Figure TR-26

Trampoline as a Vaulting Aid (Fig. TR-27 through TR-30)

Because the trampoline is approximately the same height as a horse, it can easily be used to learn and practice many vaulting skills. Two safety rules should always be enforced when using the trampoline for vaulting: (1) a mat should be draped over the end of the trampoline so no one falls through the shock cords or springs and (2) someone should always be at the opposite end and sides to assist if a student should lose her balance upon landing. When performing handspring or Yamishita vaults on the trampoline, it is sometimes helpful to have a landing mat on top of the bed of the trampoline to absorb some of the spring. The following figures show the use of the trampoline for practicing and learning beginning through advanced vaults.

Figure TR-27

265

Figure TR-28

Figure TR-29

Figure TR-30

Use of Trampoline for Learning Beam Dismounts (Fig. TR-31 and TR-32)

When using the beam for learning certain dismounts such as shown below, place the side or end of beam over the trampoline. Some beams may have to be raised slightly for a nice fit. When attempting the back (Fig. TR-31) or front (Fig. TR-32) sommie dismount onto the trampoline, make sure a spotter is standing close enough to assist if balance is lost.

Figure TR-31

267

Figure TR-32

Trampoline for Learning Some Uneven Bar Skills (Fig. TR-33)

Because of its design, the trampoline is not really very helpful in learning many uneven bar skills. However, some skills such as the cast away (Fig. TR-33) or squat stand can be learned on the frame.

Figure TR-33

The above are just a few uses for the versatile piece of equipment called the trampoline. Put your mind to work and you will be able to come up with some unique uses.

268

GYMNASTICS IN THE SCHOOL CURRICULUM AND CLASS ORGANIZATION

"What on earth am I going to do with fifty students in half a gym during the gymnastic unit?" This question is often asked by teachers confronted with the same or similar situations. It is hoped that the following suggestions can be used or varied to fit your particular needs and that they will, to some extent, offer a solution to the question above.

Planning ahead seems to be the key to success. Check to see what equipment you have, what equipment you need, and the amount of money available for purchasing equipment and supplies.

It is most likely that all apparatus cannot be purchased at one time, so the following is suggested:

1. First check into those dark corners of the equipment room; you can usually find a horse or a set of parallel bars. If there are no parallel bars, look for a horizontal bar; even if your school has the "wall flower" type, it can be put to good use.
2. Check the mats. Do you have an adequate number? Are they in good condition? Remember that you need mats to surround the apparatus as well as for tumbling.
3. Since you can use the parallel bars (by removing one bar) or the horizontal bar for learning beginning skills for the uneven parallel bar, I would suggest ordering a balance beam (one that adjusts to a low, medium, and regulation height) and a reuther board.
4. If no equipment is available, the following purchase order would be suggested: mats, beam, uneven parallel bars (plus extra bar), reuther board, horse, and trampoline. Some type of transporter should also be ordered so that equipment can be moved easily and safely.

CHAOS

Supplies such as magnesium (chalk), chalk stands, colored tape (for marking areas on mat and apparatus), spotting belts, and other safety aids, such as a beam pad, should be ordered with the equipment.

Secure information on available films (for rental and purchase), wall charts, and bulletin board material. Some of the visual aids materials can be obtained free of charge from the apparatus distributors.

Check the school library and your personal library and make a list of reference books. Order books and magazines if necessary.

EQUIPMENT

Ordering Equipment

Ordering equipment is not an easy task. Teachers or administrators should first investigate what is presently on the market, then use the following criteria as a guideline for purchasing the equipment.

1. What safety features does the apparatus have?
2. Is the apparatus durable? Does the apparatus have a guarantee?
3. Is the apparatus adaptable to your needs?
4. Is the apparatus easily moved from place to place? Can it be stored without too much difficulty?
5. Does the apparatus meet FIG specifications? (If the apparatus is to be used at any time for competition, it is essential that it be adjustable to proper heights, etc.)
6. *Will the company service the apparatus promptly and efficiently?*
7. The least important factor should be the cost of the equipment. Usually if a little more is paid for the equipment initially, chances are that it will not have to be serviced or replaced frequently.

To secure information on apparatus, obtain catalogues from district salesmen, write directly to the company, or pick up some catalogues at professional convention exhibitions. It is also advisable to discuss this matter with colleagues who have used various makes of apparatus before making a final decision.

Care of Equipment

Since gymnastic equipment is expensive initially, special care should be taken to keep it in good condition for as long as possible. If maintenance is performed, equipment can last indefinitely.

1. Check equipment before each use (refer to chapters on apparatus for details).
2. Have adequate number of students moving equipment so they do not injure themselves or damage the equipment.
3. Wash mats to clean off chalk dust, dirt, or body oils.
4. Make sure equipment is properly used; do not let balance beam be used as a clothes rack or a seat for twenty students.
5. Before each unit or once a year have a representative from the company from which the equipment was purchased (or other personnel with proper knowledge of the equipment) examine the apparatus to make certain it is in top usable condition.

GYMNASTICS IN THE SCHOOL CURRICULUM

Gymnastics should be an integral part of the school physical education curriculum, being introduced in kindergarten and offered through high school and college. The values derived from participation in gymnastics are numerous: strength, flexibility, balance, endurance, kinesthetics, agility, self-discipline, coordination, courage, self-confidence, and perseverance. The sport also allows for a great deal of creativeness and small- and large-group interaction, and it is generally challenging to students at all levels.

With more media coverage of the Olympics and other international gymnastics events, schools are being encouraged to develop or broaden their existing programs in gymnastics.

In gymnastics, individuals compete against themselves, without a teammate to help with their performance. This situation develops a competitive drive in performers and helps prepare them for our competitive way of life.

Students cannot be expected to perform skills at an intermediate level without having basics. Some provisions must be made each year or in each unit for those students with inadequate backgrounds and physical abilities. On the other hand, it is not fair to gifted students to hold them back just because a unit does not offer "on paper" skills that they are ready for.

The following is a suggested format for gymnastics K-12. Do not underestimate the ability of the the children, especially if you yourself have encountered a difficult time with gymnastics. When students start at an early age and with a solid foundation, they will be able to perform skills beyond those suggested.

GYMNASTICS IN THE SCHOOL CURRICULUM K-12

Grade	Beam	Bars	Vault	Tumbling

K-1
Boys & Girls
	Gymnastics at this level should be exploratory and should include:
	    How to get on, off, under, through, and over the apparatus.
	    How to be small, roung, big, square.
	    How to move upside down, slow, fast.
	    How to move on one body part, on two body parts, etc.
	    How to roll small, big, long.
	    How to get through space and different ways to cover distances.			

2-3
Girls
	Walking
	    forward
	    backward
	    on toes
	Chassé (gallop)
	Step hop (skip)
	Squat turn
	Toe turn
	Forward roll
		Pull over
		Cast
		Back hip circle
		Underswing
		    dismount
		Forward roll
		    dismount
			Use of board
			Squat onto mats
				Tripod
				Forward roll
				Backward roll
				Headstand
				Cartwheel

4-6
Girls
	Sissone (push
	    leap)
	Run
	Leap
	Kick turn
	Back roll
	Round-off
	    dismount
	Squat mount
	Step-on mount
		Beat-swing mount
		Pullover to high
		    bar
		Underswing to
		    stride
		Mill circle
		Front hip circle
		Sole-circle
		    dismount
			Squat
			Flank
			Straddle
				Handstand
				Handstand forward
				    roll
				Round-off
				Back extension
				Limbre
				Front walkover
				Back walkover

7 Girls	Review all skills taught in K-6			
8-12 Girls	Individualized instruction. Develop a chart similar to the following one and allow students to work at their own pace with student-teacher directed goals. Make two copies, one for the student and one for your files.			

GYMNASTICS SKILLS SHEET

Name   Schools

Skill	Date	Teacher initial	Grade
BEAM			
Forward walk			
Chassé			
Step hop			
Pas de chat			
Forte			
Sissone			
Slide			
Leap			
Squat jump			
Squat turn			
Toe turn			
Forward roll			
Backward roll			
Cartwheel			
Handstand forward roll			
Back walkover			
Squat mount			
Step-on mount			
Forward-roll mount			
Round-off dismount			
Cartwheel quarter dismount			
Handspring dismount			
Aerial dismount			
UNEVENS			
Beat-swing mount			
Pullover mount			
Front hip-circle mount			
Kip mount			
Back hip circle			
Front hip circle			
Mill circle			
Stem rise			
Pullover to high			
Kip to high			
Front seat circle			
Back seat circle			
Cast wrap			
Squat on			
Sole-circle half turn			
Underswing dismount low bar			
high bar			
Handstand quarter dismount			
Flank-cut dismount			
Hecht dismount			

Skill	Date	Teacher initial	Grade
TUMBLING			
Tripod			
Tip up			
Headstand			
Forward roll			
Backward roll			
Handstand			
Cartwheel			
Round-off			
Kip			
Back roll extension			
Back walkover			
Front walkover			
Limbre			
Front handspring			
Back handspring			
Front-handspring step out			
Round-off back handspring			
Side aerial			
Front aerial			
VAULTING			
Flank			
Squat			
Straddle			
Handspring			
TRAMPOLINE			
Seat drop			
Knee drop			
Half turn			
Full turn			
Knee-drop full turn			
Back drop			
Half-turn back drop			
Swivel hips			
Seat drop, full turn, seat drop			
Knee drop, back drop			
Knee drop, half turn, back drop			
Cradle			
Front sommie			
Back sommie			

272

NOW ABOUT THOSE FIFTY STUDENTS!

Of course, one of the best ways to handle large groups in any situation is to have assistants. One of the following may be a solution for your particular problem.

1. Train students to spot (before or after school).
2. Limit the number of skills required in the unit.
3. Use a buddy system.
4. Give a good basic course for all students, and start an after-school club or team for advanced or interested students.

Ways to Organize Students Within Groups

1. Ability grouping: beginners, intermediates, and advanced. Have a progression for each group.
2. Buddy system: pair a weak individual with a strong indicidual or have an advanced student with a beginner student.
3. Somatotype the students: have three groups—one of mesomorphs, one of endomorphs, and one of ectomorphs. Refer to glossary for definition of terms. Definitions are for extreme somatotypes; however, individuals are usually combinations of these various body structures.
4. Random grouping: first six in group one, second six in group two, etc.

Ways to Organize Large Groups in Each Area of Gymnastics

Tumbling

1. Use cross-mat tumbling technique.
   a. Number off by fours and have every fourth girl perform at one time with the person to the left acting as the spotter.
   b. File students: after one girl has almost finished performing, the second starts, etc.
   c. After students can perform skills well, give commands and have every other student perform.

Example: forward roll commands—step onto mat, squat, place hands on mat, roll.

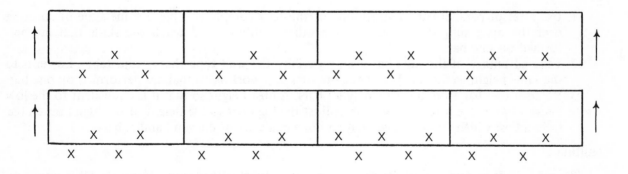

2. Arrange mats in semicircle.
   a. Apply same techniques as above or work in groups of four if mats are of adequate size.
   b. Allow students to work in these groups at their own pace with two performing and the other two acting as spotters.

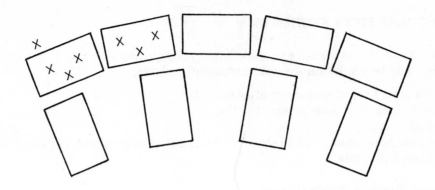

Floor Exercise

For large groups it is almost always impossible to have students perform individual routines due to limited time and space. You can revert to a mass exercise made up either in advance or created during one or two class sessions, with the students helping design the routine and floor pattern. Refer to floor exercise chapter for more suggestions.

A floor exercise mat can be made by covering carpet padding with a large piece of canvas.

Balance Beam

It is not likely that any school will have ten balance beams, so teachers must make use of improvised equipment. The following suggestions might benefit your particular situation.
1. Most gymnasiums have lines for basketball and volleyball courts. These lines can be utilized by the students to practice skills before attempting them on the beam.
2. Some gyms have stages. If yours has, use the stage as a partial beam. Even though this is a one-sided arrangement, students can get the feeling of being off the floor to some degree. Depending on the height of the stage, mounts can also be practiced here.
3. Possibly the industrial arts department in your school would agree to make a couple of low beams. This is a very inexpensive task.
4. If the gym has bleachers, use the first row as a low beam.

Uneven Parallel Bars

Girls do not need a regulation set of uneven parallel bars to begin learning skills suited to that apparatus.

1. Use a set of parallel bars; remove one of the bars completely, place some type of covering over the open support (towel or some other padding), and teach the skills that are performed on one bar.
2. Take advantage of the high bar also, especially the wall type that is adjustable. Lower it to the same height as the low bar of the unevens and work skills that are performed on one bar.
3. Remove one bar from a set of parallel bars. Adjust height so that it is equivalent to the low uneven bar; move it to the high bar. Adjust the high bar to the height of the high uneven bar (also adjust width), and you will have a homemade set of uneven parallel bars.

Vaulting

Playing leap frog is probably the most elementary form of vaulting. (Many students enjoy reverting to their childhood games.) This activity could be used as a lead-up. If vaulting equipment is not available, vault onto folded or stacked mats.

GENERAL SAFETY FACTORS

1. Make sure apparatus is in good condition and properly mantled.

274

2. Have adequate mats surrounding the equipment.
3. Arrange apparatus so that students can work without fear of falling into or onto another object.
4. Have students in proper physical condition before allowing them to work on the apparatus. (See suggested exercises.)
5. Allow students to rest when fatigued.
6. Keep interest up by varying exercises or skills on apparatus and not making requirements too difficult.
7. Teach good spotting techniques as well as mechanical techniques.
8. Make sure the area is well lit and properly ventilated.
9. Teach with a positive approach to avoid developing fear in students.
10. Have a definite skill progression for each class.

SPOTTING

Spotting is in itself an art. It is not always putting a student through an entire skill but rather giving assistance where most needed for success and to prevent injury. Spotting can be done with hand contact, mechanical devices (e.g., spotting belt), or just readiness to assist if necessary.

In all spotting work, it is the duty of the spotter to prevent the head from falling to the mat or striking any part of the apparatus. Therefore, the most common points of contact for spotting are the performer's shoulders, upper arms, back, and wrists.

In general, the spotter should stand close to the apparatus and should understand that she must sacrifice her own safety to assist the performer. Except for an occasional slap on the face with an uncontrolled hand, a spotter is seldom hurt.

The spotter should know the following about the skill she is spotting.

1. Position of the body from the beginning throughout the entire skill.
2. What part of the body produces the force or momentum to initiate movement of the skill.
3. What parts of the body control the movement of the skill, such as the hands, hips, feet, etc.
4. In what part(s) of the skill are accidents most likely to occur, and what can be done to prevent accidents or to assist the performer at that point.

Remember that giving proper assistance to students in gymnastic skills is of utmost importance maintaining their interest and in creating confidence in you as a spotter. Always be alert.

Know what to expect from your students. Have a definite skill progression and do not allow them to attempt advanced skills before they have mastered the basic skills. If there are lead-ups to skills and if the student cannot perform them, she should not be allowed to attempt the skill itself.

It might be advisable to post a chart with the skill progressions to make students aware of the necessity for learning in this particular manner.

METHODS FOR TESTING

Subjective Evaluation

1. Each skill can be analyzed and parts charted for testing. This is the most objective type of evaluation, but it is not feasible in large classes.
   Example: Forward roll
           Squat—knees together.
           Hands in front of body on mat.
           Extended legs, pushing equally with both feet.
           Bent arms and tucked head at proper time.

No loud sound when rolling onto back.
Legs together and straight when inverted.
Legs tucked at proper time.
Stand executed without loss of balance and without using hand to push to stand.
2. Rate skill as whole (0 to 4 points)
   0 (F) Failure to perform skill.
   1 (D) Performance—some phases correct, some incorrect, poor form.
   2 (C) Performance—machanics correct, poor form, skill not performed smoothly.
   3 (B) Performance—mechanically correct, form good.
   4. (A) Performance—mechanically correct with very good form and control.
3. Pass or fail grading system.
   1. Failure—unable to perform skill.
   2. Pass—able to perform skill whether mechanically correct or not and with either good or poor form.

Objective Evaluation in Gymnastics

Evaluation in physical education should not be on skill alone. There are many students who can understand and analyze movement very well but cannot perform as efficiently as others. We should try to encourage those more physically gifted to be able to understand and apply principles of movement when performing to obtain maximum results. We should not only teach the "how," but also the "why," "when," and "relationship of this movement to another."

The following are examples of test questions that can be used at the secondary (junior and senior high) level and college level (for physical education majors).

Junior-Senior High

TUMBLING

1. When performing a forward roll, where are the hands placed?
   a. Between the legs on the mat.
   b. Forward of the knees on the mat.
   c. To the side of the knees on the mat.
   d. It doesn't make any difference where the hands are placed.
2. In performing the forward roll, when is the head tucked toward the chest?
   a. When the hands are placed on the mat.
   b. Before the hands are placed on the mat.
   c. As the hips are raised and the legs extend.
   d. As the elbows bend.
3. When spotting tumbling skills, our main concern is protection of what part of the body?
   a. Head
   b. Eyes
   c. Back
   d. Arms

BALANCE BEAM

1. When working on the balance beam it is important that we have an _____ spotter.
   a. Friendly
   b. Strong
   c. Alert
   d. Passive.
2. On the beam we use which of the following types of walks?
   a. Flat-footed
   b. Dance

c. Ordinary

d. Fast

3. List three classifications of skills we learned on the beam. (Answers will depend on what the teacher covered in class.)

a. Rolls

b. Locomotor skills

c. Poses

d. Dance moves

e. Mounts

f. Dismounts

UNEVEN BARS

1. List three grips used on the unevens and beside it a skill that requires the use of that grip. Example:

GRIP   SKILL

a. Forward   a. Back hip circle

2. Proper body position in the front support position involves all but which one of the following?

a. Shoulders hunched.

b. Upper thighs on bar.

c. Arms straight.

d. Legs straight and together.

3. It is important to learn the cast (push-away) well so that we can perform other skills. Which of the following skills is not preceded by a cast?

a. Back hip circle

b. Single-leg shoot through.

c. Double-leg shoot through

d. Back hip pullover

VAULTING

1. The side of the horse closest to the reuther board is referred to as the (near) side.

2. In order to perform a good vault, the run must be executed in which of the following manners?

a. Sluggish

b. Fast all the way.

c. Slow, then fast before the hurdle.

d. Slow, but with a long stride.

3. The spotter for a squat vault should be on the far side of the horse and do which of the following?

a. Grab shoulder of performer and pull her over the horse.

b. Grasp upper arm and assist in lifting performer up and over the horse.

c. Assist only if performer needs help.

d. None of the above.

FLOOR EXERCISE

1. The time limit of a competitive routine is (60) to (90) seconds.

2. List three components of a floor exercise routine.

Example: 1. Tumbling and acrobatic skills.

2. Dance moves.

3. Variations in tempo

3. Floor exercise is performed to music in a 40 X 40 foot (12 X 12 meter) area.

College Level—Students Majoring in Physical Education

Since physical education majors are being trained for the teaching profession, they should be able to analyze and evaluate students' performance, along with having the ability to perform at least the basic skills for each sport. Therefore, the questions should be developed to evaluate their ability to comprehend and analyze movement and to recall facts and principles.

TUMBLING

1. In order to initiate movement, one must:
   a. Move the center of gravity past the base of support.
   b. Displace the center of gravity to the lower limbs.
   c. Shift the center of gravity to the lower limbs.
   d. Tilt the head forward.
2. When correcting a backward roll that was performed crooked, which of the following suggestions most likely would not be made?
   a. Keep the right elbow straight.
   b. Do not turn the head to the side.
   c. Push with the hands equally and simultaneously.
   d. Push with the hands and feet simultaneously.
3. Which of the following principles is not involved with the mechanics of executing the front handspring?
   a. Arms remaining overhead until landing.
   b. Strong push action of the forward foot after the hurdle.
   c. Head kept in normal position throughout entire skill.
   d. Legs not meeting while in the inverted position.

VAULTING

1. The most common reason for hitting the horse with the knees when attempting a squat vault is:
   a. Bringing knees to chest too late.
   b. Poor hurdle.
   c. Landing flat-footed on the board.
   d. Leaning forward from the board on takeoff.
2. When the hips pass over the horse in squat vaults:
   a. Directly beneath the shoulders.
   b. Before the shoulders.
   c. After the shoulders.
   d. None of the above.
3. Common faults of the beginning vaulter include all but one of the following;
   a. Failure to use the board quickly.
   b. Executing a hurdle that is too high.
   c. Reaching the horizontal position in preflight.
   d. Leaning forward when contacting the reuther board.

UNEVEN BARS

1. The most common mistake beginners make in performing a back hip pullover on low bar is:
   a. Insufficient kick.
   b. Allowing hips to move forward of the bar.
   c. Forcing the head back as the legs kick.
   d. Allowing the arms to extend.
2. Why is it essential to bring the body back to the bar in an arched position from the cast preceding a back hip circle?
   a. To keep the shoulders upright.
   b. To develop short axis rotation.
   c. To ensure a tighter wrap.
   d. To keep the arms from bending.
3. The most common error made by beginners on the cast is:
   a. Keeping the arms straight.
   b. Using a forward grip.
   c. Allowing the shoulders to move back of the bar.
   d. Piking as the body contacts the bar.

BALANCE BEAM

1. When spotting the backward roll, where does the spotter place her hands?
   a. On the hip area.
   b. One hand on the abdomen, the other on the lower back.
   c. One hand on the thigh, other hand on the arms.
   d. Both hands around waist and upper hip area.
2. Considering the mechanical action of the mounts below, which could not be easily transferred to another event in gymnastics?
   a. Straddle
   b. Squat
   c. Handspring
   d. Wolf
3. When performing on the beam, one should be concerned with proper body alignment for which of the following reasons?
   a. So that skills may be performed in a mechanically correct manner.
   b. For aesthetic beauty.
   c. For ease of maneuverability.
   d. So the spotter will not have to assist.

MISCELLANEOUS—ORGANIZATION QUESTION

1. You are teaching gymnastics to fifty students in half a gym (30′ by 30′). There are four activities going on simultaneously. Which of the following arrangements of apparatus would be best for the situation? Consider skills being performed and amount of space needed for various skills on each apparatus, and remember that students will rotate as a group from one activity to the next. Rotation will be counterclockwise.
   b—Apparatus arranged so there is sufficient room for mounts, dismounts, landing in vaulting, and mat arrangement around the apparatus. Also it is arranged so that students will not use the same muscle groups from one event to the other.

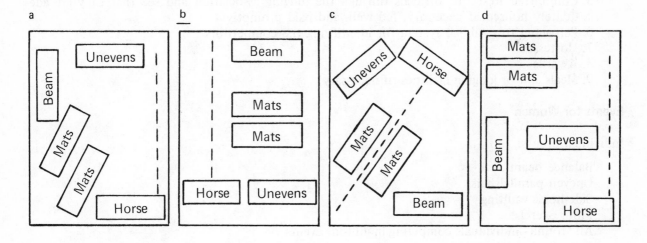

chapter eleven

ORGANIZING AND DIRECTING A GYMNASTIC MEET

A meet that appears to be running smoothly is the result of many hours of preparation. Many first meets are very hectic, take hours to complete, and leave those in charge with a negative attitude towards future gymnastic meets. Therefore, it is hoped that the following information will serve as a guideline when you are asked to organize, direct, and/or sponsor a gymnastic meet at your school or club.

PLANNING A GYMNASTIC MEET

Appoint Committees

1. Publicity
2. Equipment and supplies
3. Ticket sales; finances
4. Facilities
   a. Secure gym
   b. Secure locker room facilities—make sure there are adequate dressing and showering facilities
5. Committee to secure officials through the judging association and see that they are adequately housed, if necessary, fed well, and paid promptly
6. Personnel to establish system for identifying the competitors
7. Hostesses
8. Awards
9. Meals and/or lodging facilities (if necessary)

Events for Women

Individual events:

Balance beam
Uneven parallel bars
Side-horse vaulting
Floor exercise
All around—individuals competing in all four events

Place

The gymnasium where the meet is to be held should meet the following criteria.

1. Be large enough to accommodate equipment used.
   a. 80 feet for vaulting (could be less), 60 feet for the runway, and 10 feet for landing beyond the horse. (Judges should be situated far enough from the four corners of the horse to get a clear view.)
   b. 45 by 45 feet for floor exercise, allowing ample room for judges to be seated at each corner.

2. Have adequate light and proper temperature control. A cooler gym is preferable. Apparatus should be placed so there will not be any glare from the lights or sun.
3. Be large enough to accommodate spectators if there are to be any. In many cases it is advisable to rope off safety areas for gymnasts with sign stating, "No Spectators Allowed Beyond This Point!"
4. Be free of hazards where gymnasts must perform and await their turn before performing, such as:
   Buckled floors
   Projections from walls
   Excessive dust
   Unnecessary extension cords from the tape recorder or public address system
5. Should have adequate electrical fixtures or outlets for tape recorders, public address systems, and record players.

Time

The time of the meet will depend on many things. However, if it is possible to select a time, consider the following.

1. Number of entrants expected.
2. Age of gymnasts.
3. Traveling time involved to and from the meet.
4. Try to avoid having the meet too close to a meal unless the number of entrants is so great that you have no choice.
5. Allow at least the following period of time per performer:
   a. Beam—three minutes (judging time included)
   b. Bars—one and a half to two minutes
   c. Vaulting—two minutes
   d. Floor exercise—three minutes
6. Consider time for moving equipment, warm-up periods, intermission, judges' conferences, and presentation of awards.

Date

Try to select a date well enough in advance so there will be few or no conflicts.

Entries

Notices of meet and entry blanks should be sent out well in advance. They should contain information pertinent to the meet with any special regulations. An entry form and meet notice should contain the following.

1. Type of meet
   a. Optional
   b. Compulsory (stating which compulsories will be used)
   c. Age group
   d. Open (to anyone)
   e. Closed (usually a dual or district meet)
2. Date
3. Location
4. Time (time warm-ups start and time meet starts)
5. Sponsor
6. Sanction—if meet has to be sanctioned
7. Events
8. Fee, if any

9. Closing date for entries
10. Award system, if any
11. Notice that a physical examination is required before an individual will be allowed to compete
12. Notice that the sponsoring organization will not be responsible for accidents incurred during the meet
13. The entry blank portion should contain the following:
    a. Place for name, address, age, number (if any), and affiliation (school or club)
    b. Events to be held with a check space
    c. Place for gymnast's signature
    d. Place for coach's signature and parent's signature if the performer is a minor

Sample Notice of Meet

WOMEN'S OPEN OPTIONAL GYMNASTIC MEET
April 14, 198-
POOLESVILLE HIGH SCHOOL
POOLESVILLE, MARYLAND

Sponsor Poolesville High School Gymnastic Club
Place   Women's gymnasium
Time   Warm-ups 9:00 a.m.
           Meet 10:00 a.m.
Events   Floor exercise, balance beam, side-horse vaulting, uneven parallel bars, and all around
Entry fee $12.00 for All Around
Deadline Entries close with the meet director, Mrs. Bertha Stevens, on Monday, April 10, at 4:00 p.m.
Awards   Trophies will be given to the first three places in each event and the top three All Around.

Detach the entry below and return to meet director.

Sample Entry Blank (attached to meet notice)

WOMEN'S OPEN OPTIONAL GYMNASTIC MEET
April 14, 198-

Poolesville High School   Poolesville, Maryland

Name ————————— Age ——— Phone ————————————
                                                 area code   number

Address ————————————————————————————
        street   city   state   zip code

School or club affiliation ————————————————————

Total fee remitted: $ ——————— (All Around $12.00)

Note: I understand that the school will not be responsible for any injuries incurred during participation in this meet.

                            Gymnast's signature ————————————————

                            Coach's signature ——————————————————

                            Parent or guardian's signature ——————————————

Sample Group Entry Form

```
┌────────────────────────────────────────────────────────────────────────┐
│                     MID ATLANTIC OPEN COMPULSORY                         │
│                          CLASS I, II, III                                │
│                           April 14, 198-                                 │
│                       TRENTON STATE COLLEGE                              │
│                        TRENTON, NEW JERSEY                               │
│                                                                          │
│   Club       Southhampton                                                │
│   Address    27 Richard Rd.   Ivyland, Pa. 18974                         │
│   Phone      215-627-1719                                                │
│                                                                          │
│   Name                            Age         Level                      │
│   ──────────────────────────────────────────────────────                │
│   JoAnn Corl                      15          Class I                     │
│   Marcy Maimon                    15          Class I                     │
│   Susan Maimon                    15          Class I                     │
│   Vicki Moore                     14          Class I                     │
│   Susan Schaeffer                 12          Class I                     │
│   Tracy Lassin                    11          Class I                     │
│   Penney Hauschild                14          Class I                     │
│   Wendy Ricketts                  15          Class I                     │
│   Jennifer Hay                    15          Class I                     │
│                                                                          │
│                              Total remittance     $108.00                │
│                              (Entry fee $12.00 per person)               │
│   *This form must be accompanied with individual waiver forms.           │
└────────────────────────────────────────────────────────────────────────┘
```

Awards

Decide on quantity, quality, cost, design, etc., and order well in advance. Order extras in case of ties.

Officials

The number in parentheses will indicate the ideal number needed for an event or meet. If two or more events are held simultaneously, the number will increase accordingly.

    a. Meet director (1)
    b. Judges (4). This is the ideal situation, but two judges per event are adequate for local meets
    c. Scorers (2)
    d. Flashers (one per event)
    e. Runners (2)
    f. Announcer (1)
    g. Timer (1)

Duties of the Officials

    a. *Meet director*
   1. Responsible for conducting the meet in an orderly fashion.
   2. Must be available to answer questions that may arise in various situations.
   3. Handles any inquiries. In school or club situations, the governing body usually decides how the inquiries are to be handled.
   4. Makes decisions on matters not covered by the rules.

    b. *Superior judge* (included as one of the four judges mentioned above)
   1. Scores performances.
   2. Makes sure that the range of the other judges' scores are within legal limits.
   3. Calls conferences if she feels that the performer has not been given a realistic score.
   4. Makes sure that the judges are in the proper places and alert.

    c. *Judges*
   1. Score performers to the best of their ability.
   2. Make notations when scoring so they are able to defend scores in case of inquiry.
   3. Are alert and in the proper places.

    d. *Scorers*
   1. Sit at the head table and keep a master copy of all scores for all events.
   2. Record scores accurately.

    e. *Flasher*
   Sits beside superior judge. After scores have been turned into the head (superior) judge and they are determined to be within limits, the flasher will then by some method show the performers and audience the *average* score given by the judges.

    f. *Runners*
   Stand or sit beside judges. Take score to superior judge as quickly as possible after performance.

    g. *Announcer*
   1. Gives all directions (loudly and clearly).
   2. Informs competitors of events, warm-ups, and the line-up.
   3. Should have enough knowledge of gymnastics to inform competitors and audience of rulings or incidents that may happen and to inform audience about nature of composition of the routines they are watching.

    h. *Timers*
   Time the floor exercise and balance-beam routines to make sure they are within the time limit.

    i. *Other personnel*
   1. Physician or nurse
   2. Guides or hostesses
   3. Ticket takers
   4. Equipment movers
   5. Persons to organize contestants
   6. Electrician (optional)
   7. Photographer (optional)

Note: If any of the officials besides the judges are to be paid for their services, this should be decided in advance. Checks should be ready to issue immediately after the meet is completed. A budget, including gate receipts and fees for registration, should be kept. If at all possible, meets should be self-supporting.

ORGANIZATION AND DIRECTION

Setting Up Equipment

After entries are closed and the judges have been obtained, it is advisable to design some type of plan for setting up and moving equipment. Arrangements must be made to fit the needs of the gymnasts and other personnel involved. If it is at all possible, it is best to have all equipment set up for the warm-up period before the meet to allow the performers to adjust to the particular pieces of apparatus being used. If this is not feasible, then the gymnasts should be given a longer time to warm up on the apparatus when it is set up.

If only one event is to be running at a time, the following order is suggested.

1. Floor exercise
2. Vaulting
3. Beam
4. Bars

   or

1. Vaulting
2. Bars
3. Beam
4. Floor exercise

The floor exercise mat (or area if mat is not available) should be set up in advance to make sure it flattens out as much as possible.

For the warm-up period, the floor patterns could be as shown below.

After the warm-up period leave equipment where it is or put the horse, beam, and bars on transporters ready to move. After floor exercise is completed, have designated persons roll up the mat while others are ready to move horse and mats into position either on a diagonal or to the side of the gym. After vaulting, if the horse was moved, put it in original position or take to storage room, and move both bars and beam with mats to the center of the gym, leaving ample room for mount, dismount, and judges' seats.

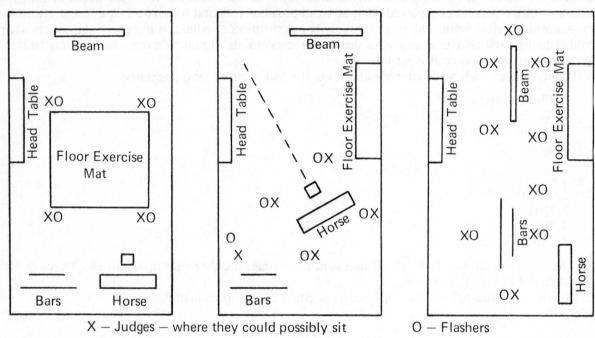

X — Judges — where they could possibly sit   O — Flashers

If two events are to run simultaneously, the following order of events and setup of apparatus is suggested.

1. Floor exercise and beam.
2. Bars and vaulting.

Warm-up   First Two Events   Second Two Events

If two events are running simultaneously, the sponsor and meet director must be prepared to decide for a gymnast if she is called to both events simultaneously. What usually happens in this case is that the gymnast selects the event to perform in first and is then either given sufficient time to rest before performing the other event or is placed at the bottom of the list.

It is also advisable to have a person responsible for making sure the performers are ready when called "on deck" (next up) or "in the hole" (third up), In meets where there are many entrants, this person should line up the performers and not allow them to wander around.

Selecting Order of Performers

After entries are in, make a list of all performers in each event. Doing one event at a time, place their names in some type of container, and as you draw them out, make up the official list. A performer should not go first or last in more than one event. In some meets, gymnasts will be rotated in teams.

Score Sheets

After drawing names for order of performances, make up score sheets for the judges, scorers, and, if possible, extras for the coaches and contestants.

Sample Score Sheet for Head Table

WOMEN'S OPEN MEET

April 14, 198-

POOLESVILLE HIGH

Event ___(Beam)___   Judge's Signature   1) _____

2) _____

3) _____

4) _____

Scores

Name	No.	Judge 1	Judge 2	Judge 3	Judge 4	Average	Place
Ramsay, Bobby	42						
Cooper, Phyllis	101						
Garvey, Pat	68						
Moser, Lorraine	7						
Shifflett, Charlotte	14						

Note: This particular type of score sheet can be used by each judge (as is done here), as well as used by the scorer for the master sheet. If extras are passed out to the audience, they can keep score also.

Individual Score Sheet for Optional Bars, Beam, and Floor Exercise

Circle one				Circle one		
Bars	Beam	Floor	Work area	Bars	Beam	Floor
Competitor #				Competitor #		
Difficulty	3.0					
Exec. & amp.	4.0					
General Comp.	.5					
Rhythm	.3					
Spacing	.2					
Dist. of elements	.2					
Connections	.5					
Gen. impression	.5					
Risk	.4					
Originality	.2					
Virtuosity	.2					
Neutral deductions				Final score		
Total						
				Judge's initial		

Individual Score Sheet for Compulsory Bars, Beam, and Floor Exercise

Circle one				Circle one		
Bars	Beam	Floor	Work area	Bars	Beam	Floor
Competitor #				Competitor #		
Exactness of parts	2.0					
Exactness of direction	.5					
Exactness of rhythm	1.5					
Elegance	1.0					
Sureness of execution	1.5					
Amplitude	1.5					
Lightness	1.0					
Coordination	1.0					
Falls				Final score		
Final score						
				Judge's initial		

Individual Score Sheet for Optional Vaulting

OPTIONAL VAULT	Vault #1	Vault #2	Optional Vault	Optional Vault
Competitor #			Competitor #	Competitor #
Vault			Second Vault	First Vault
Preflight				
First phase turn				
On horse and repulsion				
Afterflight				
Second phase turn				
Body stretch				
Dynamics				
Direction				
Balance and landing				
Spotting			Final score	Final score
Final score				
			Judge's initial	Judge's initial

Individual Score Sheet for Compulsory Vaulting

COMPULSORY VAULT	Vault #1	Vault #2	Comp. Vault	Comp. Vault
Competitor #			Competitor #	Competitor #
			Second Vault	First Vault
Preflight				
On horse and repulsion				
Afterflight				
Direction				
Dynamics				
Landing				
Spotting			Final score	Final score
Final score				
			Judge's initial	Judge's initial

Flash Cards

If commercial flash cards cannot be purchased, they can be made out of oil cloth or cardboard and can be attached to rings so they can be flipped. There should be one complete set for each flasher and a set with three rows of numbers for the head judge's flasher so the average score can be shown. An opaque projector could be used to flash groups of scores.

Miscellaneous Equipment and Materials

Typewriter for head table
Tables and chairs for scorers and announcer
Desks or chairs for flashers and judges
Adding machine
Microphone
Scratch paper for judges and scorers
Pencils
Clipboards
Chalk—magnesium
Stop watches
Tape recorder
Piano
Rope—to rope off vaulting runway and to keep spectators out of gym area.
Tape—measuring tape to measure vaulting distances and check dimensions of equipment (height, etc., if necessary), adhesive tape for gymnasts if needed
Sand or emery paper to remove chalk from bars
Extension cords
Magic markers to make signs
Mop or broom to remove excessive chalk dust from floor
First aid supplies
Record player

General Judging Procedures

New judging rules and routine requirements for women's gymnastics were instituted after the last Olympics. General changes will be discussed below; however, for specific requirements and deductions please consult the USGF Interpretations of the International Rules for Women's Gymnastics. These may be obtained from the USGF, PO Box 12713, Tucson, Arizona 85711.

Depending on the level of the meet, two to four judges rate the exercises. The judges confer after the first exercise (except finals), then arrive at the remaining scores independently. If two judges are used, the scores are averaged; if four judges are used, the high and low scores are eliminated and the two middle scores averaged. Only the averaged score is flashed to the audience and performers.

The general 10.0 breakdown is listed below. Today, however, it is possible to score above a 10.0. Refer to USGF guide for specifics.

10.0 Breakdown

4.0	Execution and amplitude
3.0	Difficulty
.5	General composition
.3	General rhythm
.2	Spacing

.2   Distribution of the elements
.5   Connections
.5   General impression
.4   Risk
.2   Virtuosity
.2   Originality

General Elements Defined

Execution and Amplitude—Correctness in technique, maximum body position, full extension of body part(s) involved.

Difficulty— Four mediums at .3 each; three superiors at .6 each.

Refer to Code of Points for A, B, C, and D elements:

A element—a movement of no difficulty or risk value

B element—a movement of medium difficulty (.3) with no risk value

C element—1) a movement of superior difficulty (.6) with no risk value

2) a movement of superior difficulty (.6) with a risk value of .1 or .2

D element—a movement of superior difficulty (.6) with a risk value of .3

General Composition—Choice of elements suited to the gymnast's body build, ability, and routine requirement.

General Rhythm—Dynamic changes in movement such as slow, fast, etc.

Spacing—Using space, level, and direction well.

Distribution of Elements—Equal distribution of A-D elements as well as distribution of dance and tumbling elements.

Connections—Level of connections used. All easy? All difficult?

General Impressions— Elegance in projection, presentation, and suitability.

Risk— A level of difficulty that exceeds the A and B classification of skills.

Originality—New or unusual combinations.

Virtuosity—Ultimate performance with charisma.

Becoming a Gymnastics Official

If you are interested in becoming a gymnastics official, you should first contact your state judging director for dates of clinics and workshops to be held during the year. If you cannot secure the name of such an individual, write to the USGF Womens Committee, PO Box 12713, Tucson, Arizona 85711.

There are various levels of officiating, and of course you must start at the bottom and work your way up. The general categories are listed below in the order in which they may be obtained. Within each category there are specific classifications which determine the level of meets that can be judged by an individual holding that particular rating. For specifics ask your state or regional judging director.

Apprentice:	Can judge local meets.
Associate:	Can judge local meets, may be asked to do Class II State.
State:	Can judge local and state meets, may be asked to do some regional meets.
Regional:	Can judge local, state, and regional meets.
National:	Can judge local, state, regional, and national meets.
Elite:	Can judge all levels plus elite.
Fig:	Can judge all levels and may be asked to do international meets.
Brevet:	Has done all levels including international and may be asked to do any level.

At the beginning level you take a written test on the Class III compulsories. After success at that level you take the test for optional judging at that level. If you passed Class III, the next year you may take the Class II test and so on. Ask your state chairman or state judging director for dates of exams, scores needed to pass, and retest dates.

Do not be discouraged if you fail the test the first time around; you will definitely not be the first to take the exams twice or maybe three times.

If you are interested only in judging high school meets, most states will require that you take only the national interscholastic exam prepared specifically for high school gymnastics. If this is your desire, then contact the state high school gymnastics chairman for specific dates of tests.

GLOSSARY

1. Aerial—Body suspended in air; performance of skill without hands, with the body usually in an arched position.
2. Arched—The back is hyperextended, shoulders relaxed and back, and abdomen forward.
3. A terre—On the floor.
4. Backbend (bridge)—Hands and feet support body while in arched position on floor. Head is tilted up and back. Back is facing floor.
5. Bent hip ascent—A position in vaulting where the body pikes in preflight, then continues with the remainder of the vault.
6. Crotch seat (straddle seat)—Beam: one leg on each side of beam, sitting facing either end. Bars: same as stride position, one leg in front of the bar, the other leg behind the bar. On the bars this position is rarely referred to as the straddle seat.
7. Dégagé—To remove or disengage.
8. Downbackward—Moving arms down to side of body, past the side of the body, then backward and upward.
9. Ectomorph—The extreme ectomorphic individual is slender and frail looking, with a large forehead, small face, and a sharp nose. She tends to have a slender neck, narrow chest, flat abdomen, and long thin limbs.
10. En dedans—Movement rearward to front position.
11. En dehors—Movement from the front to the back.
12. Endomorph—The extreme endomorphic individual has rounded contours, a predominance of weight in the abdominal, hip, and thigh area, and short thick limbs.
13. English handstand—Beam: handstand done facing the length of the beam; heels of hands together.
14. En l'air—In the air.
15. Flank—Raising the hips as high as possible and keeping the supporting arm straight, lift both legs together and straight up and over the apparatus. As legs move over apparatus, lift non-supporting arm.
16. Flip—Movement performed without hands. Body position in air is tucked. Same as sommie.
17. Foreupward—Move arms from side of body to a forward and upward position, stopping at a 45° angle.
18. Front support—Beam or bars: upper thighs resting on beam or bar with arms straight, shoulders extended, head up.
19. Inverted—Head down, legs extended upward. Example: headstand.
20. Jeté—Small hop.
21. Layout—Straight body-ascent vault: as hands contact the horse, the body is completely straight and should be at least on a 45° angle to the horse. Tumbling: refers to an aerial position where the body is completely extended while suspended in air. Movement usually revolves around the head in layout movement.
22. Long hang—Bars: hands in a forward grip, body straight and hanging from the high bar.

23. Mesomorph—The extreme mesomorphic individual has a heavy angular outline with thick, massive muscles. Her bones are prominent; the neck is long and strong; the chest is large; the waist is long and slender; and the limbs are muscular.
24. Pike—Hips flexed but legs straight and together.
25. Plié—Bending the knees. The feet may be in any of the ballet positions. Knees turn out over toes.
26. Plop—Bars: refers to the movement of the eagle catch and hecht dismount. This movement is a very explosive one in that upper and lower body forcefully moves up and back simultaneously.
27. Prone—Lying, usually on the floor or mat, full length with the face downward. This position is used for exercises such as the push-up.
28. Punch—Forcefully spring from the mat or board with slight knee bend to get maximum lift. The movement must be rapid and hard.
29. Rear arch (supine arch)—Supporting the body weight on the hands and heels. Back bend could also be referred to as a supine arch.
30. Rear sitting—Sitting on, but having back to apparatus. Example: sitting on low bar with back to high bar.
31. Semi-plié (demi-plié)—Slight knee bend.
32. Single-leg flank—Moving one leg through the flank position.
33. Split—One leg extended forward, other leg extended backward with buttocks and legs flat on floor. Upper body facing toward forward leg. Trunk may be arched backward, bent over forward leg, or held erect.
34. Squat—Tumbling: knees are brought to the chest. Jumping: heels are raised to the buttocks.
35. Stick—Vaulting: landing without having to step forward, sideward, or backward to gain balance.
36. Stoop—Upper body flexed, legs straight and together.
37. Straddle—Position in which the legs are separated sideways. Upper body may be erect or flexed, may be sitting or standing, or used in air as position in vaulting, beam, or bar work.
38. Stride—Bars: one leg extended forward of the bar, other leg in back of the bar; sitting on the bar or supported by the hands. Running: refers to length of steps.
39. Supine—Lying on back, facing upward.
40. Swan—Bars: body arched and balanced on the upper thighs. Arms overhead or obliquely sideways. Vaulting: same as hecht, going over horse with body in arched position, face down.
41. Tendu—Snapping one foot to the other foot.
42. Tour—turn.
43. Tuck—Knees bent and close to the chest. Examples: tuck jump and position in air for front or back sommie.

SKILLS WITH MULTIPLE NAMES

Tumbling

1. Forward roll—front roll
2. Headstand—head balance
3. Handstand—hand balance
4. Front limbre—front over
5. Tip-up—knee elbow stand—turk stand—frog hand balance
6. Somersault—sommie—flip—aerial (Refer to glossary for clarification, as these terms are used incorrectly in many instances.)
7. Back roll extension—back roll to handstand snap down
8. Snap down—mule kick—handstand snap down to stoop
9. Back handspring—flip flop

Balance Beam

1. Straddle seat—crotch seat
2. V seat—V sit—balance seat—piked seat
3. Step-on mount—single-leg squat mount
4. Arabesque—scale
5. Windy—kick through handstand making half turn on one arm to stand
6. English handstand dismount—handstand snapdown dismount

Uneven Parallel Bars

1. Cast from high bar to hip circle on low—flying hip circle—cast rotate from high to low—cast wrap
2. Single-leg stem rise—single-leg kip to high
3. Mill circle—stride-leg rotate—crotch circle
4. Stride support—split support
5. Cast—push away

Note: There are many other skills with multiple names; however, the above are most frequently disputed.

ADDITIONAL RESOURCE MATERIALS

Allison, June. *Advanced Gymnastics for Women.* London: Stanley, Paul & Co., 1963.

Aziz, J. A. *How to Teach Gymnastics—Tumbling and Balancing.* J. A. Aziz, 551 Chiddington Ave., London, Ontario, Canada.

Babbitt, D., and Zivic, T. *Manual for Coaches of Women's Gymnastics.* Ontario, Canada: Dept. of Athletics, York University, 1964.

Baley, James. *Handbook of Gymnastics in the Schools.* Boston: Allyn & Bacon, 1974.

Bowers, Carolyn; Fie, Jackie; and Kjeldsen, Kitty. *Judging and Coaching Womens Gymnastics.* Palo Alto, Calif.: Mayfield Publishing Co., 1972.

Claus, M. *Better Gymnastics for Boys.* New York: Dodd, Mead & Co., 1970.

Cochrane, Tuovi. *International Gymnastics for Girls and Women.* Reading, Mass.: Addison Wesley, 1969.

Davis, H. *Beginning Gymnastics for College Women.* Austin, Tex.: Jenkins Publishing Co., 1970.

Drury, Blanche, and Schmid, Andrea. *Gymnastics for Women.* 4th ed. Palo Alto, Calif.: Mayfield Publishing Co., 1976.

Edwards, Bannie. *Tumbling.* Philadelphia: W. B. Saunders, 1969.

Endo, Frank (distributor for all current Japanese gymnastics texts), 12200 S. Berendo Ave., Los Angeles, Calif. 90044.

Fogel, S. *Gymnastic Handbook.* Englewood Cliffs, N.J.: Prentice Hall, 1971.

Frederick, A. B. *Gymnastics for Women.* Dubuque, Iowa: William C. Brown, 1966.

—*Gymnastics for Men.* Dubuque, Iowa: William C. Brown, 1969.

—*212 Ideas for Making Low Cost Physical Education Equipment.* Danville, Ill.: School Aid Co., 1972.

Gault, Jim, and Grant, Jack. *The World of Women's Gymnastics.* Millbrae, Calif.: Celestial Arts, 1976.

Hartley, Sandra. *Training and Conditioning for Women's Competitive Gymnastics.* Sandra Hartley, The University of Alberta, Edmonton 7, Canada.

Hennessy, Jeff. *The Trampoline as I See It.* Lafayette, La.: International Publishing Co., 1969.

Holmes, B., and Kalakian, L. *Men's Gymnastics.* Boston: Allyn & Bacon, 1972.

Hughes, E. *Gymnastics for Girls.* New York: Ronald Press, 1971.

—*Gymnastics for Men.* New York: Ronald Press, 1966.

Huval, Lloyd. *Physical Education Gymnastics for Men and Women.* Sarasota, Fla.: Omni Press Co., 1975.

Kaneko, Akimoto. *Olympic Gymnastics.* New York: Sterling Publishing Co., 1976.

Kaywell, Grace. *Ballet for Gymnastics.* Santa Monica, Calif.: Sundby Publications, 1966.

Keeney, Chuck. *Trampolining Illustrated.* New York: Ronald Press, 1961.

Kjeldsen, Kitty. *Women's Gymnastics.* Boston: Allyn & Bacon, 1975.

Loken, Newt, and Willoughby, Robert. *Complete Book of Gymnastics.* 3rd ed. Englewood Cliffs, N.J.: Prentice Hall, 1977.

O'Quinn, Garland. *Gymnastics for Elementary School Children.* Manchaca, Tex.: Sterling Swift, 1973.

Pechal, Mildred. *Artistic Gymnastics—Floor Exercise.* Waldwick, N.J.: Hoctor Dance Records, 1964.

Price, Hartley, et al. *Gymnastics and Tumbling.* New York: Avco, 1972.

Ryser, Otto. *Manual for Tumbling and Apparatus Stunts.* 6th ed. Dubuque, Iowa: William C. Brown, 1968.

Schmid, Andrea. *Modern Rhythmic Gymnastics.* Palo Alto, Calif.: Mayfield Publishing Co., 1976.

Sjursen, Helen. *Skills for Women's Gymnastics.* Waldwick, N.J.: Hoctor Records, 1970.

Stewart, Hik. *Competitive Gymnastics.* 2nd ed. London: Stanley, Paul & Co., 1971.

Szypula, George. *Tumbling and Balancing for All.* East Lansing: Michigan State University, 1977.

Tonry, Don. *Gymnastics ABC Illustrated.* Northbridge, Mass.: Gymnastic Aids.

Vincent, Bill. *Gymnastic Routines for Men.* Philadelphia: W. B. Saunders, 1972.

Wachtel, Erna, and Loken, Newt. *Girls Gymnastics.* Chicago: Sterling Publishing Co., 1967.

Weaver, Ernestine. *Gymnastics for Girls and Women.* Englewood Cliffs, N.J.: Prentice Hall, 1968.

PERIODICALS

Gymnast of America, PO Box 1310, Durango, Colo. 81301.
Gymnastics World, World Publications, Box 366, Mountain View, Calif. 94040.
International Gymnast, Sundby Publications, 410 Broadway, Santa Monica, Calif. 90401.

ORGANIZATIONS

NAGWS   1201 Sixteenth St., Washington, D.C. 20036. Has gymnastics guide and other related pamphlets.

USGF   PO Box 12713, Tucson, Ariz. 85711. The prime source of current rules publications for national and international competition.

INDEX

301